VOICES IN DISSENT

Books by Arthur A. Ekirch, Jr.

THE IDEA OF PROGRESS IN AMERICA, 1815-1860
THE DECLINE OF AMERICAN LIBERALISM
THE CIVILIAN AND THE MILITARY
MAN AND NATURE IN AMERICA
THE AMERICAN DEMOCRATIC TRADITION: A HISTORY

VOICES
IN
DISSENT

AN ANTHOLOGY OF INDIVIDUALIST THOUGHT
IN THE UNITED STATES

Selected and Edited by
ARTHUR A. EKIRCH, JR.

New York: THE CITADEL PRESS

TO
My Students and Colleagues
at the
American University

CONTENTS

CONTENTS 7

PREFACE

The selections here brought together include conservative as well as radical pieces. Their authors, however, may all fairly be characterized as possessing a high degree of individuality. In one way or another, they challenged what seemed to be reigning popular opinions or beliefs. Since some readers may want to question my choices, I wish to explain that I intentionally avoided spokesmen for organized party or group interests. Furthermore I sought out views which, although distinctive and unorthodox, are not merely esoteric or quixotic. Most of the essays included have had some influence on the course of history. Yet, in their own time, the authors may have jeopardized their social or political position by stating their honest convictions.

In making the selections, I strove to find pieces that are readable, excising or abridging where necessary, but indicating in every instance the omissions and source of the complete text. I have also provided short biographical introductions. These purposely have been kept brief so that the reader will not be distracted from the text itself. Finally, I hope that others, too, may discover the intellectual joy and stimulation that I have gained from reading and rereading these voices in dissent.

ARTHUR A. EKIRCH, JR.

SOURCES AND ACKNOWLEDGMENTS

1. Benjamin Rush, "A Plan of a Peace-Office for the United States." From *Essays, Literary, Moral and Philosophical* (first published in 1798; second edition, Philadelphia, 1806), pp. 183-88.

2. Thomas Paine, "The Age of Reason." From *The Complete Writings of Thomas Paine*, edited by Philip S. Foner (New York: The Citadel Press, 1945), I. pp. 463-69.

3. Fisher Ames, "The Dangers of American Liberty." From *The Works of Fisher Ames* (first published in 1809; Boston, 1854), II, pp. 382-83, 386, 392-99.

4. John Randolph, "Speech on Preparedness and War." From *The Annals of Congress*, Twelfth Congress, First Session (December 9 and 10, 1811), pp. 422, 441-42, 447-50, 454-55.

5. Daniel Webster, "Speech on the Conscription Bill." From *The Letters of Daniel Webster*, edited by C. H. Van Tyne (New York, 1902), pp. 56, 60-68.

6. William Ellery Channing, "On the Annexation of Texas to the United States." From *The Works of William E. Channing* (Boston, 1888), pp. 756-58, 761-66.

7. Orestes A. Brownson, "The Laboring Classes." From *Boston Quarterly Review*, III (July, 1840), pp. 368-75, 390-95.

8. William Lloyd Garrison, "No Compromise With Slavery." From *Selections from the Writings and Speeches of William Lloyd Garrison* (Boston, 1852), pp. 136-42.

9. Charles Sumner, "The True Grandeur of Nations." From *Orations and Speeches* (Boston, 1850), I, pp. 47-54, 66-67, 119-27.

10. Theodore Parker, "The True Idea of a Christian Church." From *Theodore Parker: An Anthology*, edited by H. S. Commager (Boston: Beacon Press, 1960), pp. 83-88. Copyright © 1960 by Henry Steele Commager. Reprinted by permission of the Beacon Press.

11. Henry David Thoreau, "Civil Disobedience." From *The Writings of Henry David Thoreau* (Manuscript Edition, Boston and New York: Houghton Mifflin, 1906), IV, pp. 356-61, 369-76, 386-87.

12. Lysander Spooner, "Limitations Imposed Upon the Majority." From *An Essay on the Trial by Jury* (Boston, 1852), pp. 206-7, 214-21.

13. Caleb Sprague Henry, "The Historical Destination of the Human Race." From *Considerations on Some of the Elements and Conditions of Social Welfare and Human Progress* (New York, 1861), pp. 216-17, 221-41.

14. Benjamin R. Curtis, "Executive Power." From *Executive Power* (Boston, 1862), pp. 12-15, 20-25.

15. Henry George, "What the Railroad Will Bring Us." From *The Overland Monthly*, I (October, 1868), pp. 298-306.

16. William Graham Sumner, "The Case of the Forgotten Man Farther Considered." From *What Social Classes Owe to Each Other* (first published in 1883; Caldwell, Idaho: Caxton, 1961), pp. 116-26, 129-31.

17. William Graham Sumner, "The Conquest of the United States by Spain." From *The Conquest of the United States by Spain* (Boston, 1899), pp. 3-5, 8-10, 23-32.

18. Robert G. Ingersoll, "What Is Religion." From *The Works of Robert G. Ingersoll* (Dresden Edition, New York, 1900), IV, pp. 495-508.

19. W.E.B. Du Bois, "The Souls of Black Folk." From *The Souls of Black Folk: Essays and Sketches* (Chicago, 1903), pp. 1-12.

20. Washington Gladden, "Shall Ill-Gotten Gains Be Sought for Christian Purposes?" From *The New Idolatry and Other Discussions* (New York, 1905), pp. 72-77, 81-84.

21. Robert M. La Gollette, "Speech on the Declaration of War Against Germany." From the *Congressional Record*, Sixty-fifth Congress, First Session (April 4, 1917), pp. 223-28, 234.

22. Randolph Bourne, "The War and the Intellectuals." From *His-

tory of a Literary Radical and Other Papers by Randolph Bourne, with an Introduction by Van Wyck Brooks (New York: Russell and Russell, 1956), pp. 205-22.

23. Oliver Wendell Holmes, "Abrams Versus United States." From *Abrams et al. v. United States,* 250 U.S. pp. 616, 624-31.

24. André Siegfried, "Puritan Resistance to Freedom of Thought." From *America Comes of Age,* translated from the French by H. H. Hemming and Doris Hemming (New York: Harcourt, Brace, 1927), pp. 54-58, 64-69. Reprinted by permission of Harcourt, Brace & World, Inc.

25. Ralph Borsodi, "This Ugly Civilization." From *This Ugly Civilization* (New York: Simon and Schuster, 1929), pp. 1-6.

26. Walter Lippmann, "Planning in Time of Peace." From *An Inquiry into the Principles of the Good Society* (Boston: Little, Brown, 1937), pp. 91-105. Copyright © 1936, 1937, 1943 by Walter Lippmann. Reprinted by permission of Little, Brown & Co.

27. Robert M. Hutchins, "The Path to War—We Are Drifting into Suicide." From a radio address, January 23, 1941, published in *Vital Speeches of the Day,* VII (February 15, 1941), pp. 258-61.

28. Caleb Foote, "Have We Forgotten Justice?" From *Fellowship,* VIII (May, 1942), 79-81.

29. Clyde Eagleton, "The Beam in Our Own Eye." From *Harper's Magazine,* CXCII (June, 1946), 481-85.

30. Russell Kirk, "Conscription ad Infinitum." From *South Atlantic Quarterly,* XLV (July, 1946), 313-19.

31. Robert A. Taft, "Equal Justice Under Law." From an address delivered at Kenyon College, Gambier, Ohio, October 5, 1946, published in *Vital Speeches of the Day,* XIII (November 1, 1946), pp. 44-48.

32. Henry Miller, "Remember to Remember." From *The Air-Conditioned Nightmare,* II (New York: New Directions, 1947), preface pp. xviii-xxii, xxxii-xxxvii. Copyright © 1947 by New Directions. Reprinted by permission of New Directions.

33. Charles A. Beard, "President Roosevelt and the Coming of the War." From *President Roosevelt and the Coming of the War 1941* (New Haven: Yale University Press, 1948), pp. 573-80. Reprinted by permission of Yale University Press.

34. Edward C. Kirkland, "Intellectual Freedom in a Time of Crisis." From *The Key Reporter,* XV (Spring, 1950), pp. 2-3.

35. William O. Douglas, "Dennis Versus United States." From *Dennis et al. v. United States,* 341 U.S. 494, pp. 581-91.

36. Henry Steele Commager, "Guilt—and Innocence—by Association." From *New York Times Magazine* (November 8, 1953), pp. 13, 66 ff.

37. C. Wright Mills, "The Permanent War Economy." From *The Causes of World War Three* (New York: Simon and Schuster, 1958), pp. 56-64. Copyright © 1958 by C. Wright Mills. Reprinted by permission of Simon and Schuster, Inc.

38. Erich Fromm, "May Man Prevail?" From *May Man Prevail?* (Garden City, New York: Doubleday, 1961), pp. 248-52. Copyright © 1961 by Erich Fromm. Reprinted by permission of Doubleday & Co., Inc.

VOICES IN DISSENT

1. BENJAMIN RUSH

A Plan of a Peace-Office for the United States
(1792)

Benjamin Rush (1745-1813), physician and humanitarian reformer, was born near Philadelphia. After
completing his medical education at the University
of Edinburgh, Rush became one of the best known
doctors in America. He was an enthusiastic reformer
who espoused the causes of public education, anti-
slavery, women's rights, temperance, and peace. A
friend of both John Adams and Thomas Jefferson,
he served as Treasurer of the United States Mint
from 1797 until his death. His "Plan of a Peace-
Office" was first printed obscurely in 1792 in Benjamin Banneker's *Almanac for 1793*, but it was little
known until 1798, when Rush published it in his
Essays.

Among the defects which have been pointed out in the federal
constitution by its antifederal enemies, it is much to be lamented
that no person has taken notice of its total silence upon the subject of an office of the utmost importance to the welfare of the
United States, that is, an *office* for promoting and preserving
perpetual *peace* in our country.

It is hoped that no objection will be made to the establishment
of such an office, while we are engaged in a war with the Indians,
for as the *War-Office* of the United States was established in the

time of peace, it is equally reasonable that a *Peace-Office* should be established in the *time of war.*

The plan of this office is as follows:

I. Let a Secretary of the Peace be appointed to preside in this office, who shall be perfectly free from all the present absurd and vulgar European prejudices upon the subject of government; let him be a genuine republican and a sincere Christian, for the principles of republicanism and Christianity are no less friendly to universal and perpetual peace, than they are to universal and equal liberty.

II. Let a power be given to this Secretary to establish and maintain free-schools in every city, village and township of the United States; and let him be made responsible for the talents, principles, and morals, of all his schoolmasters. Let the youth of our country be carefully instructed in reading, writing, arithmetic, and in the doctrines of a religion of some kind: the Christian religion should be preferred to all others; for it belongs to this religion exclusively to teach us not only to cultivate peace with men, but to forgive, nay more—to love our very enemies. It belongs to it further to teach us that the Supreme Being alone possesses a power to take away human life, and that we rebel against his laws, whenever we undertake to execute death in any way whatever upon any of his creatures.

III. Let every family in the United States be furnished at the public expense, by the Secretary of this office, with a copy of an American edition of the BIBLE. This measure has become the more necessary in our country, since the banishment of the bible, as a school-book, from most of the schools in the United States. Unless the price of this book be paid for by the public, there is reason to fear that in a few years it will be met with only in courts of justice or in magistrates' offices; and should the absurd mode of establishing truth by kissing this sacred book fall into disuse, it may probably, in the course of the next generation, be seen only as a curiosity on a shelf in a public museum.

IV. Let the following sentence be inscribed in letters of gold over the doors of every State and Court house in the United States. THE SON OF MAN CAME INTO THE WORLD, NOT TO DESTROY MEN'S LIVES, BUT TO SAVE THEM.

V. To inspire a veneration for human life, and an horror at the shedding of human blood, let all those laws be repealed which authorize juries, judges, sheriffs, or hangmen to assume the resentments of individuals and to commit murder in cold blood in any case whatever. Until this reformation in our code of penal jurisprudence takes place, it will be vain to attempt to introduce universal and perpetual peace in our country.

VI. To subdue that passion for war, which education, added to human depravity, have made universal, a familiarity with the instruments of death, as well as all military shows, should be carefully avoided. For which reason, militia laws should every where be repealed, and military dresses and military titles should be laid aside: reviews tend to lessen the horrors of a battle by connecting them with the charms of order; militia laws generate idleness and vice, and thereby produce the wars they are said to prevent; military dresses fascinate the minds of young men, and lead them from serious and useful professions; were there no *uniforms,* there would probably be no armies; lastly, military titles feed vanity, and keep up ideas in the mind which lessen a sense of the folly and miseries of war.

VII. In the last place, let a large room, adjoining the federal hall, be appropriated for transacting the business and preserving all the records of this *office.* Over the door of this room let there be a sign, on which the figures of a LAMB, a DOVE, and an OLIVE BRANCH should be painted, together with the following inscriptions in letter of gold: PEACE ON EARTH—GOOD-WILL TO MEN. AH! WHY WILL MEN FORGET THAT THEY ARE BRETHREN?

Within this apartment let there be a collection of ploughshares and pruning-hooks made out of swords and spears; and on each of the walls of the apartment, the following pictures as large as the life:

1. A lion eating straw with an ox, and an adder playing upon the lips of a child.

2. An Indian boiling his venison in the same pot with a citizen of Kentucky.

3. Lord Cornwallis and Tippoo Saib, under the shade of a syca-more-tree in the East Indies, drinking Madeira wine together out of the same decanter.

4. A group of French and Austrian soldiers dancing arm and arm, under a bower erected in the neighbourhood of Mons.

5. A St. Domingo planter, a man of color, and a native of Africa, legislating together in the same colonial assembly.

To complete the entertainment of this delightful apartment, let a group of young ladies, clad in white robes, assemble every day at a certain hour, in a gallery to be erected for the purpose, and sing odes and hymns, and anthems in praise of the blessings of peace.

One of these songs should consist of the following lines.

> Peace o'er the world her olive wand extends,
> And white-rob'd innocence from heaven descends;
> All crimes shall cease, and ancient frauds shall fail,
> Returning justice lifts aloft her scale.

In order more deeply to affect the minds of the citizens of the United States with the blessings of peace, by *contrasting* them with the evils of war, let the following inscriptions be painted upon the sign which is placed over the door of the War Office:

1. An office for butchering the human species.
2. A Widow and Orphan making office.
3. A broken bone making office.
4. A Wooden leg making office.
5. An office for creating public and private vices.
6. An office for creating a public debt.
7. An office for creating speculators, stock Jobbers, and Bankrupts.
8. An office for creating famine.
9. An office for creating pestilential diseases.
10. An office for creating poverty, and the destruction of liberty, and national happiness.

In the lobby of this office let there be painted representations of all the common military instruments of death, also human skulls, broken bones, unburied and putrefying dead bodies, hospitals crowded with sick and wounded Soldiers, villages on fire, mothers in besieged towns eating the flesh of their children, ships sinking in the ocean, rivers dyed with blood, and extensive plains without a tree or fence, or any other object, but the ruins of deserted farm houses.

Above this group of woeful figures—let the following words be inserted, in red characters to represent human blood,

"NATIONAL GLORY."

2. THOMAS PAINE

The Age of Reason
(1794)

Thomas Paine (1737-1809) is famous both for his role in the American and French Revolutions and for his advocacy of Deism. His celebrated pamphlet *Common Sense* aroused American sentiments for independence, and a generation later his *Rights of Man* served as an eloquent defense of the principles of the French Revolution. Reared in England as a Quaker, Paine became profoundly impressed by the scientific thought of the eighteenth-century Enlightenment. His Deist beliefs were expressed in *The Age of Reason,* a notable attack on all revealed religion, which he published while under the proscription of the Reign of Terror in France.

It has been my intention for several years past to publish my thoughts upon religion. I am well aware of the difficulties that attend the subject; and from that consideration had reserved it to a more advanced period of life. I intended it to be the last offering I should make to my fellow-citizens of all nations, and that at a time when the purity of the motive that induced me to it could not admit of a question, even by those who might disapprove the work. The circumstance that has now taken place in France of the total abolition of the whole order of priesthood and of everything appertaining to compulsive articles of faith, has not only precipitated my intention, but rendered a work of this kind exceedingly necessary, lest in the general wreck of superstition, of false systems of government and false theology, we lose sight of morality, of humanity and of the theology that is true.

As several of my colleagues, and others of my fellow-citizens of France, have given me the example of making their voluntary and individual profession of faith, I also will make mine; and I do this with all that sincerity and frankness with which the mind of man communicates with itself.

I believe in one God, and no more; and I hope for happiness beyond this life.

I believe in the equality of man; and I believe that religious duties consist in doing justice, loving mercy, and endeavoring to make our fellow-creatures happy.

But, lest it should be supposed that I believe many other things in addition to these, I shall, in the progress of this work, declare the things I do not believe, and my reasons for not believing them.

I do not believe in the creed professed by the Jewish Church, by the Roman Church, by the Greek Church, by the Turkish Church, by the Protestant Church, nor by any church that I know of. My own mind is my own church.

All national institutions of churches, whether Jewish, Christian, or Turkish, appear to me no other than human inventions, set up to terrify and enslave mankind, and monopolize power and profit.

I do not mean by this declaration to condemn those who believe otherwise; they have the same right to their belief as I have to mine. But it is necessary to the happiness of man that he be mentally faithful to himself. Infidelity does not consist in believing, or in disbelieving; it consists in professing to believe what he does not believe.

It is impossible to calculate the moral mischief, if I may so express it, that mental lying has produced in society. When a man has so far corrupted and prostituted the chastity of his mind as to subscribe his professional belief to things he does not believe he has prepared himself for the commission of every other crime.

He takes up the trade of a priest for the sake of gain, and, in order to qualify himself for that trade, he begins with perjury. Can we conceive anything more destructive to morality than this?

Soon after I had published the pamphlet "Common Sense," in America, I saw the exceeding probability that a revolution in the system of government would be followed by a revolution in the system of religion. The adulterous connection of church and state, wherever it has taken place, whether Jewish, Christian, or Turkish, has so effectually prohibited by pains and penalties every discussion upon established creeds, and upon first principles of religion, that until the system of government should be changed, those subjects could not be brought fairly and openly before the world; but that whenever this should be done, a revolution in the system of religion would follow. Human inventions and priest-craft would be detected, and man would return to the pure, un-mixed and unadulterated belief of one God, and no more.

Every national church or religion has established itself by pre-tending some special mission from God, communicated to certain individuals. The Jews have their Moses; the Christians their Jesus Christ, their apostles and saints; and the Turks their Mahomet, as if the way to God was not open to every man alike.

Each of those churches show certain books, which they call *revelation,* or the Word of God. The Jews say that their Word of God was given by God to Moses, face to face; the Christians say that their Word of God came by divine inspiration; and the Turks say that their Word of God (the Koran) was brought by an angel from heaven. Each of those churches accuse the other of unbelief; and for my own part, I disbelieve them all.

As it is necessary to affix right ideas to words, I will, before I proceed further into the subject, offer some observations on the word *revelation*. Revelation, when applied to religion, means something communicated *immediately* from God to man.

No one will deny or dispute the power of the Almighty to make such a communication, if He pleases. But admitting, for the sake of a case, that something has been revealed to a certain person, and not revealed to any other person, it is a revelation to that person only. When he tells it to a second person, a second to a third, a third to a fourth, and so on, it ceases to be a revelation to all those persons. It is a revelation to the first person only, and *hearsay* to every other, and consequently they are not obliged to believe it.

It is a contradiction in terms and ideas to call anything a revelation that comes to us at second hand, either verbally or in writing. Revelation is necessarily limited to the first communication—after this, it is only an account of something which that person says was a revelation made to him; and though he may find himself obliged to believe it, it cannot be incumbent upon me to believe it in the same manner; for it was not a revelation to *me,* and I have only his word for it that it was made to him. When Moses told the children of Israel that he received the two tables of the commandments from the hand of God, they were not obliged to believe him, because they had no other authority for it than his telling them so; and I have no other authority for it than some historian telling me so. The commandments carry no internal evidence of divinity with them; they contain some good moral precepts, such as any man qualified to be a lawgiver, or a legislator, could produce himself, without having recourse to supernatural intervention.

When I am told that the Koran was written in heaven and brought to Mahomet by an angel, the account comes too near the same kind of hearsay evidence and second hand authority as the former. I did not see the angel myself, and, therefore, I have a right not to believe it.

When also I am told that a woman, called the Virgin Mary, said, or gave out, that she was with child without any cohabitation with a man, and that her betrothed husband, Joseph, said that an angel told him so, I have a right to believe them or not; such a circumstance required a much stronger evidence than their bare word for it; but we have not even this—for neither Joseph nor Mary wrote any such matter themselves: it is only reported by others that *they said so*—it is hearsay upon hearsay, and I do not choose to rest my belief upon such evidence.

It is, however, not difficult to account for the credit that was given to the story of Jesus Christ being the Son of God. He was born at a time when the heathen mythology had still some fashion and repute in the world, and that mythology had prepared the people for the belief of such a story. Almost all the extraordinary men that lived under the heathen mythology were reputed to be the sons of some of their gods. It was not a new thing, at that time, to believe a man to have been celestially begotten; the intercourse of gods with women was then a matter of familiar opinion.

Their Jupiter, according to their accounts, had cohabited with hundreds: the story, therefore, had nothing in it either new, wonderful or obscene; it was conformable to the opinions that then prevailed among the people called Gentiles, or Mythologists, and it was those people only that believed it.

The Jews, who had kept strictly to the belief of one God, and no more, and who had always rejected the heathen mythology, never credited the story.

It is curious to observe how the theory of what is called the Christian Church sprung out of the tail of the heathen mythology. A direct incorporation took place, in the first instance, by making the reputed founder to be celestially begotten. The trinity of gods that then followed was no other than a reduction of the former plurality, which was about twenty or thirty thousand; the statue of Mary succeeded the statue of Diana of Ephesus; the deification of heroes changed into the canonization of saints; the Mythologists had gods for everything; the Christian Mythologists had saints for everything: the Church became as crowded with the one as the Pantheon had been with the other, and Rome was the place of both. The Christian theory is little else than the idolatry of the ancient Mythologists, accommodated to the purposes of power and revenue; and it yet remains to reason and philosophy to abolish the amphibious fraud.

Nothing that is here said can apply, even with the most distant disrespect, to the real character of Jesus Christ. He was a virtuous and an amiable man. The morality that he preached and practiced was of the most benevolent kind; and though similar systems of morality had been preached by Confucius, and by some of the Greek philosophers, many years before; by the Quakers since; and by many good men in all ages, it has not been exceeded by any.

Jesus Christ wrote no account of himself, of his birth, parentage, or anything else; not a line of what is called the New Testament is of his writing. The history of him is altogether the work of other people; and as to the account given of his resurrection and ascension, it was the necessary counterpart to the story of his birth. His historians, having brought him into the world in supernatural manner, were obliged to take him out again in the same manner, or the first part of the story must have fallen to the ground.

The wretched contrivance with which this latter part is told exceeds every thing that went before it. The first part, that of the miraculous conception, was not a thing that admitted of publicity; and therefore the tellers of this part of the story had this advantage, that though they might not be credited, they could not be detected. They could not be expected to prove it, because it was not one of those things that admitted of proof, and it was impossible that the person of whom it was told could prove it himself.

But the resurrection of a dead person from the grave, and his ascension through the air, is a thing very different as to the evidence it admits of, to the invisible conception of a child in womb. The resurrection and ascension, supposing them to have taken place, admitted of public and ocular demonstration, like that of the ascension of a balloon, or the sun at noon day, to all Jerusalem at least.

A thing which everybody is required to believe requires that the proof and evidence of it should be equal to all, and universal; and as the public visibility of this last related act was the only evidence that could give sanction to the former part, the whole of it falls to the ground because that evidence never was given. Instead of this, a small number of persons, not more than eight or nine, are introduced as proxies for the whole world to say they saw it, and all the rest of the world are called upon to believe it. But it appears that Thomas did not believe the resurrection, and, as they say, would not believe without having ocular and manual demonstration himself. *So neither will I,* and the reason is equally as good for me, and for every other person, as for Thomas.

It is in vain to attempt to palliate or disguise this matter. The story, so far as relates to the supernatural part, has every mark of fraud and imposition stamped upon the face of it. Who were the authors of it is as impossible for us now to know as it is for us to be assured that the books in which the account is related were written by the persons whose names they bear; the best surviving evidence we now have respecting this affair is the Jews. They are regularly descended from the people who lived in the times this resurrection and ascension is said to have happened, and they say, *it is not true.* It has long appeared to me a strange inconsistency to cite the Jews as proof of the truth of the story. It is the same as if a man were to say, I will prove the truth of what I have told you by producing the people who say it is false.

That such a person as Jesus Christ existed, and that he was crucified, which was the mode of execution at that day, are historical relations strictly within the limits of probability. He preached most excellent morality and the equality of man; but he preached also against the corruptions and avarice of the Jewish priests; and this brought upon him the hatred and vengeance of the whole order of priesthood.

The accusation which those priests brought against him was that of sedition and conspiracy against the Roman government, to which the Jews were then subject and tributary; and it is not improbable that the Roman government might have some secret apprehension of the effects of his doctrine, as well as the Jewish priests; neither is it improbable that Jesus Christ had in contemplation the delivery of the Jewish nation from the bondage of the Romans. Between the two, however, this virtuous reformer and revolutionist lost his life.

3. FISHER AMES

The Dangers of American Liberty
(1805)

Fisher Ames (1758-1808), conservative Federalist, was born in Dedham, Massachusetts, and graduated from Harvard College in 1774. As a member of the U. S. House of Representatives in the 1790's, he was a staunch supporter of Alexander Hamilton's economic program. His speech in defense of Jay's Treaty in 1796 is commonly regarded as one of the greatest addresses ever delivered in the halls of Congress. An implacable opponent of Jeffersonian principles, Ames pessimistically predicted that it was the fate of all popular democracies to degenerate eventually into military despotisms.

A democracy cannot last. Its nature ordains that its next change shall be into a military despotism, of all known governments, perhaps, the most prone to shift its head, and the slowest to mend its vices. The reason is, that the tyranny of what is called the people, and that by the sword, both operate alike to debase and corrupt, till there are neither men left with the spirit to desire liberty, nor morals with the power to sustain justice. Like the burning pestilence that destroys the human body, nothing can subsist by its dissolution but vermin.

A military government may make a nation great, but it cannot make them free. . . .

A democracy is so like an army that no one will be at a loss in applying these observations. The great spring of action with the people in a democracy is their fondness for one set of men, the men who flatter and deceive, and their outrageous aversion to another, most probably those who prefer their true interest to their favor.

A mob is no sooner gathered together than it instinctively feels the want of a leader, a want that is soon supplied. They may not obey him as long, but they obey him as implicitly, and will as readily fight and burn, or rob and murder, in his cause, as the soldiers will for their general.

As the Roman provinces were held in subjection by Roman troops, so every American State is watched with jealousy, and ruled with despotic rigor by the partisans of the faction that may happen to be in power. The successive struggles to which our licentiousness may devote the country, will never be of state against state, but of rival factions diffused over our whole territory. Of course, the strongest army, or that which is best commanded, will prevail, and we shall remain subject to one indivisible bad government.

This conclusion may seem surprising to many; but the event of the Roman republic will vindicate it on the evidence of history. . . .

They are certainly blind who do not see that we are descending from a supposed orderly and stable republican government into a licentious democracy, with a progress that baffles all means to resist, and scarcely leaves leisure to deplore its celerity. The institutions and the hopes that Washington raised are nearly prostrate; and his name and memory would perish, if the rage of his enemies had any power over history. But they have not—history will give scope to her vengeance, and posterity will not be defrauded.

But if our experience had not clearly given warning of our approaching catastrophe, the very nature of democracy would inevitably produce it.

A government by the passions of the multitude, or, no less correctly, according to the vices and ambition of their leaders, is a democracy. We have heard so long of the indefeasible sovereignty of the people, and have admitted so many specious theories of the rights of man, which are contradicted by his nature and experience, that few will dread at all, and fewer still will dread as they ought, the evils of an American democracy. They will not believe them near, or they will think them tolerable or temporary. Fatal delusion!

When it is said, there may be a tyranny of the *many* as well as of the *few,* every democrat will yield at least a cold and speculative assent; but he will at all times act, as if it were a thing incomprehensible, that there should be any evil to be apprehended in the uncontrolled power of the people. He will say arbitrary power may make a tyrant, but how can it make its possessor a slave?

In the first place, let it be remarked the power of individuals is a very different thing from their liberty. When I vote for the man I prefer, he may happen not to be chosen; or he may disappoint my expectations if he is; or he may be outvoted by others in the public body to which he is elected. I may then hold and exercise all the power that a citizen can have or enjoy, and yet such laws may be made and such abuses allowed as shall deprive me of all liberty. I may be tried by a jury, and that jury may be culled and picked out from my political enemies by a federal marshal. Of course, my life and liberty may depend on the good pleasure of the man who appoints that marshal. I may be assessed arbitrarily for my faculty, or upon conjectural estimation of my property, so that all I have shall be at the control of the government, whenever its displeasure shall exact the sacrifice. I may be told that I am a federalist, and as such bound to submit, in all cases whatsoever, to the will of the majority, as the ruling faction ever pretend to be. My submission may be tested by my resisting or obeying commands that will involve me in disgrace, or drive me to despair. I may become a fugitive, because the ruling party have made me afraid to stay at home; or, perhaps, while I remain at home, they may, nevertheless, think fit to inscribe my name on the list of emigrants and proscribed persons.

All this was done in France, and many of the admirers of French examples are impatient to imitate them. All this time the people may be told, they are the freest in the world; but what ought my opinion to be? What would the threatened clergy, the aristocracy of wealthy merchants, as they have been called already, and thirty thousand more in Massachusetts, who vote for Governor Strong, and whose case might be no better than mine, what would they think of their condition? Would they call it liberty? Surely, here is oppression sufficient in extent and degree to make the government that inflicts it both odious and terrible; yet this and a thousand times more than this was practised in France, and will be repeated as often as it shall please God in his wrath to deliver a people to the dominion of their licentious passions.

The people, as a body, cannot deliberate. Nevertheless, they will feel an irresistible impulse to act, and their resolutions will be dictated to them by their demagogues. The consciousness, or the opinion, that they possess the supreme power, will inspire inordinate passions; and the violent men, who are the most forward to gratify those passions, will be their favorites. What is called the government of the people is in fact too often the arbitrary power of such men. Here, then, we have the faithful portrait of democracy. What avails the boasted power of individual citizens? or of what value is the will of the majority, if that will is dictated by a committee of demagogues, and law and right are in fact at the mercy of a victorious faction? To make a nation free, the crafty must be kept in awe, and the violent in restraint. The weak and the simple find their liberty arise not from their own individual sovereignty, but from the power of law and justice over all. It is only by the due restraint of others, that I am free.

Popular sovereignty is scarcely less beneficent than awful, when it resides in their courts of justice; there its office, like a sort of human providence, is to warn, enlighten, and protect; when the people are inflamed to seize and exercise it in their assemblies, it is competent only to kill and destroy. Temperate liberty is like the dew, as it falls unseen from its own heaven; constant without excess, it finds vegetation thirsting for its refreshment, and imparts to it the vigor to take more. All nature, moistened with blessings, sparkles in the morning ray. But democracy is a water-spout that bursts from the clouds, and lays the ravaged earth bare to its rocky foundations. The labors of man lie whelmed with his hopes beneath masses of ruin, that bury not only the dead but their monuments.

It is the almost universal mistake of our countrymen, that democracy would be mild and safe in America. They charge the horrid excesses of France not so much to human nature, which will never act better, when the restraints of government, morals, and religion are thrown off, but to the characteristic cruelty and wickedness of Frenchmen.

The truth is, and let it humble our pride, the most ferocious of all animals, when his passions are roused to fury and are uncontrolled, is man; and of all goverments, the worst is that which never fails to excite, but was never found to restrain those passions, that is, democracy. It is an illuminated hell, that in the midst of remorse, horror, and torture, rings with festivity; for experience shows, that one joy remains to this most malignant description of the damned, the power to make others wretched. When a man looks round and sees his neighbors mild and merciful, he cannot feel afraid of the abuse of their power over him; and surely if they oppress me, he will say, they will spare their own liberty, for that is dear to all mankind. It is so. The human heart is so constituted, that a man loves liberty as naturally as himself. Yet liberty is a rare thing in the world, though the love of it is so universal.

Before the French Revolution, it was the prevailing opinion of our countrymen, that other nations were not free, because their despotic governments were too strong for the people. Of course, we were admonished to detest all existing governments, as so many lions in liberty's path; and to expect by their downfall the happy opportunity, that every emancipated people would embrace, to secure their own equal rights forever. France is supposed to have had this opportunity, and to have lost it. Ought we not then to be convinced, that something more is necessary to preserve liberty than to love it? Ought we not to see that when the people have destroyed all power but their own, they are the nearest possible to a despotism, the more uncontrolled for being new, and tenfold the more cruel for its hypocrisy?

The steps by which a people must proceed to change a government, are not those to enlighten their judgment or to soothe their passions. They cannot stir without following the men before them, who breathe fury into their hearts and banish nature from them. On whatever grounds and under whatever leaders the contest may be commenced, the revolutionary work is the same, and the characters of the agents will be assimilated to it. A revolution is a mine that must explode with destructive violence. The men who were once peaceable like to carry firebrands and daggers too long. Thus armed, will they submit to salutary restraint? How will you bring them to it? Will you undertake to reason down fury? Will you satisfy revenge without blood? Will you preach banditti into habits of self-denial? If you can, and in times of violence and anarchy, why do you ask any other guard than sober reason for your life and property in times of peace and order, when men are most disposed to listen to it? Yet even at such times, you impose restraints; you call out for your defence the whole array of law, with its instruments of punishment and terror; you maintain ministers to strengthen force with opinion, and to make religion the auxiliary of morals. With all this, however, crimes are still perpetrated; society is not any too safe or quiet. Break down all these fences; make what is called law an assassin; take what it ought to protect, and divide it; extinguish, by acts of rapine and vengeance, the spark of mercy in the heart; or, if it should be found to glow there, quench it in that heart's blood; make your people scoff at their morals, and unlearn an education to virtue; displace the Christian sabbath by a profane one, for a respite once in ten days from the toils of murder, because men, who first shed blood for revenge, and proceed to spill it for plunder, and in the progress of their ferocity, for sport, want a festival—what sort of society would you have? Would not rage grow with its indulgence? The coward fury of a mob rises in proportion as there is less resistance; and their inextinguishable thirst for slaughter grows more ardent as more blood is shed to slake it. In such a state is liberty to be gained or guarded from violation? It could not be kept an hour from the daggers of those who, having seized despotic power, would claim it as their lawful prize. I have written the history of France. Can we look back upon it without terror, or forward without despair?

The nature of arbitrary power is always odious; but it cannot be long the arbitrary power of the multitude. There is, probably, no form of rule among mankind, in which the progress of the government depends so little on the particular character of those who administer it. Democracy is the creature of impulse and violence; and the intermediate stages towards the tyranny of one are so quickly passed, that the vileness and cruelty of men are displayed with surprising uniformity. There is not time for great talents to act. There is no sufficient reason to believe, that we should conduct a revolution with much more mildness than the French. If a revolution find the citizens lambs, it will soon make them carnivorous, if not cannibals. We have many thousands of the Paris and St. Domingo assassins in the United States, not as fugitives, but as patriots, who merit reward, and disdain to take any but power. In the progress of our confusion, these men will effectually assert their claims and display their skill. There is no governing power in the state but party. The moderate and thinking part of the citizens are without power or influence; and it must be so, because all power and influence are engrossed by a factious combination of men, who can overwhelm uncombined individuals with numbers, and the wise and virtuous with clamor and fury.

It is indeed a law of politics, as well as of physics, that a body in action must overcome an equal body at rest. The attacks that have been made on the constitutional barriers proclaim, in a tone that would not be louder from a trumpet, that party will not tolerate any resistance to its will. All the supposed independent orders of the commonwealth must be its servile instruments, or its victims. We should experience the same despotism in Massachusetts, New Hampshire, and Connecticut, but the battle is not yet won. It will be won; and they who already display the temper of their Southern and French allies, will not linger or reluct in imitating the worst extremes of their example.

What, then, is to be our condition?

Faction will inevitably triumph. Where the government is both stable and free, there may be parties. There will be differences of opinion, and the pride of opinion will be sufficient to generate contests, and to inflame them with bitterness and rancor.

There will be rivalships among those whom genius, fame, or station have made great, and these will deeply agitate the state without often hazarding its safety. Such parties will excite alarm, but they may be safely left, like the elements, to exhaust their fury upon each other.

The object of their strife is to get power *under* the government; for, where that is constituted as it should be, the power *over* the government will not seem attainable, and, of course, will not be attempted.

But in democratic states there will be factions. The sovereign power being nominally in the hands of all, will be effectively within the grasp of a few; and therefore, by the very laws of our nature, a few will combine, intrigue, lie, and fight to engross it to themselves. All history bears testimony, that this attempt has never yet been disappointed.

Who will be the associates? Certainly not the virtuous, who do not wish to control the society, but quietly to enjoy its protection. The enterprising merchant, the thriving tradesman, the careful farmer, will be engrossed by the toils of their business, and will have little time or inclination for the unprofitable and disquieting pursuits of politics. It is not the industrious, sober husbandman, who will plough that barren field; it is the lazy and dissolute bankrupt, who has no other to plough. The idle, the ambitious, and the needy will band together to break the hold that law has upon them, and then to get hold of law. Faction is a Hercules, whose first labor is to strangle this lion, and then to make armor of his skin. In every democratic state, the ruling faction will have law to keep down its enemies; but it will arrogate to itself an undisputed power over law. If our ruling faction has found any impediments, we ask, which of them is now remaining? And is it not absurd to suppose, that the conquerors will be contented with half the fruits of victory?

We are to be subject, then, to a despotic faction, irritated by the resistance that has delayed, and the scorn that pursues their triumph, elate with the insolence of an arbitrary and uncontrollable domination, and who will exercise their sway, not according to the rules of integrity or national policy, but in conformity with their own exclusive interests and passions.

This is a state of things which admits of progress, but not of reformation; it is the beginning of a revolution, which must advance. Our affairs, as first observed, no longer depend on counsel. The opinion of a majority is no longer invited or permitted to control our destinies, or even to retard their consummation. The men in power may, and no doubt will give place to some other faction, who will succeed, because they are abler men, or possibly, in candor we say it, because they are worse. Intrigue will for some time answer instead of force, or the mob will supply it. But by degrees force only will be relied on by those who are *in,* and employed by those who are *out.* The vis major will prevail, and some bold chieftain will conquer liberty, and triumph and reign in her name.

Yet it is confessed, we have hopes that this event is not very near. We have no cities as large as London or Paris; and of course the ambitious demagogues may find the ranks of their standing army too thin to rule by them alone. It is also worth remark, that our mobs are not, like those of Europe, excitable by the cry of no bread. The dread of famine is everywhere else a power of political electricity, that glides through all the haunts of filth, and vice, and want in a city, with incredible speed, and in times of insurrection rives and scorches with a sudden force, like heaven's own thunder. Accordingly, we find the sober men of Europe more afraid of the despotism of the rabble than of the government.

But as in the United States we see less of this description of low vulgar, and as in the essential circumstance alluded to, they are so much less manageable by their demagogues, we are to expect that our affairs will be long guided by courting the mob, before they are violently changed by employing them. While the passions of the multitude can be conciliated to confer power and to overcome all impediments to its action, our rulers have a plain and easy task to perform. It costs them nothing but hypocrisy. As soon, however, as rival favorites of the people may happen to contend by the practice of the same arts, we are to look for the sanguinary strife of ambition. Brissot will fall by the hand of Danton, and he will be supplanted by Robespierre. The revolution will proceed in exactly the same way, but not with so rapid a pace, as that of France.

4. JOHN RANDOLPH

Speech on Preparedness and War
(1811)

John Randolph (1773-1833) of Roanoke served Virginia as a Member of Congress for over a quarter
century. At first a staunch Jeffersonian, he later broke
with his party, chiefly because he was bitterly opposed to the increasingly bellicose tone of its foreign
policy in the decade before the War of 1812. A his-
trionic, but able, Congressman and orator, Randolph's
brilliance at times seemed to hover on the edge of in-
sanity, and his sarcastic wit made him a host of enemies.

In the days of terror, we shrunk at standing armies; and what is
the object now—defence? Who? Freemen who would not defend
themselves. He would ask, if seven millions of Americans were
to be protected in their lives and liberties by ten thousand vaga-
bonds who were fit food for gunpowder? It would be necessary
to know the ulterior views of the committee on this point. It would
be proper, before a vote was taken on this resolution, to know for
what purpose these additional troops were wanted. The House
ought not to commit itself on a question of such magnitude without
detailed information. He was as much opposed to raising standing
armies now, as he had been in the reign of terror. He had seen
too much of the corruptions attendant on these establishments,
in the course of the investigation in which he was now engaged,

not to disclaim all share in the creation of them. The people of the United States could defend themselves, if necessary, and had no idea of resting their defence on mercenaries, picked up from brothels and tippling houses—pickpockets who have escaped from Newgate, &c., and sought refuge in this asylum of oppressed humanity. He contended that this resolution contained an unconstitutional proposition, and that the standing army now in the service of the United States was maintained in the very teeth of that part of the Constitution which declares that no money for the support of a standing army should be appropriated for more than two years. He again called for information as to the object of the army now proposed to be raised; declaring, that, if the President should say they were necessary for the protection of New Orleans, to be employed against the Indians, or to repel incursions from Canada (although this seemed not to be much thought of), he should not refuse to grant them. He declared the report to be a negative position, which could not be combatted except to disadvantage. He wished to know the Constitutional resources of the committee, and expressed a hope that the remarks he had made would draw out the talents of that body. . . .

It was a question, as it had been presented to the House, of peace or war. In that light it had been argued; in no other light could he consider it, after the declarations made by members of the Committee of Foreign Relations. Without intending any disrespect to the Chair, he must be permitted to say, that if the decision yesterday was correct, "That it was not in order to advance any arguments against the resolution, drawn from topics before other committees of the House," the whole debate, nay, the report itself on which they were acting, was disorderly; since the increase of the military force was a subject at that time in agitation by the select committee raised on that branch of the President's Message. But it was impossible that the discussion of a question broad as

the wide ocean of our foreign concerns—involving every consideration of interest, of right, of happiness and of safety at home—
touching, in every point, all that was dear to freemen, "their lives,
their fortunes, and their sacred honor!"—could be tied down by
the narrow rules of technical routine. The Committee of Foreign
Relations had indeed decided that the subject of arming the militia
(which he had pressed upon them as indispensable to the public
security) did not come within the scope of their authority. On
what ground, he had been and still was unable to see, they had
felt themselves authorized (when that subject was before another
committee) to recommend the raising of standing armies, with a
view (as had been declared) of immediate war—a war not of
defence, but of conquest, of aggrandizement, of ambition; a war
foreign to the interest of this country, to the interests of humanity
itself.

He knew not how gentlemen, calling themselves Republicans,
could advocate such a war. What was their doctrine in 1798-9,
when the command of the army—that highest of all possible trusts
in any Government, be the form what it may—was reposed in
the bosom of the Father of his Country, the sanctuary of a nation's
love, the only hope that never came in vain! When other worthies
of the Revolution—Hamilton, Pinckney, and the younger Washington—men of tried patriotism, of approved conduct and valor,
of untarnished honor, held subordinate command under him!
Republicans were then unwilling to trust a standing army, even
to his hands who had given proof that he was above all human
temptation. Where now is the Revolutionary hero to whom you
are about to confide this sacred trust? To whom will you confide
the charge of leading the flower of our youth to the Heights of
Abraham? Will you find him in the person of an acquitted felon?
What! then you were unwilling to vote an army where such men
as had been named held high command! when WASHINGTON

himself was at the head—did you then show such reluctance, feel such scruples; and are you now nothing loth, fearless of every consequence? Will you say that your provocations were less then than now? When your direct commerce was interdicted—your Ambassadors hooted with derision from the French Court—tribute demanded—actual war waged upon you!

Those who opposed the army then, were indeed denounced as the partisans of France; as the same men—some of them at least—are now held up as the advocates of England; those firm and undeviating Republicans, who then dared, and now dare, to cling to the ark of the Constitution, to defend it even at the expense of their fame, rather than surrender themselves to the wild projects of mad ambition! There was a fatality attending plenitude of power. Soon or late, some mania seizes upon its possessors—they fall from dizzy height through the giddiness of their own heads. Like a vast estate, heaped up by the labor and industry of one man, which seldom survives the third generation—power, gained by patient assiduity, by a faithful and regular discharge of its attendant duties, soon gets above its own origin. Intoxicated with their own greatness the Federal party fell. Will not the same causes produce the same effects now, as then? Sir, you may raise this army, you may build up this vast structure of patronage, this mighty apparatus of favoritism; but—"lay not the flattering unction to your souls"—you will never live to enjoy the succession. You sign your political death warrant. . . .

This war of conquest, a war for the acquisition of territory and subjects, is to be a new commentary on the doctrine that Republics are destitute of ambition—that they are addicted to peace, wedded to the happiness and safety of the great body of their people. But it seems this is to be a holiday campaign—there is to be no expense of blood, or treasure, on our part—Canada is to conquer herself—she is to be subdued by the principles of fraternity. The people of that country are first to be seduced from their allegiance, and converted into traitors, as preparatory to the making them good citizens. Although he must acknowledge that some of our flaming patriots were thus manufactured, he did not think the process would hold good with a whole community. It was a dangerous experiment. We were to succeed in the French mode by the system of fraternization—all is French! but how dreadfully it might be retorted on the Southern and Western slaveholding States. He detested this subornation of treason. No—if he must have them, let them fall by the valor of our arms, by fair, legitimate conquest; not become the victims of treacherous seduction.

He was not surprised at the war spirit which was manifesting itself in the gentlemen from the South. In the year 1805-6, in a struggle for the carrying trade of belligerent colonial produce, this country had been most unwisely brought into collision with the great Powers of Europe. By a series of most impolitic and ruinous measures, utterly incomprehensible to every rational, sober-minded man, the Southern planters, by their own votes, had succeeded in knocking down the price of cotton to seven cents, and of tobacco (a few choice crops excepted) to nothing— and in raising the price of blankets (of which a few would not be amiss in a Canadian campaign), coarse woolens, and every article of first necessity, three or four hundred per cent. And now that, by our own acts, we have brought ourselves into this unprecedented condition, we must get out of it in any way, but by an acknowledgement of our own want of wisdom and forecast. But is war the true remedy? Who will profit by it? Speculators—a few lucky merchants, who draw prizes in the lottery—commissaries and contractors. Who must suffer by it? The people. It is their blood, their taxes, that must flow to support it. . . .

Our people will not submit to be taxed for this war of conquest and dominion. The Government of the United States was not calculated to wage offensive foreign war—it was instituted for the common defence and general welfare; and whosoever should embark it in a war of offence, would put it to a test which it was by no means calculated to endure. Make it out that Great Britain had instigated the Indians on the late occasion, and he was ready for battle; but not for dominion. He was unwilling, however, under present circumstances, to take Canada, at the risk of the Constitution—to embark in a common cause with France and be dragged at the wheels of the car of some Burr or Bonaparte. For a gentleman from Tennessee or Genesee, or Lake Champlain, there may be some prospect of advantage. Their hemp would bear a great price by the exclusion of foreign supply. In that too the great importers were deeply interested. The upper country on the Hudson and the Lakes would be enriched by the supplies for the troops, which they alone could furnish. They would have the exclusive market: to say nothing of the increased preponderance from the acquistion of Canada and that section of the Union, which the Southern and Western States had already felt so severely in the apportionment bill. . . .

But before this miserable force of ten thousand men was raised to take Canada, he begged them to look at the state of defence at home—to count the cost of the enterprise before it was set on foot, not when it might be too late—when the best blood of the country should be spilt, and nought but empty coffers left to pay the cost. Are the bounty lands to be given in Canada? It might lessen his repugnance to that part of the system, to granting these lands, not to those miserable wretches who sell themselves to slavery for a few dollars and a glass of gin, but in fact to the clerks in our offices, some of whom, with an income of fifteen hundred or two thousand dollars, lived at the rate of four or five thousand, and yet grew rich—who perhaps at that moment were making out blank assignments for these land rights.

He would beseech the House, before they ran their heads against this post, Quebec, to count the cost. His word for it, Virginia planters would not be taxed to support such a war—a war which must aggravate their present distresses; in which they had not the remotest interest. Where is the Montgomery, or even the Arnold, or the Burr, who is to march to Point Levi?

He called upon those professing to be Republicans to make good the promises held out by their Republican predecessors when they came into power—promises, which for years afterwards they had honestly, faithfully fulfilled. We had vaunted of paying off the national debt, of retrenching useless establishments; and yet had now become as infatuated with standing armies, loans, taxes, navies, and war, as ever were the Essex Junto. What Republicanism is this?

5. DANIEL WEBSTER

Speech on the Conscription Bill
(1814)

Daniel Webster (1782-1852), the famous Massachusetts statesman and orator, was born in New Hampshire and graduated from Dartmouth College, which
he ably defended in a celebrated legal case before the
Supreme Court. A successful lawyer and popular
patriotic speaker, Webster became the Whig Party
spokesman for a conservative, nationalistic, high-
tariff point of view, critical of both Southern slave-
holders and Northern abolitionists. As a younger man
just entering politics, he joined his fellow New Eng-
landers in opposition to the War of 1812, refusing
to vote war taxes. His speech in the House of Representatives, vigorously attacking President Madison's
proposal for military conscription, was not printed in
the *Annals of Congress* and went unpublished for
almost a century.

After the best reflection which I have been able to bestow on
the subject of the bill before you, I am of [the] opinion that its
principles are not warranted by any provision of the Constitution. . . .

Let us examine the nature and extent of the power, which is
assumed by the various military measures before us. In the present
want of men and money, the Secretary of War has proposed to

Congress a Military Conscription. For the conquest of Canada, the people will not enlist; and if they would, the Treasury is exhausted, and they could not be paid. Conscription is chosen as the most promising instrument, both of overcoming reluctance to the Service, and of subduing the difficulties which arise from the deficiencies of the Exchequer. The administration asserts the right to fill the ranks of the regular army by compulsion. It contends that it may now take one out of every twenty-five men, and any part or the whole of the rest, whenever its occasions require. Persons thus taken by force, and put into an army, may be compelled to serve there, during the war, or for life. They may be put on any service, at home or abroad, for defence or for invasion, according to the will and pleasure of Government. This power does not grow out of any invasion of the country, or even out of a state of war. It belongs to Government at all times, in peace as well as in war, and is to be exercised under all circumstances, according to its mere discretion. This, Sir, is the amount of the principle contended for by the Secretary of War.

Is this, Sir, consistent with the character of a free Government? Is this civil liberty? Is this the real character of our Constitution? No, Sir, indeed it is not. The Constitution is libelled, foully libelled. The people of this country have not established for themselves such a fabric of despotism. They have not purchased at a vast expense of their own treasure and their own blood a Magna Charta to be slaves. Where is it written in the Constitution, in what article or section is it contained, that you may take children from their parents, and parents from their children, and compel them to fight the battles of any war, in which the folly or the wickedness of Government may engage it? Under what conceal-ment has this power lain hidden, which now for the first time comes forth, with a tremendous and baleful aspect, to trample down and destroy the dearest rights of personal liberty? Who will show me any constitutional injunction, which makes it the duty of the American people to surrender every thing valuable in life, and even life itself, not when the safety of their country and its liberties may demand the sacrifice, but whenever the purposes of an ambitious and mischievous Government may require it? . . .

Congress having, by the Constitution a power to raise armies, the Secretary contends that no restraint is to be imposed on the exercise of this power, except such as is expressly stated in the written letter of the instrument. In other words, that Congress may execute its powers, by any means it chooses, unless such means are particularly prohibited. But the general nature and object of the Constitution impose as rigid a restriction on the means of exercising power, as could be done by the most explicit injunctions. It is the first principle applicable to such a case, that no construction shall be admitted which impairs the general nature and character of the instrument. A free constitution of Government is to be construed upon free principles, and every branch of its provisions is to receive such an interpretation as is full of its general spirit. No means are to be taken by implication, which would strike us absurdly, if expressed. And what would have been more absurd, than for this constitution to have said, that to secure the great blessings of liberty it gave to Government an uncontrolled power of military conscription? Yet such is the absurdity which it is made to exhibit, under the commentary of the Secretary of War. . . .

If the Secretary of War has proved the right of Congress to enact a law enforcing a draft of men out of the Militia into the regular army, he will at any time be able to prove, quite as clearly, that Congress has power to create a Dictator. The arguments which have helped him in one case, will equally aid him in the other. The same reason of a supposed or possible state necessity, which is urged now, may be repeated then, with equal pertinency and effect.

Sir, in granting Congress the power to raise armies, the People have granted all the means which are ordinary and usual, and which are consistent with the liberties and security of the People themselves; and they have granted no others. To talk about the unlimited power of the Government over the means to execute its authority, is to hold a language which is true only in regard to despotism. The tyranny of Arbitrary Government consists as much in its means as in its ends; and it would be a ridiculous and absurd constitution which should be less cautious to guard against abuses in the one case than in the other. All the means and instruments which a free Government exercises, as well as the ends and objects which it pursues, are to partake of its own essential character, and to be conformed to its genuine spirit. A free Government with arbitrary means to administer it is a contradiction; a free Government without adequate provision for personal security is an absurdity; a free Government, with an uncontrolled power of military conscription, is a solecism, at once the most ridiculous and abominable that ever entered into the head of man.

Sir, I invite the supporters of the measures before you to look to their actual operation. Let the men who have so often pledged their own fortunes and their own lives to the support of this war, look to the wanton sacrifice which they are about to make of their lives and fortunes. They may talk as they will about substitutes, and compensations, and exemptions. It must come to the draft at last. If the Government cannot hire men voluntarily to fight its battles, neither can individuals. If the war should continue, there will be no escape, and every man's fate, and every man's life will come to depend on the issue of the military draft. Who shall describe to you the horror which your orders of Conscription shall create in the once happy villages of this country? Who shall describe the distress and anguish which they will spread over those hills and valleys, where men have heretofore been accustomed to labor, and to rest in security and happiness. Anticipate the scene, Sir, when the class shall assemble to stand its draft, and to throw the dice for blood. What a group of wives and mothers, and sisters, of helpless age and helpless infancy, shall gather round the theatre of this horrible lottery, as if the stroke of death were to fall from Heaven before their eyes, on a father, a brother, a son or an husband. And in a majority of cases, Sir, it will be the stroke of death. Under present prospects of the continuance of the war, not one half of them on whom your conscription shall fall, will ever return to tell the tale of their sufferings. They will perish of disease and pestilence, or they will leave their bones to whiten in fields beyond the frontier. Does the lot fall on the father of a family? His children, already orphans, shall see his face no more. When they behold him for the last time, they shall see him lashed and fettered, and dragged away from his own threshold, like a felon and an outlaw. Does it fall on a son, the hope and the staff of aged parents? That hope shall fail them. On that staff they shall lean no longer. They shall not enjoy the happiness of dying before their children. They shall totter to their grave, bereft of their offspring, and unwept by any who inherit their blood. Does it fall on a husband? The eyes which watch his parting steps may swim in tears forever. She is a wife no longer. There is no relation so tender or so sacred, that, by these accursed measures, you do not propose to violate it. There is no happiness so perfect, that you do not propose to destroy it. Into the paradise of domestic life you enter, not indeed by temptations and sorceries, but by open force and violence. . . .

Nor is it, Sir, for the defence of his own house and home, that he who is the subject of military draft is to perform the task allotted to him. You will put him upon a service equally foreign to his interests and abhorrent to his feelings. With his aid you are to push your purpose of conquest. The battles which he is to fight are the battles of invasion; battles which he detests perhaps and abhors, less from the danger and the death that gather over them, and the blood with which they drench the plain, than from the principles in which they have their origin. Fresh from the peaceful pursuits of life, and yet a soldier but in name, he is to be opposed to veteran troops hardened under every scene, inured to every privation and disciplined in every service. If, Sir, in this strife he fall—if, while ready to obey every rightful command of Government, he is forced from home against right, not to contend for the defence of his country, but to prosecute a miserable and detestable project of invasion, and in that strife he fall, 'tis murder. It may stalk above the cognizance of human law, but in the sight of Heaven it is murder; and though millions of years may roll away, while his ashes and yours lie mingled together in the earth, the day will yet come, when his spirit and the spirits of his children must be met at the bar of omnipotent justice. May God, in his compassion, shield me from any participation in the enormity of this guilt.

I would ask, Sir, whether the supporters of these measures have well weighed the difficulties of their undertaking. Have they considered whether it will be found easy to execute laws, which bear such marks of despotism on their front, and which will be so productive of every sort and degree of misery in their execution? For one, Sir, I hesitate not to say, that they can not be executed. No law professedly passed for the purpose of compelling a service in the regular army, nor any law, which under color of military draft, shall compel men to serve in the army, not for the emergencies mentioned in the Constitution, but for long periods, and for the general objects of war, can be carried into effect. In my opinion, it ought not to be carried into effect. The operation of measures thus unconstitutional and illegal ought to be prevented, by a resort to other measures which are both constitutional and legal. It will be the solemn duty of the State Governments to protect their own authority over their own Militia, and to interpose between their citizens and arbitrary power. These are among the objects for which the State Governments exist; and their highest obligations bind them to the preservation of their own rights and the liberties of their people. I express these sentiments here, Sir, because I shall express them to my constituents. Both they and myself live under a Constitution which teaches us, that "the doctrine on non-resistance against arbitrary power and oppression, is absurd, slavish, and destructive of the good and happiness of mankind." With the same earnestness with which I now exhort you to forbear from these measures, I shall exhort them to exercise their unquestionable right of providing for the security of their own liberties.

In my opinion, Sir, the sentiments of the free population of this country are greatly mistaken here. The nation is not yet in a temper to submit to conscription. The people have too fresh and strong a feeling of the blessings of civil liberty to be willing thus to surrender it. You may talk to them as much as you please, of the victory and glory to be obtained in the Enemy's Provinces; they will hold those objects in light estimation, if the means be a forced military service. You may sing to them the song of Canada Conquests in all its variety, but they will not be charmed out of the remembrance of their substantial interests, and true happiness. Similar pretences, they know, are the graves in which the liberties of other nations have been buried, and they will take warning.

Laws, Sir, of this nature can create nothing but opposition. If you scatter them abroad, like the fabled serpents' teeth, they will spring up into armed men. A military force cannot be raised, in this manner, but by the means of a military force. If administration has found that it can not form an army without conscription, it will find, if it ventures on these experiments, that it can not enforce conscription without an army. The Government was not constituted for such purposes. Framed in the spirit of liberty, and in the love of peace, it has no powers which render it able to enforce such laws. The attempt, if we rashly make it, will fail; and having already thrown away our peace, we may thereby throw away our Government.

Allusions have been made, Sir, to the state of things in New England, and, as usual, she has been charged with an intention to dissolve the Union. The charge is unfounded. She is much too wise to entertain such purposes. She has had too much experience, and has too strong a recollection of the blessings which the Union is capable of producing under a just administration of Government. It is her greatest fear, that the course at present pursued will destroy it, by destroying every principle, every interest, every sentiment, and every feeling, which have hitherto contributed to uphold it. Those who cry out that the Union is in danger are themselves the authors of that danger. They put its existence to hazard by measures of violence, which it is not capable of enduring. They talk of dangerous designs against Government, when they are overthrowing the fabric from its foundations. They alone, Sir, are friends to the union of the States, who endeavor to maintain the principles of civil liberty in the country, and to preserve the spirit in which the Union was framed.

6. WILLIAM ELLERY CHANNING

On the Annexation of Texas to the United States
(1837)

William Ellery Channing (1780-1842), the leading
Unitarian clergyman of the early nineteenth century,
exercised as much influence through his writings and
public speeches as he did from the pulpit. Ever interested in politics, he was a pioneer opponent of war
and slavery. In an open letter to Henry Clay on the
Texas question in 1837, Channing stigmatized the
agitation for annexation as a false patriotism, fraught
with the danger of war, and motivated by the desire
to extend and perpetuate slavery.

Having thus considered the grievances of the Texans, I now proceed to consider the real and great causes of the revolt. These are
matters of notoriety, so as to need no minute exposition. The first
great cause was the unbounded, unprincipled spirit of land speculation, which so tempting a prize as Texas easily kindled in multitudes in the United States, where this mode of gambling is too
common a vice. Large grants of land in Texas were originally made
to individuals, chiefly citizens of our country, who, in many cases,
transferred their claims to joint-stock companies in some of our
cities. . . .

We have here one explanation of the zeal with which the Texan
cause was embraced in the United States. From this country the

great impulse has been given to the Texan revolution; and a principal motive has been, the unappeasable hunger for Texan land. An interest in that soil, whether real or fictitious, has been spread over our country. Thus "the generous zeal for freedom," which has stirred and armed so many of our citizens to fight for Texas, turns out to be a passion for unrighteous spoil.

I proceed to another cause of the revolt; and this was, the resolution to throw Texas open to slave-holders and slaves. Mexico, at the moment of throwing off the Spanish yoke, gave a noble testimony of her loyalty to free principles, by decreeing, "that no person thereafter should be born a slave or introduced as such into the Mexican States; that all slaves then held should receive stipulated wages, and be subject to no punishment but on trial and judgment by the magistrate." The subsequent acts of the government carried out fully these constitutional provisions. It is matter of deep grief and humiliation, that the emigrants from this country, whilst boasting of superior civilization, refused to second this honorable policy, intended to set limits to one of the greatest social evils. Slaves were brought into Texas with their masters from the neighboring States of this country. One mode of evading the laws was, to introduce slaves under formal indentures for long periods, in some cases it is said for ninety-nine years. By a decree of the State Legislature of Coahuila and Texas, all indentures for a longer period than ten years were annulled, and provision was made for the freedom of children born during this apprenticeship. This settled, invincible purpose of Mexico to exclude slavery from her limits, created as strong a purpose to annihilate her authority in Texas. By this prohibition, Texas was virtually shut against emigration from the Southern and Western portions of this country; and it is well known that the eyes of the South and West had for some time been turned to this province, as a new market for slaves, as a new field for slave labor, and as a vast accession of political power to the slave-holding States. That such views were prevalent, we know; for, nefarious as they are, they found their way into the public prints. The project of dismembering a neighboring republic, that slave-holders and slaves might overspread a region which had been consecrated to a free population, was discussed in newspapers as cooly as if it were a matter of obvious right and unquestionable humanity. A powerful interest was thus created for severing from Mexico her distant province. We have here a powerful incitement to the Texan revolt, and another explanation of the eagerness with which men and money were thrown from the United States into that region to carry on the war of revolution. . . .

It is full time that we should lay on ourselves serious, resolute restraint. Possessed of a domain vast enough for the growth of ages, it is time for us to stop in the career of acquisition and conquest. Already endangered by our greatness, we cannot advance without imminent peril to our institutions, union, prosperity, virtue, and peace. Our former additions of territory have been justified by the necessity of obtaining outlets for the population of the South and West. No such pretext exists for the occupation of Texas. We cannot seize upon or join to ourselves that territory, without manifesting and strengthening the purpose of setting no limits to our empire. We give ourselves an impulse, which will and must precipitate us into new invasions of our neighbors' soil. Is it by pressing forward in this course that we are to learn self-restraint? Is cupidity to be appeased by gratification? Is it by unrighteous grasping that an impatient people will be instructed how to hem themselves within the rigid bounds of justice?

Texas is a country conquered by our citizens; and the annexation of it to our Union will be the beginning of conquests which, unless arrested and beaten back by a just and kind Providence, will stop only at the Isthmus of Darien. Henceforth, we must cease to cry, Peace, peace. Our Eagle will whet, not gorge, its appetite on its first victim; and will snuff a more tempting quarry, more alluring blood, in every new region which opens southward. To annex Texas is to declare perpetual war with Mexico. That word, *Mexico,* associated in men's minds with boundless wealth, has already awakened rapacity. Already it has been proclaimed that the Anglo-Saxon race is destined to the sway of this magnificent realm, that the rude form of society which Spain established there is to yield and vanish before a higher civilization. Without this exposure of plans of rapine and subjugation, the result, as far as our will can determine it, is plain. Texas is the first step to Mexico. . . .

Have we counted the cost of establishing and making perpetual these hostile relations with Mexico? Will wars, begun in rapacity, carried on so far from the centre of confederation, and, of consequence, little checked or controlled by Congress, add strength to our institutions, or cement our union, or exert a healthy moral influence on rulers or people? What limits can be set to the atrocities of such conflicts? What limits to the treasures which must be lavished on such distant borders? What limits to the patronage and power which such distant expeditions must accumulate in the hands of the Executive? Are the blood and hard-earned wealth of the older States to be poured out like water to protect and revenge a new people, whose character and condition will plunge them into perpetual wrongs?

Is the time never to come when the neighborhood of a more powerful and civilized people will prove a blessing, instead of a curse, to an inferior community? It was my hope, when the Spanish colonies of this continent separated themselves from the mother country, and, in admiration of the United States, adopted republican institutions, that they were to find in us friends to their freedom, helpers to their civilization. If ever a people were placed by Providence in a condition to do good to a neighboring state, we of this country sustained such a relation to Mexico. That nation, inferior in science, arts, agriculture, and legislation, looked to us with a generous trust. She opened her ports and territories to our farmers, mechanics, and merchants. We might have conquered her by the only honorable arms—by the force of superior intelligence, industry, and morality. We might silently have poured in upon her our improvements, and by the infusion of our population have assimilated her to ourselves. Justice, good-will, and profitable intercourse might have cemented a lasting friendship. And what is now the case? A deadly hatred burns in Mexico towards this country. No stronger national sentiment now binds her scattered provinces together than dread and detestation of republican America. She is ready to attach herself to Europe for defence from the United States. All the moral power which we might have gained over Mexico we have thrown away; and suspicion, dread, and abhorrence have supplanted respect and trust.

I am aware that these remarks are met by a vicious reasoning, which discredits a people among whom it finds favor. It is some-times said that nations are swayed by laws as unfailing as those which govern matter; that they have their destinies; that their character and position carry them forward irresistibly to their goal; that the stationary Turk must sink under the progressive civilization of Russia, as inevitably as the crumbling edifice falls to the earth; that, by a like necessity, the Indians have melted before the white man, and the mixed, degraded race of Mexico must melt before the Anglo-Saxon. Away with this vile sophistry! There is no necessity for crime. There is no fate to justify rapacious nations, any more than to justify gamblers and robbers in plunder. We boast of the progress of society, and this progress consists in the substitution of reason and moral principle for the sway of brute force. It is true that more civilized must always exert a great power over less civilized communities in their neighborhood. But it may and should be a power to enlighten and improve, not to crush and destroy. We talk of accomplishing our destiny. So did the late conqueror of Europe; and destiny consigned him to a lonely rock in the ocean, the prey of an ambition which destroyed no peace but his own.

Hitherto I have spoken of the annexation of Texas as embroiling us with Mexico; but it will not stop here. It will bring us into collision with other states. It will, almost of necessity, involve us in hostility with European powers. Such are now the connections of nations, that Europe must look with jealousy on a country whose ambition, seconded by vast resources, will seem to place within her grasp the empire of the New World. And not only general considerations of this nature, but the particular relation of certain foreign states to this continent, must tend to destroy the peace now happily subsisted between us and the kingdoms of Europe. . . .

It is of great and manifest importance that we should use every just means to separate this continent from the politics of Europe, that we should prevent, as far as possible, all connection, except commercial, between the Old and the New World, that we should give to foreign states no occasion or pretext for insinuating themselves into our affairs. For this end, we should maintain towards our sister republics a more liberal policy than was ever adopted by nation towards nation. We should strive to appease their internal divisions, and to reconcile them to each other. We should even make sacrifices to build up their strength. Weak and divided, they cannot but lean upon foreign support. No pains should be spared to prevent or allay the jealousies which the great superiority of this country is suited to awaken. By an opposite policy we shall favor foreign interference. By encroaching on Mexico we shall throw her into the arms of European states, shall compel her to seek defense in transatlantic alliance. How plain is it, that alliance with Mexico will be hostility to the United States, that her defenders will repay themselves by making her subservient to their views, that they will monopolize her trade, and control her resources. And with what face can we resist the aggressions of others on our neighbor, if we give an example of aggression? Still more, if by our advances we put the colonies of England in new peril, with what face can we oppose her occupation of Cuba? Suppose her, with that magnificent island in her hands, to command the Mexican Gulf and the mouths of the Mississippi; will the Western States find compensation for this formidable neighborhood in the privilege of flooding Texas with slaves?

Thus, wars with Europe and Mexico are to be entailed on us by the annexation of Texas. And is war the policy by which this country is to flourish? Was it for interminable conflicts that we formed our Union? Is it blood, shed for plunder, which is to consolidate our institutions? Is it by collision with the greatest maritime power that our commerce is to gain strength? Is it by arming against ourselves the moral sentiments of the world that we are to build up national honor? Must we of the North buckle on our armor to fight the battle of slavery; to fight for a possession which our moral principles and just jealousy forbid us to incorporate with our confederacy? In attaching Texas to ourselves, we provoke hostilities, and at the same time expose new points of attack to our foes. Vulnerable at so many points, we shall need a vast military force. Great armies will require great revenues, and raise up great chieftains. Are we tired of freedom, that we are prepared to place it under such guardians? Is the republic bent on dying by its own hands? Does not every man feel that, with war our habit, our institutions cannot be preserved? If ever a country were bound to peace, it is this. Peace is our great interest. In peace our resources are to be developed, the true interpretation of the Constitution to be established, and the interfering claims of liberty and order to be adjusted. In peace we are to discharge our great debt to the human race, and to diffuse freedom by manifesting its fruits. A country has no right to adopt a policy, however gainful, which, as it may foresee, will determine it to a career of war. A nation, like an individual, is bound to seek, even by sacrifices, a position which will favor peace, justice, and the exercise of a beneficent influence on the world. A nation provoking war by cupidity, by encroachment, and, above all, by efforts to propagate the curse of slavery, is alike false to itself, to God, and to the human race. . . .

By this act, slavery will be spread over regions to which it is now impossible to set limits. Texas, I repeat it, is but the first step of aggressions. I trust, indeed, that Providence will beat back and humble our cupidity and ambition. But one guilty success is often suffered to be crowned, as men call it, with greater, in order that a more awful retribution may at length vindicate the justice of God, and the rights of the oppressed. Texas, smitten with slavery, will spread the infection beyond herself. We know that the tropical regions have been found most propitious to this pestilence; nor can we promise ourselves that its expulsion from them for a season forbids its return. By annexing Texas, we may send this scourge to a distance, which, if now revealed, would appall us, and through these vast regions every cry of the injured will invoke wrath on our heads.

By this act, slavery will be perpetuated in the old States, as well as spread over new. It is well known that the soil of some of the old States has become exhausted by slave cultivation. Their neighborhood to communities which are flourishing under free labor forces on them perpetual arguments for adopting this better system. They now adhere to slavery, not on account of the wealth which it extracts from the soil, but because it furnishes men and women to be sold in newly settled and more southern districts. It is by slave-breeding and slave-selling that these States subsist. Take away from them a foreign market, and slavery would die. Of consequence, by opening a new market, it is prolonged and invigorated. By annexing Texas, we shall not only create it where it does not exist, but breathe new life into it, where its end seemed to be near. States, which might and ought to throw it off, will make the multiplication of slaves their great aim and chief resource.

Nor is the worst told. As I have before intimated—and it cannot be too often repeated—we shall not only quicken the domestic slave-trade, we shall give a new impulse to the foreign. This, indeed, we have pronounced in our laws to be felony; but we make our laws cobwebs, when we offer to rapacious men strong motives for their violation. Open a market for slaves in an unsettled country, with a sweep of sea-coast, and at such a distance from the seat of government that laws may be evaded with impunity, and how can you exclude slaves from Africa? It is well known that cargoes have been landed in Louisiana. What is to drive them from Texas? In incorporating this region with the Union to make it a slave country, we send the kidnapper to prowl through the jungles, and to dart, like a beast of prey, on the defenceless villages of Africa; we chain the helpless, despairing victims; crowd them into the fetid, pestilential slave-ship; expose them to the unutterable cruelties of the middle passage, and, if they survive it, crush them with perpetual bondage.

I now ask whether, as a people, we are prepared to seize a neighboring territory for the end of extending slavery? I ask whether, as a people, we can stand forth in the sight of God, in the sight of the nations, and adopt this atrocious policy? Sooner perish! Sooner be our name blotted out from the record of nations! . . .

7. ORESTES A. BROWNSON

The Laboring Classes
(1840)

Orestes A. Brownson (1803-1876) was a radical reformer and associate of the New England transcendentalists. An early follower of Robert Owen's Utopian Socialism, he also sought spiritual refuge in a
variety of religious denominations, finally establishing
his own church in Boston in 1836. Two years later
he founded the *Boston Quarterly Review.* During
the 1830's Brownson was an enthusiastic supporter
of Jacksonian Democracy and of the cause of the
working-man. But, disillusioned by the Whig triumph
of 1840, he became progressively more conservative,
supporting Calhoun for President and joining the
Catholic Church in 1844.

In regard to labor two systems obtain; one that of slave labor, the
other that of free labor. Of the two the first is, in our judgment,
except so far as the feelings are concerned, decidedly the least oppressive. If the slave has never been a free man, we think, as a
general rule, his sufferings are less than those of the free laborer
at wages. As to actual freedom one has just about as much as the
other. The laborer at wages has all the disadvantages of freedom
and none of its blessings, while the slave, if denied the blessings,
is freed from the disadvantages. We are no advocates of slavery,
we are as heartily opposed to it as any modern abolitionist can be;

but we say frankly that, if there must always be a laboring population distinct from proprietors and employers, we regard the slave
system as decidedly preferable to the system at wages. It is no
pleasant thing to go days without food, to lie idle for weeks, seeking work and finding none, to rise in the morning with a wife and
children you love, and know not where to procure them a
breakfast, and to see constantly before you no brighter prospect
than the alms-house. Yet these are no unfrequent incidents in the
lives of our laboring population. Even in seasons of general prosperity, when there was only the ordinary cry of "hard times," we
have seen hundreds of people in a not very populous village, in a
wealthy portion of our common country, suffering for the want of
the necessaries of life, willing to work, and yet finding no work
to do. Many and many is the application of a poor man for work,
merely for his food, we have seen rejected. These things are little
thought of, for the applicants are poor; they fill no conspicuous
place in society, and they have no biographers. But their wrongs
are chronicled in heaven. It is said there is no want in this country.
There may be less than in some other countries. But death by
actual starvation in this country is, we apprehend, no uncommon
occurrence. The sufferings of a quiet, unassuming but useful class
of females in our cities, in general sempstresses, too proud to beg
or to apply to the alms-house, are not easily told. They are industrious; they do all that they can find to do; but yet the little there
is for them to do, and the miserable pittance they receive for it, is
hardly sufficient to keep soul and body together. And yet there
is a man who employs them to make shirts, trousers, &c., and
grows rich on their labors. He is one of our respectable citizens,
perhaps is praised in the newspapers for his liberal donations to
some charitable institution. He passes among us as a pattern of
morality, and is honored as a worthy Christian. And why should
he not be, since our *Christian* community is made up of such as he,

and since our clergy would not dare question his piety, lest they should incur the reproach of infidelity, and lose their standing, and their salaries? Nay, since our clergy are raised up, educated, fashioned, and sustained by such as he? Not a few of our churches rest on Mammon for their foundation. The basement is a trader's shop.

We pass through our manufacturing villages, most of them appear neat and flourishing. The operatives are well dressed, and we are told, well paid. They are said to be healthy, contented, and happy. This is the fair side of the picture; the side exhibited to distinguished visitors. There is a dark side, moral as well as physical. Of the common operatives, few, if any, by their wages, acquire a competence. A few of what Carlyle terms not inaptly the *body-servants* are well paid, and now and then an agent or an overseer rides in his coach. But the great mass wear out their health, spirits, and morals, without becoming one whit better off than when they commenced labor. The bills of mortality in these factory villages are not striking, we admit, for the poor girls when they can toil no longer go home to die. The average life, working life we mean, of the girls that come to Lowell, for instance, from Maine, New Hampshire, and Vermont, we have been assured, is only about three years. What becomes of them then? Few of them ever marry; fewer still ever return to their native places with reputations unimpaired. "She has worked in a Factory," is almost enough to damn to infamy the most worthy and virtuous girl. We know no sadder sight on earth than one of our factory villages presents, when the bell at break of day, or at the hour of breakfast, or dinner, calls out its hundreds or thousands of operatives. We stand and look at these hard working men and women hurrying in all directions and ask ourselves, where go the proceeds of their labors? The man who employs them, and for whom they are toiling as so many slaves, is one of our city nabobs, revelling in luxury; or he is a member of our legislature, enacting laws to put money in his own pocket; or he is a member of Congress, contending for a high Tariff to tax the poor for the benefit of the rich; or in these times he is shedding crocodile tears over the deplorable condition of the poor laborer, while he docks his wages twenty-five per cent.; building miniature log cabins, shouting Harrison and "hard cider." And this man too would fain pass for a Christian and a republican. He shouts for liberty, stickles for equality, and is horrified at a Southern planter who keeps slaves.

One thing is certain; that of the amount actually produced by the operative, he retains a less proportion than it costs the master to feed, clothe, and lodge his slave. Wages is a cunning device of the devil, for the benefit of tender consciences, who would retain all the advantages of the slave system, without the expense, trouble, and odium of being slave-holders.

Messrs. Thome and Kimball, in their account of emancipation in the West Indies, establish the fact that the employer may have the same amount of labor done, twenty-five per cent. cheaper than the master. What does this fact prove, if not that wages is a more successful method of taxing labor than slavery? We really believe our Northern system of labor is more oppressive, and even more mischievous to morals, than the Southern. We, however, war against both. We have no toleration for either system. We would see the slave a man, but a free man, not a mere operative at wages. This he would not be were he now emancipated. Could the abolitionists effect all they propose, they would do the slave no service. Should emancipation work as well as they say, still it would do the slave no good. He would be a slave still, although with the title and cares of a freeman. If then we had no constitutional objections to abolitionism, we could not, for the reason here implied, be abolitionists.

The slave system, however, in name and form, is gradually disappearing from Christendom. It will not subsist much longer. But its place is taken by the system of labor at wages, and this system, we hold, is no improvement upon the one it supplants. Nevertheless the system of wages will triumph. It is the system which in name sounds honester than slavery, and in substance is more profitable to the master. It yields the wages of iniquity, without its opprobrium. It will therefore supplant slavery, and be sustained—for a time.

Now, what is the prospect of those who fall under the operation of this system? We ask, is there a reasonable chance that any considerable portion of the present generation of laborers, shall ever become owners of a sufficient portion of the funds of production, to be able to sustain themselves by laboring on their own capital, that is, as independent laborers? We need not ask this question, for everybody knows there is not. Well, is the condition of a laborer at wages the best that the great mass of the working-people ought to be able to aspire to? Is it a condition—nay can it be made a condition—with which a man should be satisfied; in which he should be contented to live and die?

In our own country this condition has existed under its most favorable aspects, and has been made as good as it can be. It has reached all the excellence of which it is susceptible. It is now not improving but growing worse. The actual condition of the working-man today, viewed in all its bearings, is not so good as it was fifty years ago. If we have not been altogether misinformed, fifty years ago, health and industrious habits, constituted no mean stock in trade, and with them almost any man might aspire to competence and independence. But it is so no longer. The wilderness has receded, and already the new lands are beyond the reach of the mere laborer, and the employer has him at his mercy. If the present relation subsist, we see nothing better for him in reserve than what he now possesses, but something altogether worse.

We are not ignorant of the fact that men born poor become wealthy, and that men born to wealth become poor; but this fact does not necessarily diminish the numbers of the poor, nor augment the numbers of the rich. The relative numbers of the two classes remain, or may remain, the same. But be this as it may; one fact is certain, no man born poor has ever, by his wages, as a simple operative, risen to the class of the wealthy. Rich he may have become, but it has not been by his own manual labor. He has in some way contrived to tax for his benefit the labor of others. He may have accumulated a few dollars which he has placed at usury, or invested in trade; or he may, as a master work-man, obtain a premium on his journeymen; or he may have from a clerk passed to a partner, or from a workman to an overseer. The simple market wages for ordinary labor, has never been adequate to raise him from poverty to wealth. This fact is decisive of the whole controversy, and proves that the system of wages must be supplanted by some other system, or else one half of the human race must forever be the virtual slaves of the other.

Now the great work for this age and the coming, is to raise up the laborer, and to realize in our own social arrangements and in the actual condition of all men, that equality between man and man, which God has established between the rights of one and those of another. In other words, our business is to emancipate the proletaries, as the past has emancipated the slaves. This is our work. There must be no class of our fellow men doomed to toil through life as mere workmen at wages. If wages are tolerated it must be, in the case of the individual operative, only under such conditions that by the time he is of a proper age to settle in life, he shall have accumulated enough to be an independent laborer on his own capital—on his own farm or in his own shop. Here is our work. How is it to be done?

Reformers in general answer this question, or what they deem its equivalent, in a manner which we cannot but regard as very unsatisfactory. They would have all men wise, good, and happy; but in order to make them so, they tell us that we want not external changes, but internal; and therefore instead of declaiming against society and seeking to disturb existing social arrangements, we should confine ourselves to the individual reason and conscience; seek merely to lead the individual to repentance, and to reformation of life; make the individual a practical, a truly religious man, and all evils will either disappear, or be sanctified to the spiritual growth of the soul.

This is doubtless a capital theory, and has the advantage that kings, hierarchies, nobilities—in a word, all who fatten on the toil and blood of their fellows—will feel no difficulty in supporting it. Nicholas of Russia, the Grand Turk, his Holiness the Pope, will hold us their especial friends for advocating a theory, which secures to them the odor of sanctity even while they are sustaining by their anathemas or their armed legions, a system of things of which the great mass are and must be the victims. If you will only allow me to keep thousands toiling for my pleasure or my profit, I will even aid you in your pious efforts to convert their souls. I am not cruel; I do not wish either to cause, or to see suffering; I am therefore disposed to encourage your labors for the souls of the working-man, providing you will secure to me the products of his bodily toil. So far as the salvation of his soul will not interfere with my income, I hold it worthy of being sought; and if a few thousand dollars will aid you, Mr. Priest, in reconciling him to God, and making fair weather for him hereafter, they are at your service. I shall not want him to work for me in the world to come, and I can indemnify myself for what your salary costs me, by paying him less wages. A capital theory this, which one may advocate without incurring the reproach of a disorganizer, a Jacobin, a leveller, and without losing the friendship of the rankest aristocrat in the land.

This theory, however, is exposed to one slight objection, that of being condemned by something like six thousand years' experience. For six thousand years its beauty has been extolled, its praises sung, and its blessings sought, under every advantage which learning, fashion, wealth, and power can secure; and yet under its practical operations, we are assured, that mankind, though totally depraved at first, have been growing worse and worse ever since.

For our part, we yield to none in our reverence for science and religion; but we confess that we look not for the regeneration of the race from priests and pedagogues. They have had a fair trial. They cannot construct the temple of God. They cannot conceive its plan, and they know not how to build. They daub with untempered mortar, and the walls they erect tumble down if so much as a fox attempt to go up thereon. In a word they always league with the people's masters, and seek to reform without disturbing the social arrangements which render reform necessary. They would change the consequents without changing the antecedents, secure to men the rewards of holiness, while they continue their allegiance to the devil. We have no faith in priests and pedagogues. They merely cry peace, peace, and that too when there is no peace, and can be none.

We admit the importance of what Dr. Channing in his lectures on the subject we are treating recommends as "self-culture." Self-culture is a good thing, but it cannot abolish inequality, nor restore men to their rights. As a means of quickening moral and intellectual energy, exalting the sentiments, and preparing the laborer to contend manfully for his rights, we admit its importance, and insist as strenuously as any one on making it as universal as possible; but as constituting in itself a remedy for the vices of the social state, we have no faith in it. As a means it is well, as the end it is nothing.

The truth is, the evil we have pointed out is not merely individual in its character. It is not, in the case of any single indi-

vidual, of any one man's procuring, nor can the efforts of any
one man, directed solely to his own moral and religious perfection,
do aught to remove it. What is purely individual in its nature,
efforts of individuals to perfect themselves, may remove. But the
evil we speak of is inherent in all our social arrangements, and
cannot be cured without a radical change of those arrangements.
Could we convert all men to Christianity in both theory and
practice, as held by the most enlightened sect of Christians among
us, the evils of our social state would remain untouched. Continue
our present system of trade, and all its present evil consequences
will follow, whether it be carried on by your best men or your
worst. Put your best men, your wisest, most moral, and most
religious men, at the head of your paper money banks, and the
evils of the present banking system will remain scarcely diminished.
The only way to get rid of its evils is to change the system, not
its managers. The evils of slavery do not result from the personal
characters of slave masters. They are inseparable from the system,
let who will be masters. . . .

Under the influence of the Church, our efforts are not directed
to the reorganization of society, to the introduction of equality
between man and man, to the removal of the corruptions of the
rich, and the wretchedness of the poor. We think only of saving
our own souls, as if a man must not put himself so out of the
case, as to be willing to be damned before he can be saved. Paul
was willing to be accursed from Christ, to save his brethren from
the vengeance which hung over them. But nevertheless we think
only of saving our own souls; or if perchance our benevolence is
awakened, and we think it desirable to labor for the salvation of
others, it is merely to save them from imaginary sins and the
tortures of an imaginary hell. The redemption of the world is
understood to mean simply the restoration of mankind to the favor
of God in the world to come. Their redemption from the evils of

inequality, of factitious distinctions, and iniquitous social institutions, counts for nothing in the eyes of the Church. And this is its condemnation.

We cannot proceed a single step, with the least safety, in the great work of elevating the laboring classes, without the exaltation of sentiment, the generous sympathy and the moral courage which Christianity alone is fitted to produce or quicken. But it is lamentable to see how, by means of the mistakes of the Church, the moral courage, the generous sympathy, the exaltation of sentiment, Christianity does actually produce or quicken, is perverted, and made efficient only in producing evil, or hindering the growth of good. Here is wherefore it is necessary on the one hand to condemn in the most pointed terms the Christianity of the Church, and to bring out on the other hand in all its clearness, brilliancy, and glory the Christianity of Christ.

Having, by breaking down the power of the priesthood and the Christianity of the priests, obtained an open field and freedom for our operations, and by preaching the true Gospel of Jesus, directed all minds to the great social reform needed, and quickened in all souls the moral power to live for it or to die for it; our next resort must be to government, to legislative enactments. Government is instituted to be the agent of society, or more properly the organ through which society may perform its legitimate functions. It is not the master of society; its business is not to control society, but to be the organ through which society effects its will. Society has never to petition government; government is its servant, and subject to its commands.

Now the evils of which we have complained are of a social nature. That is, they have their root in the constitution of society as it is, and they have attained to their present growth by means of social influences, the action of government, of laws, and of systems and institutions upheld by society, and of which individuals are the slaves. This being the case, it is evident that they are to be removed only by the action of society, that is, by government, for the action of society is government.

But what shall government do? Its first doing must be an *un*doing. There has been thus far quite too much government, as well as government of the wrong kind. The first act of government we want, is a still further limitation of itself. It must begin by circumscribing within narrower limits its powers. And then it must proceed to repeal all laws which bear against the laboring classes, and then to enact such laws as are necessary to enable them to maintain their equality. We have no faith in those systems of elevating the working classes, which propose to elevate them without calling in the aid of the government. We must have government, and legislation expressly directed to this end.

But again what legislation do we want so far as this country is concerned? We want first the legislation which shall free the government, whether State or Federal, from the control of the Banks. The Banks represent the interest of the employer, and therefore of necessity interests adverse to those of the employed; that is, they represent the interests of the business community in opposition to the laboring community. So long as the government remains under the control of the Banks, so long it must be in the hands of the natural enemies of the laboring classes, and may be made, nay, will be made, an instrument of depressing them yet lower. It is obvious then that, if our object be the elevation of the laboring classes, we must destroy the power of the Banks over the government, and place the government in the hands of the laboring classes themselves, or in the hands of those, if such there be, who have an identity of interest with them. But this cannot be done so long as the Banks exist. Such is the subtle influence of credit, and such the power of capital, that a banking system like ours, if sustained, necessarily and inevitably becomes the real and efficient government of the country. We have been struggling for ten years in this country against the power of the Banks, struggling to free merely the Federal government from their grasp, but with humiliating success. At this moment, the contest is almost doubtful—not indeed in our mind, but in the minds of a no small portion of our countrymen. The partisans of the Banks count on certain victory. The Banks discount freely to build "log cabins," to purchase "hard cider," and to defray the expense of manufacturing enthusiasm for a cause which is at war with the interests of the people. That they will succeed, we do not for one moment believe; but that they could maintain the struggle so long, and be as strong as they now are, at the end of ten years' constant hostility, proves but all too well the power of the Banks, and their fatal influence on the political action of the community. The present character, standing, and resources of the Bank party, prove to a demonstration that the Banks must be destroyed, or the laborer not elevated. Uncompromising hostility to the whole banking system should therefore be the motto of every working-man, and of every friend of Humanity. The system must be destroyed. On this point there must be no misgiving, no subterfuge, no palliation. The system is at war with the rights and interest of labor, and it must go. Every friend of the system must be marked as an enemy to his race, to his country, and especially to the laborer. No matter who he is, in what party he is found, or what name he bears, he is, in our judgment, no true democrat, as he can be no true Christian.

Following the destruction of the Banks, must come that of all monopolies, of all PRIVILEGE. There are many of these. We cannot specify them all; we therefore select only one, the greatest of them all, the privilege which some have of being born rich while others are born poor. It will be seen at once that we allude to the hereditary descent of property, an anomaly in our American system, which must be removed, or the system itself will be destroyed. We cannot now go into a discussion of this subject, but we promise to resume it at our earliest opportunity. We only say now, that as we have abolished hereditary monarchy and hereditary nobility, we must complete the work by abolishing hereditary property. A man shall have all he honestly acquires, so long as he himself belongs to the world in which he acquires it. But his power over his property must cease with his life, and his property must then become the property of the state, to be disposed of by some equitable law for the use of the generation which takes his place. Here is the principle without any of its details, and this is the grand legislative measure to which we look forward. We see no means of elevating the laboring classes which can be effectual without this. And is this a measure to be easily carried? Not at all. It will cost infinitely more than it cost to abolish either hereditary monarchy or hereditary nobility. It is a great measure, and a startling one. The rich, the business community, will never voluntarily consent to it, and we think we know too much of human nature to believe that it will ever be effected peaceably. It will be effected only by the strong arm of physical force. It will come, if it ever come at all, only at the conclusion of war, the like of which the world as yet has never witnessed, and from which, however inevitable it may seem to the eye of philosophy, the heart of Humanity recoils with horror.

We are not ready for this measure yet. There is much previous work to be done, and we should be the last to bring it before the legislature. The time, however, has come for its free and full discussion. It must be canvassed in the public mind, and society prepared for acting on it. No doubt they who broach it, and especially they who support it, will experience a due share of contumely and abuse. They will be regarded by the part of the community they oppose, or may be thought to oppose, as "graceless varlets," against whom every man of substance should set his face. But this is not, after all, a thing to disturb a wise man, nor to deter a true man from telling his whole thought. He who is worthy of the name of man, speaks what he honestly believes the interests of his race demand, and seldom disquiets himself about what may be the consequences to himself. Men have, for what they believed the cause of God or man, endured the dungeon, the scaffold, the stake, the cross, and they can do it again, if need be. This subject must be freely, boldly, and fully discussed, whatever may be the fate of those who discuss it.

8. WILLIAM LLOYD GARRISON

No Compromise with Slavery
(*c.* 1840)

William Lloyd Garrison (1805-1879) was one of the
first reformers to demand the immediate abolition of
slavery. In the *Liberator,* which he founded in 1831,
Garrison wrote: "I am in earnest—I will not equivo-
cate—I will not excuse—I will not retreat a single
inch—and *I will be heard.*" Though he antagonized
the more moderate antislavery spokesmen who preferred to work through the established churches and
political parties, his fiery speeches helped to arouse
the conscience of the nation in regard to slavery and
to draw young men and women into the abolitionist
crusade.

Cost what it may, every slave on the American soil must be
liberated from his chains. Nothing is to be put in competition, on
the score of value, with the price of his liberty; for whatever conflicts with the rights of man must be evil, and therefore intrinsically worthless. Are we to be intimidated from defending his
cause by the fear of consequences? Is it, then, safe to do wrong?
Has a just God so ordered it, that the strong may oppress the
weak, the rich defraud the poor, the merciless torture the innocent,
not only without guilt, but with benefit to mankind? Is there no
similitude between the seed that is sown, and the harvest which
it brings forth? Have cause and effect ceased to retain an indis-

soluble connection with each other? On such a plea, what crime may not be committed with impunity? what deed of villainy may not demand exemption from rebuke? what system of depravity may not claim protection against the assaults of virtue?

Let not those who say, that the path of obedience is a dangerous one, claim to believe in the living and true God. They deny his omniscience, omnipresence, omnipotence. It is his will, that the bands of wickedness should be loosed, the heavy burdens of tyranny undone, the oppressed set free. They reject it as absurd, impracticable, dangerous. It is his promise, that the results of emancipation shall be noon-day light for darkness, health for disease, fertility for barrenness, prosperity like a spring of water whose waters fail not, the building up of old waste places, the restoring of paths to dwell in, the glory of the Lord for a reward, and his guidance continually! They affirm, that the promise is worthless, and to disregard it is a duty. They exalt the Spirit of Evil above all that is called God, and raise an Ephesian clamor against those who will not fall down and worship it. Yet they put on the garb of religion; they extol faith, hope, charity; they build and dedicate temples of worship, in the name of Christ; they profess to be the disciples of Him who came to proclaim liberty to the captives, and the opening of the prison to them that are bound. Unblushing hypocrites! think not, by your pious dissembling, to hide your iniquity from the pure in heart, or to "circumvent God"! Impious contemners of Divine wisdom and goodness! from your companionship, the spirits of the free shrink with horror!

For more than two centuries, slavery has polluted the American soil. It has grown with the growth, and strengthened with the strength of the Republic. Its victims have multiplied, from a single cargo of stolen Africans, to three millions of native-born inhabitants. In our colonial state, it was deemed compatible with loyalty to the mother country. In our revolutionary struggle for independence, it exchanged the sceptre of monarchy for the star-spangled banner of republicanism, under the folds of which it has found ample encouragement and protection. From the days of the Puritans down to the present time, it has been sanctified by the religion, and upheld by the patriotism of the nation. From the adoption of the American Constitution, it has declared war and made peace, instituted and destroyed national banks and tariffs, controlled the army and navy, prescribed the policy of the government, ruled in both Houses of Congress, occupied the Presidential chair, governed the political parties, distributed offices of trust and emolument among its worshippers, fettered Northern industry and enterprise, and trampled liberty of speech and of conscience in the dust.

It has exercised absolute mastery over the American Church. In her skirts is found "the blood of the souls of the poor innocents." With the Bible in their hands, her priesthood have attempted to prove that slavery came down from God out of Heaven. They have become slave-owners and dealers in human flesh. They have justified robbery, adultery, barbarity, man-stealing and murder, on a frightful scale. They have been among the foremost to crush the sacred cause of emancipation, to cover its advocates with infamy, to oppose the purification of the Church. They have become possessors of the flock, whom they slay, "and hold themselves not guilty; and they that sell them say, Blessed be the Lord, for I am rich: and their own shepherds pity them not."

If slavery be thus entwined around the civil, social, and pecuniary interests of the Republic—if the religious sects and political parties are banded together for its safety from internal revolt and external opposition—if the people, awed by its power and corrupted by its influence, are basely bending their knees at its footstool—is it wonderful that Church and State are shaken to their foundations by the rallying cry of Liberty, "To the rescue!" in behalf of imbruted humanity? Or should it be accounted marvellous, that they who have sternly resolved to effect the utter overthrow of this frightful usurpation are subjected to persecution, reproach, loss of character, and the hazard of life? Constituting the "forlorn hope" in the struggling cause of freedom, they must be prepared to meet all the vicissitudes of the conflict, and to make whatever sacrifices may be needed to achieve the victory. Hereafter, when the song of jubilee shall be sung by those for whose deliverance they toiled so devotedly, their deeds and their memories shall be covered with a halo of glory, and held in grateful remembrance by enfranchised millions.

Slavery must be overthrown. No matter how numerous the difficulties, how formidable the obstacles, how strong the foes to be vanquished—slavery must cease to pollute the land. No matter, whether the event be near or remote, whether the task-master willingly or unwillingly relinquish his arbitrary power, whether by a peaceful or a bloody process—slavery must die. No matter, though, to effect it, every party should be torn by dissensions, every sect dashed into fragments, the national compact dissolved, the land filled with the horrors of a civil and a servile war—still, slavery must be buried in the grave of infamy, beyond the possibility of a resurrection. If the State cannot survive the anti-slavery agitation, then let the State perish. If the Church must be cast down by the strugglings of Humanity to be free, then let the Church fall, and its fragments be scattered to the four winds of heaven, never more to curse the earth. If the American Union cannot be maintained, except by immolating human freedom on the altar of tyranny, then let the American Union be consumed by a living thunderbolt, and no tear be shed over its ashes. If the Republic must be blotted out from the roll of nations, by proclaiming liberty to the captives, then let the Republic sink beneath the waves of oblivion, and a shout of joy, louder than the voice of many waters, fill the universe at its extinction.

Against this declaration, none but traitors and tyrants will raise an outcry. It is the mandate of Heaven, and the voice of God. It has righteousness for its foundation, reason for its authority, and truth for its support. It is not vindictive but merciful, not violent but pacific, not destructive but preservative. It is simply asserting the supremacy of right over wrong, of liberty over slavery, of God over man. It is only raising the standard of rectitude from the dust, and placing it on the eternal throne.

The Party or Sect that will suffer by the triumph of justice cannot exist with safety to mankind. The State that cannot tolerate universal freedom must be despotic; and no valid reason can be given why despotism should not at once be hurled to the dust. The Church that is endangered by the proclamation of eternal truth, and that trades in slaves and souls of men, is "the habitation of devils, and the hold of every foul spirit, and a cage of every unclean and hateful bird; therefore shall her plagues come in one day, death, and mourning, and famine; and she shall be utterly burned with fire; for strong is the Lord God who judgeth her." The Union that can be perpetuated only by enslaving a portion of the people is "a covenant with death, and an agreement with hell," and destined to be broken in pieces as a potter's vessel. When judgment is laid to the line, and righteousness to the plummet, the hail shall sweep away the refuge of lies, and the waters shall overflow the hiding-place. The Republic that depends for its stability on making war against the government of God and the rights of man, though it exalt itself as the eagle, and set its nest among the stars, shall be cast into the bottomless deep, and the loss of it shall be a gain to the world.

There must be no compromise with slavery—none whatever. Nothing is gained, every thing is lost, by subordinating principle to expediency. The spirit of freedom must be inexorable in its demand for the instant release of all who are sighing in bondage, nor abate one jot or tittle of its righteous claims. By one remorseless grasp, the rights of humanity have been taken away; and by one strong blow, the iron hand of usurpation must be made to relinquish its hold. The apologist for oppression becomes himself the oppressor. To palliate crime is to be guilty of its perpetration. To ask for a postponement of the case, till a more convenient season, is to call for a suspension of the moral law, and to assume that it is right to do wrong, under present circumstances. Talk not of other questions to be settled, of other interests to be secured, of other objects to be attained before the slave can have his fetters broken. Nothing can take precedence of the question of liberty. No interest is so momentous as that which involves "the life of the soul"; no object so glorious as the restoration of a man to himself. It is idle to talk of human concerns, where there are not human beings. Slavery annihilates manhood, and puts down in its crimson ledger as chattels personal, those who are created in the image of God. Hence, it tramples under foot whatever pertains to human safety, human prosperity, human happiness. Hence, too, its overthrow is the primary object to be sought, in order to secure private advantage and promote the public weal.

In the present struggle, the test of character is as infallible as it is simple. He that is with the slaveholder is against the slave: he that is with the slave is against the slaveholder. He that thinks, speaks, acts, on the subject of slavery, in accordance with the feelings and wishes of the tyrant, does every thing to perpetuate the thralldom of his victims. When was it ever known for tyranny to devise and execute effective measures for its own overthrow? Or for the oppressor and the oppressed to be agreed on the great question of equal rights? Who talks of occupying neutral ground between these hostile parties? of reconciling them, by prolonging the sufferings of the one, and the cruelty of the other? of mutually satisfying them as to the means and the plan by which the rod and the chain shall be broken? I tell such vain babbler, or crafty hypocrite, that he is acting the part of a fool or a knave. Impossibilities are impossibilities; and to propose their adoption, as the only rational methods by which to dethrone injustice, is an insult to human intelligence. Slavery cannot be conquered by flattery or stratagem. Its dying throes will convulse the land and sea.

Abolitionists! friends of liberty! remember that the foe with whom you are in conflict is full "of all deceivableness of unrighteousness," and will resort to every artifice to make you quit the field. Put on the whole armor of God; so shall you be invulnerable and invincible; so shall no weapon against you prosper. The war admits of no parley. No flag of truce must be sent or received by you; you must neither give nor take any quarters. As Samuel hewed Agag in pieces, so, with the battle-axe of Truth, you must cleave Slavery to the ground, and give its carcass to the fowls of the air. May Heaven re-inspire your hearts, give new vigor to your arms, direct your blows aright, fill the breast of the enemy with dismay, and grant you a splendid victory!

9. CHARLES SUMNER

The True Grandeur of Nations
(1845)

Charles Sumner (1811-1874), United States Senator
from Massachusetts during the era of the Civil War,
slowly made his reputation as a scholarly lawyer and
reformer. The turning point of his career was his
Fourth of July oration in 1845, in which he outraged
his conservative Whig friends but thrilled his audience. Boston newspapers noted that the speech fell
like an avalanche on the military guests seated in uniform in the front row. Five years later Sumner was
sent to the Senate by a coalition of Free Soilers and
Democrats. A champion of peace and emancipation,
he pursued both causes in a highly personal, and
often rather erratic, way, antagonizing both friend
and foe even though few doubted his sincerity or his
idealism.

I have already alluded, in the early part of this Address, to some
of the obstacles encountered by the advocate of Peace. One of these
is the warlike tone of the literature, by which our minds are
formed. The world has supped so full with battles, that all its
inner modes of thought, and many of its rules of conduct seem to
be incarnadined with blood; as the bones of swine, fed on madder,
are said to become red. But I now pass this by, though a fruitful
theme, and hasten to other topics. I propose to consider in suc-

cession, very briefly, some of those prejudices, which are most powerful in keeping alive the *custom* of War.

One of the most important of these is the prejudice in its favor founded on the *belief in its necessity*. When War is called a necessity, it is meant, of course, that its object cannot be attained in any other way. Now I think that it has already appeared with distinctness, approaching demonstration, that the professed object of War, which is justice between nations, is in no respect promoted by War; that force is not justice, nor in any way conducive to justice; that the eagles of victory can be the emblems only of successful force, and not of established right. Justice can be obtained only by the exercise of the reason and judgment; but these are silent in the din of arms. Justice is without passion; but War lets loose all the worst passions of our nature, while "Chance, high arbiter, more embroils the fray." The age has passed in which a nation, within the enchanted circle of civilization, can make war upon its neighbor, for any professed purpose of booty or vengeance. It does "naught in hate, but all in *honor*." There are professions of tenderness even which mingle with the first mutterings of the dismal strife. As if conscience-struck at the criminal abyss into which they are madly plunging, each of the great litigants seeks to fix on the other the charge of hostile aggression, and to assume to itself the ground of defending some right; some stolen Texas; some distant, worthless Oregon. Like Pontius Pilate, it vainly washes its hands of innocent blood, and straightway allows a crime at which the whole heavens are darkened, and two kindred countries are severed, as the veil of the Temple was rent in twain.

The various modes, proposed for the determination of international disputes, are Negotiation, Mediation, Arbitration, and a Congress of Nations—all of them practicable and calculated to secure peaceful justice. These may be employed at any time under the existing Law of Nations. *But the very law itself, which sanctions War, may be changed*—as regards two or more nations by treaty between them, and as regards all the Christian nations by general consent. If nations can agree together, in the solemn provisions of International Law, to establish War as an Arbiter of Justice between them, they can also agree together to abolish this Arbitrament, and to establish peaceful *substitutes;* precisely as similar substitutes have been established by the municipal law in order to determine controversies among individuals. A system of Arbitration may be instituted by treaties, or a Congress of Nations may be charged with the high duty of organizing an *Ultimate Tribunal* instead of "these battles" for the decision of international controversies. The will only is required in order to succeed in this work.

Let it not be said, then, that War is a *necessity;* and may our country aim at the True Glory of taking the lead in disowning the revolting system of *International* LYNCH LAW, and in proclaiming peaceful *substitutes* therefor, as the only proper modes of determining justice between nations! Such a Glory, unlike the earthly fame of battles, shall be immortal as the stars, dropping perpetual light upon the souls of men!

Another prejudice in favor of War is founded on *the practice of nations,* past and present. There is no crime or enormity in morals, which may not find the support of human example, often on an extended scale. But it cannot be urged in our day, that we are to look for a standard of duty in the conduct of vain, mistaken, fallible man. It is not in the power of man, by any subtle alchemy, to transmute wrong into right. Because War is according to the practice of the world, it cannot follow that it is right. For ages the world worshipped false gods; but these gods were not less false, because all bowed before them. At this moment the larger portion of mankind are Heathen; but Heathenism is not true. It was once the *practice* of nations to slaughter prisoners of war; but even the Spirit of War recoils now from this bloody sacrifice. . . .

There is a topic which I approach with diffidence; but in the spirit of frankness. It is the influence which War, though condemned by Christ, has derived from the *Christian Church*. When Constantine on one of his marches, at the head of his army, beheld the luminous trophy of the cross in the sky right above the meridian sun, inscribed with these words, *By this conquer,* had his soul been penetrated by the true spirit of Him, whose precious symbol it was, he would have found in it no inspiration to the spear and the sword. He would have received the lesson of self-sacrifice, as from the lips of the Saviour, and would have learned that by no earthly weapons of battle can any true victory be won. The pride of conquest would have been rebuked, and the bauble sceptre of Empire would have fallen from his hands. *By this conquer;* that is, by patience, suffering, forgiveness of evil, by all those virtues of which the cross is the affecting token, *conquer;* and the victory shall be greater than any in the annals of Roman conquests; it may not find a place in the records of man; but it shall appear in the register of everlasting life.

The Christian Church, after the first centuries of its existence, failed to discern the peculiar spiritual beauty of the faith which it professed. Like Constantine, it found new incentives to War in the religion of Peace; and such has been its character, let it be said fearlessly, even to our own day. The Pope of Rome, the asserted head of the Church, the Viceregent of Christ on earth, whose seal is a fisherman, on whose banner is a LAMB before the HOLY CROSS, assumed the command of armies, often mingling the thunders of battle with the thunders of the Vatican. The dagger which projected from the sacred vestments of the Archbishop de Retz, as he appeared in the streets of Paris, was called by the crowd "the Archbishop's Missal." We read of mitred prelates in armor of proof, and seem still to catch the jingle of the golden spurs of the bishops in the streets of Cologne. The sword of knighthood was consecrated by the Church; and priests were often the expert masters in military exercises. I have seen at the gates of the Papal Palace in Rome, a constant guard of Swiss soldiers; I have seen, too, in our own streets a show, as incongruous and as inconsistent, a pastor of a Christian church swelling by his presence the pomp of a military parade! Ay! more than this; some of us have heard, within a few short weeks, in a Christian pulpit, from the lips of an eminent Christian divine, a sermon in which we are encouraged to *serve the God of Battles, and, as citizen soldiers, to fight for Peace*—a sentiment in unhappy harmony with the profane language of the British peer, when, in addressing the House of Lords, he said, *"The best road to Peace, my Lords, is War;* War carried on in the same manner in which we are taught to worship our Creator, namely, with all our souls, with all our minds, with all our hearts, and with all our strength"; but which surely can find no support in the Religion of Him who has expressly enjoined, when one cheek is smitten to turn the other, and to which we listen with pain and mortification from the lips of one, who has voluntarily become a minister of Christian truth; alas! in his mind inferior to that of the Heathen, who declared that he *preferred the unjustest peace to the justest war. . . .*

There is still another influence which stimulates War, and interferes with the natural attractions of Peace; I refer to a selfish and exaggerated *love of country,* leading to its physical aggrandizement, and political exaltation, at the expense of other countries, and in disregard of the principles of True Greatness. Our minds, nursed by the literature of antiquity, have imbibed the narrow sentiment of heathen patriotism. Exclusive love for the land of birth, was a part of the religion of Greece and Rome. It is an indication of the lowness of their moral nature, that this sentiment was so material as well as exclusive in its character. . . .

It has been a part of the policy of rulers, to encourage this exclusive patriotism; and the people of modern times have all been quickened by the feeling of antiquity. I do not know that any one nation is in a condition to reproach another with this patriotic selfishness. All are selfish. Men are taught to live, not for mankind, but only for a small portion of mankind. The pride, vanity, ambition, brutality even, which we rebuke in individuals, are accounted virtues when displayed in the name of country. . . .

And here let us review the field over which we have passed. We have beheld War, sanctioned by International Law, as a mode of determining *justice* between Nations, elevated into an *established custom,* defined and guarded by a complex code, known as the Laws of War; we have detected its origin in an appeal, not to the moral and intellectual part of man's nature, in which alone is Justice, but in appeal to that low part of his nature, which he has in common with the beasts; we have contemplated its infinite miseries to the human race; we have weighed its sufficiency as a mode of determing justice between nations, and found that it is a rude appeal to force, or a gigantic game of chance, in which God's children are profanely dealt with as a pack of cards, while, in its unnatural wickedness, it is justly likened to the monstrous and impious *custom* of *Trial by Battle,* which disgraced the dark ages—thus showing that, in this period of boastful civilization, justice between nations is determined by the same rules of barbarous, brutal violence, which once controlled the relations between individuals. We have next considered the various prejudices by which War is sustained; found on a false belief in its necessity; on the practice of nations, past and present; on the infidelity of the Christian Church; on a false idea of honor; on an exaggerated idea of the duties of patriotism; and finally, that monster prejudice, which draws its vampire life from the vast Preparations in time of peace for War—especially dwelling, at this stage, upon the thriftless, irrational, and unchristian character of these Preparations—hailing also the auguries of their overthrow, and catching a vision of the surpassing good that will be achieved, when the boundless means, thus barbarously employed, shall be dedicated by our Republic to the works of Peace, opening the serene path to that righteousness which exalteth a Nation.

And now, if it be asked why, on this National Anniversary, in considering the TRUE GRANDEUR OF NATIONS, I have dwelt, thus singly and exclusively, on War, it is, because War is utterly and irreconcilably inconsistent with True Greatness. . . . The True Greatness of Nations is in those qualities which constitute the True Greatness of the individual. It is not in extent of territory, or in vastness of population, or in wealth; not in fortifications, or armies, or navies; not in the phosphorescent glare of fields of battle, not in Golgothas, though covered by monuments that kiss the clouds; for all these are the creatures and representatives of those qualities in our nature, which are unlike any thing in God's nature. . . .

The True Greatness of a Nation cannot be in triumphs of the intellect alone. Literature and art may enlarge the sphere of its influence; they may adorn it; but they are in their nature but accessories. *The True Grandeur of Humanity is in moral elevation, sustained, enlightened, and decorated by the intellect of man.* The surest tokens of this Grandeur, in a State, are that Christian Beneficence, which diffuses the greatest happiness among the greatest number, and that passionless, God-like Justice, which controls the relations of the State to other States, and to all the people committed to its charge.

But War crushes, with bloody heel, all beneficence, all happiness, all justice, all that is God-like in man. It suspends every commandment of the Decalogue. It sets at naught every principle of the Gospel. It silences all law, human as well as divine, except only that blasphemous code of its own, the *Laws of War*. If, in its dismal annals, there is any cheerful passage, be assured that it is not inspired by a martial Fury. Let it not be forgotten—let it ever be borne in mind, as you ponder this theme—that the virtues, which shed their charm over its horrors, are all borrowed of Peace; they are emanations of the Spirit of Love, which is so strong in the heart of man, that it survives the rudest assaults. The flowers of gentleness, of kindliness, of fidelity, of humanity, which flourish, in unregarded luxuriance, in the rich meadows of Peace, receive unwonted admiration when we discern them in War, like violets, shedding their perfume on the perilous edges of the precipice, beyond the smiling borders of civilization. God be praised for all the examples of magnanimous virtue, which he has vouchsafed to mankind! . . .

Far be from us, fellow-citizens, on this Festival, the pride of national victory, and the illusions of national freedom, in which we are too prone to indulge. None of you make rude boasts of individual prosperity, individual possessions, individual power, or individual bravery. But there can be only one and the same rule, whether in morals or in conduct, for nations and individuals; and our country will act wisely, and in the spirit of True Greatness, by emulating, in its public behavior, the reserve and modesty which are universally commended in private life. Let it cease to vaunt itself and to be puffed up; but rather brace itself, by firm resolves and generous aspirations, to the duties before it. We have but half done, when we have made ourselves free. Let not the scornful taunt, wrung from the bitter experience of the early French revolution, be directed at us: "They wish to be *free;* but know not how to be *just.*" Freedom is not an end in itself, but a means only—a means of securing Justice and Beneficence, in which alone is happiness, the real end and aim of Nations, as of every human heart. It becomes us to inquire earnestly, if there is not much to be done by which these can be advanced. If I have succeeded in impressing, on your minds, the truths, which I have endeavored to uphold today, you will be ready, as faithful citizens, alike of our own Republic, and of the universal Christian Commonwealth, to join in efforts to abolish the Arbitrament of War, to suppress International *Lynch Law,* and to induce the Disarming of the Nations, as measures indispensable to the establishment of Permanent Peace—that grand, comprehensive blessing, at once the child and parent of all those *guardian virtues,* without which there can be no National Honor, no National Glory, no True Grandeur of Nations!

10. THEODORE PARKER

The True Idea of a Christian Church
(1846)

Theodore Parker (1810-1860) was probably the most radical of the New England Unitarian clergy, many of whom he alienated by his unconventional theology. Parker believed that the Christian Church should be an instrument of social reform and good works, and he himself became increasingly a part of the anti-slavery movement during the 'forties and 'fifties. Though possessed of wide-ranging scholarly and liter-ary interests, unlike many of his friends among the transcendentalists, he remained active as a minister to his congregation.

A Christian church should be a means of reforming the world, of forming it after the pattern of Christian ideas. It should therefore bring up the sentiments of the times, the ideas of the times, and the actions of the times, to judge them by the universal standard. In this way it will learn much and be a living church, that grows with the advance of men's sentiments, ideas, and actions, and while it keeps the good of the past will lose no brave spirit of the present day. It can teach much; now moderating the fury of men, then quickening their sluggish steps. We expect the sins of commerce to be winked at in the street; the sins of the state to be applauded on election days and in a Congress, or on the fourth of July; we are used to hear them called the righteousness of the nation. There they are often measured by the avarice or the ambition of greedy men. You expect them to be tried by passion, which looks only to immediate results and partial ends. Here they are to be measured by Conscience and Reason, which look to permanent results and universal ends; to be looked at with reference to the Laws of God, the everlasting ideas on which alone is based the welfare of the world. Here they are to be examined in the light of Christianity itself. If the church be true, many things which seem gainful in the street and expedient in the senate-house, will here be set down as wrong, and all gain which comes therefrom seen to be but a loss. If there be a public sin in the land, if a lie invade the state, it is for the church to give the alarm; it is here that it may war on lies and sins; the more widely they are believed in and practiced, the more are they deadly, the more to be opposed. Here let no false idea or false action of the public go without exposure or rebuke. But let no noble heroism of the times, no noble man pass by without due honor. . . .

A Christian church should be a society for promoting true sentiments and ideas. If it would lead, it must go before men; if it would be looked up to, it must stand high.

That is not all: it should be a society for the promotion of good works. . . .

Here are the needy who ask not so much your gold, your bread, or your cloth, as they ask also your sympathy, respect, and counsel; that you assist them to help themselves, that they may have gold won by their industry, not begged out of your benevolence. It is justice more than charity they ask. Every beggar, every pauper, born and bred amongst us, is a reproach to us, and condemns our civilization. For how has it come to pass that in a land of abundance here are men, for no fault of their own, born into want, living in want, and dying of want? And that, while we pretend to a religion which says all men are brothers! There is a horrid wrong somewhere.

Here too are the drunkard, the criminal, the abandoned person, sometimes the foe of society, but far oftener the victim of society. Whence come the tenants of our alms-houses, jails, the victims of vice in all our towns? Why, from the lowest rank of the people; from the poorest and most ignorant! Say rather from the most neglected, and the public sin is confessed, and the remedy hinted at. What have the strong been doing all this while, that the weak have come to such a state? Let them answer for themselves.

Now for all these ought a Christian church to toil. It should be a church of good works; if it is a church of good faith it will be so. Does not Christianity say the strong should help the weak? Does not that mean something? It once did. Has the Christian fire faded out from those words, once so marvellously bright? Look round you, in the streets of your own Boston! See the ignorant, men and women with scarce more than the stature of men and women; boys and girls growing up in ignorance and the low civilization which comes thereof, the barbarians of Boston. Their character will one day be a blot and a curse to the nation, and who is to blame? Why, the ablest and best men, who might have had it otherwise if they would. Look at the poor, men of small ability, weak by nature, born into a weak position, therefore doubly weak; men whom the strong use for their purpose, and then cast them off as we throw away the rind of an orange after we have drunk its generous juice. Behold the wicked, so we call the weak men that are publicly caught in the cobweb of the law; ask why they became wicked; how we have aimed to reform them; what we have done to make them respect themselves, to believe in goodness, in man and God? and then say if there is not something for Christian men to do, something for a Christian church to do! Every alms-house in Massachusetts shows that the churches have not done their duty, that the Christians lie lies when they call Jesus "master" and men "brothers"! Every jail is a monument, on which it is writ in letters of iron that we are still heathens, and the gallows, black and hideous, the embodiment of death, the last argument a "Christian" state offers to the poor wretches it trained up to be criminals, stands there, a sign of our infamy; and while it lifts its horrid arm to crush the life out of some miserable man, whose blood cries to God against Cain in the nineteenth century, it lifts that same arm as an index of our shame.

Is that all? Oh, no! Did not Jesus say, resist not evil—with evil? Is not war the worst form of that evil; and is there on earth a nation so greedy of war; a nation more reckless of provoking it; one where the war-horse so soon conducts his foolish rider into fame and power? The "heathen" Chinese might send their missionaries to America, and teach us to love men! Is that all? Far from it. Did not Christ say, whatsoever you would that men should do unto you, do you even so unto them; and are there not three million brothers of yours and mine in bondage here, the hopeless sufferers of a savage doom; debarred from the civilization of our age, the barbarians of the nineteenth century; shut out from the pretended religion of Christendom, the heathens of a Christian land; chained down from the liberty unalienable in man, the slaves of a Christian republic? Does not a cry of indignation ring out from every legislature in the North; does not the press war with its million throats, and a voice of indignation go up from East and West, out from the hearts of freemen? Oh, no. There is none of that cry against the mightiest sin of this age. The rock of Plymouth, sanctified by the feet which led a nation's way to freedom's large estate, provokes no more voice than the rottenest stone in all the mountains of the West. The few that speak a manly word for truth and everlasting right, are called fanatics; bid be still, lest they spoil the market! Great God! and has it come to this, that men are silent over such a sin? 'Tis even so. Then it must be that every church which dares assume the name of Christ, that dearest name to men, thunders and lightens on this hideous wrong! That is not so. The church is dumb, while the state is only silent; while the servants of the people are only asleep, "God's ministers" are dead!

In the midst of all these wrongs and sins, the crimes of men, society, and the state, amid popular ignorance, pauperism, crime, and war, and slavery too—is the church to say nothing, do nothing; nothing for the good of such as feel the wrong, nothing to save them who do the wrong? Men tell us so, in word and deed; that way alone is "safe"! If I thought so, I would never enter the church but once again, and then to bow my shoulders to their manliest work, to heave down its strong pillars, arch and dome, and roof and wall, steeple and tower, though like Samson I buried myself under the ruins of that temple which profaned the worship of God most high, of God most loved. I would do this in the name of man; in the name of Christ I would do it; yes, in the dear and blessed name of God.

It seems to me that a church which dares name itself Christian, the Church of the Redeemer, which aspires to be a true church, must set itself about all this business, and be not merely a church of theology, but of religion; not of faith only, but of works; a just church by its faith bringing works into life. It should not be a church termagant, which only peevishly scolds at sin, in its anile way; but a church militant against every form of evil, which not only censures, but writes out on the walls of the world the brave example of a Christian life, that all may take pattern therefrom. Thus only can it become the church triumphant. . . .

The church that is to lead this century will not be a church creeping on all fours; mewling and whining, its face turned down, its eyes turned back. It must be full of the brave, manly spirit of the day, keeping also the good of times past. There is a terrific

energy in this age, for man was never so much developed, so much
the master of himself before. Great truths, moral and political,
have come to light. They fly quickly. The iron prophet of type
publishes his visions, of weal or woe, to the near and far. This
marvellous age has invented steam, and the magnetic telegraph,
apt symbols of itself, before which the miracles of fable are but
an idle tale. It demands, as never before, freedom for itself, usefulness in its institutions; truth in its teachings, and beauty in its
deeds. Let a church have that freedom, that usefulness, truth, and
beauty, and the energy of this age will soon be on its side. But
the church which did for the fifth century, or the fifteenth, will
not do for this. What is well enough at Rome, Oxford, or Berlin,
is not well enough for Boston. It must have our ideas, the smell of
our ground, and have grown out of the religion in our soul. The
freedom of America must be there before this energy will come;
the wisdom of the nineteenth century before its science will be on
the churches' side, else that science will go over to the "infidels."

Our churches are not in harmony with what is best in the present
age. Men call their temples after their old heroes and saints—
John, Paul, Peter, and the like. But we call nothing else after the
old names; a school of philosophy would be condemned if called
Aristotelian, Platonic, or even Baconian. We out-travel the past in
all but this. In the church it seems taught there is no progress
unless we have all the past on our back; so we despair of having
men fit to call churches by. We look back and not forward. We
think the next saint must talk Hebrew like the old ones, and repeat
the same mythology. So when a new prophet comes we only stone
him.

A church that believes only in past inspiration will appeal to
old books as the standard of truth and source of light; will be
antiquarian in its habits; will call its children by the old names;
and war on the new age, not understanding the man-child born

to rule the world. A church that believes in inspiration now will appeal to God; try things by reason and conscience; aim to surpass the old heroes; baptize its children with a new spirit, and using the present age will lead public opinion, and not follow it. Had Christ looked back for counsel, he might have founded a church fit for Abraham or Isaac to worship in, not for ages to come, or the age then. He that feels he is near to God, does not fear to be far from men; if before, he helps lead them on! if above, to lift them up. Let us get all we can can from the Hebrews and others of old time, and that is much; but still let us be God's free men, not the Gibeonites of the past.

Let us have a church that dares imitate the heroism of Jesus; seek inspiration as he sought it; judge the past as he; act on the present like him; pray as he prayed; work as he wrought; live as he lived. Let our doctrines and our forms fit the soul, as the limbs fit the body, growing out of it, growing with it. Let us have a church for the whole man: truth for the mind; good works for the hands; love for the heart; and for the soul, that aspiring after perfection, that unfaltering faith in God which, like lightning in the clouds shines brightest when elsewhere it is most dark. Let our church fit man, as the heavens fit the earth!

11. HENRY DAVID THOREAU

Civil Disobedience
(1849)

Henry David Thoreau (1817-1862), next to Emerson the leading light among the New England transcendentalists, was a flintier, more uncompromising individualist than his fatherly mentor. A member of the Harvard class of 1837 which heard Emerson's Phi Beta Kappa address, *The American Scholar,* Thoreau then returned home to spend most of his life in Concord, Massachusetts. There, in the midst of his idyllic sojourn at Walden Pond in the summer of 1845, he was arrested for not having paid his poll tax. His night in the local jail led him to write the classic protest which became known as his *Essay on Civil Disobedience,* and in which he also made clear his feelings in regard to slavery and the Mexican War.

I heartily accept the motto, "That government is best which governs least"; and I should like to see it acted up to more readily and systematically. Carried out, it finally amounts to this, which also I believe—"That government is best which governs not at all"; and when men are prepared for it, that will be the kind of government which they will have. Government is at best but an expedient; but most governments are usually, and all governments are sometimes, inexpedient. The objections which have been brought against a standing army, and they are many and weighty, and deserve to prevail, may also at last be brought against a standing government. The standing army is only an arm of the standing government. The government itself, which is only the mode which people have chosen to execute their will, is equally liable to be abused and perverted before the people can act through it. Witness the present Mexican war, the work of comparatively a few individuals using the standing government as their tool; for, in the outset, the people would not have consented to this measure.

This American government—what is it but a tradition, though a recent one, endeavoring to transmit itself unimpaired to posterity, but each instant losing some of its integrity? It has not the vitality and force of a single living man; for a single man can bend it to his will. It is a sort of wooden gun to the people themselves. But it is not the less necessary for this; for the people must have some complicated machinery or other, and hear its din, to satisfy that idea of government which they have. Governments show thus how successfully men can be imposed on, even impose on themselves, for their own advantage. It is excellent, we must all allow; yet this government never of itself furthered any enterprise, but by the alacrity with which it got out of its way. *It* does not keep the country free. *It* does not settle the West. *It* does not educate. The character inherent in the American people has done all that has been accomplished; and it would have done somewhat more, if the government had not sometimes got in its way. For government is an expedient by which men would fain succeed in letting one another alone; and, as has been said, when it is most expedient, the governed are most let alone by it. Trade and commerce, if they were not made of india-rubber, would never manage to bounce over the obstacles which legislators are continually putting in their way; and, if one were to judge these men wholly by the effects of their actions, and not partly by their intentions, they would deserve to be classed and punished with those mischievous persons who put obstructions on the railroads.

But, to speak practically and as a citizen, unlike those who call themselves no-government men, I ask for, not at once no government, but *at once* a better government. Let every man make known what kind of government would command his respect, and that will be one step toward obtaining it.

After all, the practical reason why, when the power is once in the hands of the people, a majority are permitted, and for a long period continue, to rule, is not because they are most likely to be in the right, nor because this seems fairest to the minority, but because they are physically the strongest. But a government in which the majority rule in all cases cannot be based on justice, even as far as men understand it. Can there not be a government in which majorities do not virtually decide right and wrong, but conscience? —in which majorities decide only those questions to which the rule of expediency is applicable? Must the citizen even for a moment, or in the least degree, resign his conscience to the legislator? Why has every man a conscience, then? I think that we should be men first, and subjects afterward. It is not desirable to cultivate a respect for the law, so much as for the right. The only obligation which I have a right to assume, is to do at any time what I think right. It is truly enough said, that a corporation has no conscience: but a corporation of conscientious men is a corporation *with* a conscience. Law never made men a whit more just; and, by means of their respect for it, even the well-disposed are daily made the agents of injustice. A common and natural result of an undue respect for law is, that you may see a file of soldiers, colonel, captain, corporal, privates, powder—monkeys and all, marching in admirable order over hill and dale to the wars, against their wills, aye, against their common sense and consciences, which makes it very steep marching indeed, and produces a palpitation of the heart. They have no doubt that it is a damnable business in which they are concerned; they are all peaceably inclined. Now, what are they? Men at all? or small moveable forts and magazines, at the service of some unscrupulous man in power? Visit the Navy Yard, and behold a marine, such a man as an American government can make, or such as it can make a man with its black arts, a mere shadow and reminiscence of humanity, a man laid out alive and standing, and already, as one may say, buried under arms with funeral accompaniments, though it may be,

> Not a drum was heard, nor a funeral note,
> As his corse to the ramparts we hurried;
> Not a soldier discharged his farewell shot
> O'er the grave where our hero we buried.

The mass of men serve the State thus, not as men mainly, but as machines, with their bodies. They are the standing army, and the militia, jailers, constables, *posse comitatus,* &c. In most cases there is no free exercise whatever of the judgment or the moral sense; but they put themselves on a level with wood and earth and stones; and wooden men can perhaps be manufactured that will serve the purpose as well. Such command no more respect than men of straw, or a lump of dirt. They have the same sort of worth only as horses and dogs. Yet such as these even are commonly esteemed good citizens. Others—as most legislators, politicians, lawyers, ministers, and officeholders—serve the State chiefly with their heads; and, as they rarely make any moral distinctions, they are as likely to serve the devil, without *intending* it, as God. A very few —as heroes, patriots, martyrs, reformers in the great sense, and *men*—serve the State with their consciences also, and so necessarily resist it for the most part; and they are commonly treated as enemies by it. A wise man will only be useful as a man, and will not submit to be "clay," and "stop a hole to keep the wind away," but leave that office to his dust at least:

> I am too high-born to be propertied,
> To be a secondary at control,
> Or useful serving-man and instrument
> To any sovereign state throughout the world.

He who gives himself entirely to his fellow-men appears to them useless and selfish; but he who gives himself partially to them is pronounced a benefactor and philanthropist.

How does it become a man to behave toward this American government today? I answer that he cannot without disgrace be associated with it. I cannot for an instant recognize that political organization as *my* government which is the *slave's* government also.

All men recognize the right of revolution; that is, the right to refuse allegiance to, and to resist, the government, when its tyranny or its inefficiency are great and unendurable. But almost all say that such is not the case now. But such was the case, they think, in the Revolution of '75. If one were to tell me that this was a bad government because it taxed certain foreign commodities brought to its ports, it is most probable that I should not make an ado about it, for I can do without them. All machines have their friction; and possibly this does enough good to counterbalance the evil. At any rate, it is a great evil to make a stir about it. But when the friction comes to have its machine, and oppression and robbery are organized, I say, let us not have such a machine any longer. In other words, when a sixth of the population of a nation which has undertaken to be the refuge of liberty are slaves, and a whole country is unjustly overrun and conquered by a foreign army, and subjected to military law, I think that it is not too soon for honest men to rebel and revolutionize. What makes this duty the more urgent is the fact, that the country so overrun is not our own, but ours is the invading army. . . .

I do not hesitate to say, that those who call themselves Abolitionists should at once effectually withdraw their support, both in person and property, from the government of Massachusetts, and not wait till they constitute a majority of one, before they suffer the right to prevail through them. I think that it is enough if they have God on their side, without waiting for that other one. Moreover, any man more right than his neighbors, constitutes a majority of one already.

I meet this American government, or its representative the State government, directly, and face to face, once a year—no more —in the person of its tax-gatherer; this is the only mode in which a man situated as I am necessarily meets it; and it then says distinctly, Recognize me; and the simplest, the most effectual, and, in the present posture of affairs, the indispensable mode of treating with it on this head, of expressing your little satisfaction with and love for it, is to deny it then. My civil neighbor, the tax-gatherer, is the very man I have to deal with—for it is, after all, with men and not with parchment that I quarrel—and he has voluntarily chosen to be an agent of the government. How shall he ever know well what he is and does as an officer of the government, or as a man, until he is obliged to consider whether he shall treat me, his neighbor, for whom he has respect, as a neighbor and well-disposed man, or as a maniac and disturber of the peace, and see if he can get over this obstruction to his neighborliness without a ruder and more impetuous thought or speech corresponding with his action? I know this well, that if one thousand, if one hundred, if ten men whom I could name—if ten *honest* men only —aye, if *one* HONEST man, in this State of Massachusetts, *ceasing to hold slaves,* were actually to withdraw from this copartnership, and be locked up in the county jail therefor, it would be the abolition of slavery in America. For it matters not how small the beginning may seem to be: what is once well done is done for ever. But we love better to talk about it: that we say is our mission. Reform keeps many scores of newspapers in its service, but not one man. If my esteemed neighbor, the State's ambassador, who will devote his days to the settlement of the question of human rights in the Council Chamber, instead of being threatened with the prisons of Carolina, were to sit down the prisoner of Massachusetts, that State which is so anxious to foist the sin of slavery upon her sister—though at present she can discover only an act of inhospitality to be the ground of quarrel with her—the Legislature would not wholly waive the subject the following winter.

Under a government which imprisons any man unjustly, the true place for a just man is also a prison. The proper place today, the only place which Massachusetts has provided for her freer and less desponding spirits, is in her prisons, to be put out and locked out of the State by her own act, as they have already put themselves out by their principles. It is there that the fugitive slave, and the Mexican prisoner on parole, and the Indian come to plead the wrongs of his race, should find them; on that separate, but more free and honorable ground, where the State places those who are not *with* her, but *against* her—the only house in a slave-state in which a free man can abide with honor. If any think that their influence would be lost there, and their voices no longer afflict the ear of the State, that they would not be as an enemy within its walls, they do not know by how much truth is stronger than error, nor how much more eloquently and effectively he can combat injustice who has experienced a little in his own person. Cast your whole vote, not a strip of paper merely, but your whole influence. A minority is powerless while it conforms to the majority; it is not even a minority then; but it is irresistible when it clogs by its whole weight. If the alternative is to keep all just men in prison, or give up war and slavery, the State will not hesitate which to choose. If a thousand men were not to pay their tax-bills this year, that would not be a violent and bloody measure, as it would be to pay them, and enable the State to commit violence and shed innocent blood. This is, in fact, the definition of a peaceable revolution, if any such is possible. If the tax-gatherer, or any other public officer, asks me, as one has done, "But what shall I do?" my answer is, "If you really wish to do anything, resign your office." When the subject has refused allegiance, and the officer has resigned his office, then the revolution is accomplished. But even suppose blood should flow. Is there not a sort of blood shed when the conscience is wounded? Through this wound a man's real manhood and immortality flow out, and he bleeds to an everlasting death. I see this blood flowing now.

I have contemplated the imprisonment of the offender, rather than the seizure of his goods—though both will serve the same purpose—because they who assert the purest right, and consequently are most dangerous to a corrupt State, commonly have not spent much time in accumulating property. To such the State renders comparatively small service, and a slight tax is wont to appear exorbitant, particularly if they are obliged to earn it by special labor with their hands. If there were one who lived wholly without the use of money, the State itself would hesitate to demand it of him. But the rich man—not to make any invidious comparison—is always sold to the institution which makes him rich. Absolutely speaking, the more money, the less virtue; for money comes between a man and his objects, and obtains them for him; and it was certainly no great virtue to obtain it. It puts to rest many questions which he would otherwise be taxed to answer; while the only new question which it puts is the hard but superfluous one, how to spend it. Thus his moral ground is taken from under his feet. The opportunities of living are diminished in proportion as what are called the "means" are increased. The best thing a man can do for his culture when he is rich is to endeavor to carry out those schemes which he entertained when he was poor. Christ answered the Herodians according to their condition. "Show me the tribute-money," said he—and one took a penny out of his pocket. If you use money which has the image of Caesar on it, and which he has made current and valuable, that is, *if you are men of the State,* and gladly enjoy the advantages of Caesar's government, then pay him back some of his own when he demands it. "Render therefore to Caesar that which is Caesar's, and to God those things which are God's," leaving them no wiser than before as to which was which; for they did not wish to know.

When I converse with the freest of my neighbors, I perceive that, whatever they may say about the magnitude and seriousness of the question, and their regard for the public tranquility, the long and the short of the matter is, that they cannot spare the protection of the existing government, and they dread the consequences to their property and families of disobedience to it. For my own part, I should not like to think that I ever rely on the protection of the State. But, if I deny the authority of the State when it presents its tax-bill, it will soon take and waste all my property, and so harass me and my children without end. This is hard. This makes it impossible for a man to live honestly and at the same time comfortably in outward respects. It will not be worth the while to accumulate property; that would be sure to go again. You must hire or squat somewhere, and raise but a small crop, and eat that soon. You must live within yourself, and depend upon yourself, always tucked up and ready for a start, and not have many affairs. A man may grow rich in Turkey even, if he will be in all respects a good subject of the Turkish government. Confucius said: "If a State is governed by the principles of reason, poverty and misery are subjects of shame; if a State is not governed by the principles of reason, riches and honors are the subjects of shame." No: until I want the protection of Massachusetts to be extended to me in some distant Southern port, where my liberty is endangered, or until I am bent solely on building up an estate at home by peaceful enterprise, I can afford to refuse allegiance to Massachusetts, and her right to my property and life. It costs me less in every sense to incur the penality of disobedience to the State, than it would to obey. I should feel as if I were worth less in that case.

Some years ago, the State met me in behalf of the Church, and commanded me to pay a certain sum toward the support of a clergyman whose preaching my father attended, but never I myself. "Pay," it said, "or be locked up in the jail." I declined to pay. But, unfortunately, another man saw fit to pay it. I did not see why the schoolmaster should be taxed to support the priest, and not the priest the schoolmaster; for I was not the State's schoolmaster, but I supported myself by voluntary subscription. I did not see why the lyceum should not present its tax-bill, and have the State to back its demand, as well as the Church. However, at the request of the selectmen, I condescended to make some such statement as this in writing:—"Know all men by these presents, that I, Henry Thoreau, do not wish to be regarded as a member of any incorporated society which I have not joined." This I gave to the town-clerk; and he has it. The State, having thus learned that I did not wish to be regarded as a member of that church, has never made a like demand on me since; though it said that it must adhere to its original presumption that time. If I had known how to name them, I should then have signed off in detail from all the societies which I never signed on to; but I did not know where to find a complete list.

I have paid no poll-tax for six years. I was put into a jail once on this account, for one night; and, as I stood considering the

walls of solid stone, two or three feet thick, the door of wood and
iron, a foot thick, and the iron grating which strained the light,
I could not help being struck with the foolishness of that institution which treated me as if I were mere flesh and blood and bones,
to be locked up. I wondered that it should have concluded at length
that this was the best use it could put me to, and had never thought
to avail itself of my services in some way. I saw that, if there was a
wall of stone between me and my townsmen, there was still a more
difficult one to climb or break through, before they could get to be
as free as I was. I did not for a moment feel confined, and the
walls seemed a great waste of stone and mortar. I felt as if I alone
of all my townsmen had paid my tax. They plainly did not know
how to treat me, but behaved like persons who are underbred. In
every threat and in every compliment there was a blunder; for they
thought that my chief desire was to stand the other side of that
stone wall. I could not but smile to see how industriously they
locked the door on my meditations, which followed them out again
without let or hinderance, and *they* were really all that was dangerous. As they could not reach me, they had resolved to punish
my body; just as boys, if they cannot come at some person against
whom they have a spite, will abuse his dog. I saw that the State
was half-witted, that it was timid as a lone woman with her silver
spoons, and that it did not know its friends from its foes, and I
lost all my remaining respect for it, and pitied it.

Thus the State never intentionally confronts a man's sense,
intellectual or moral, but only his body, his senses. It is not armed
with superior wit or honesty, but with superior physical strength.
I was not born to be forced. I will breathe after my own fashion.
Let us see who is the strongest. What force has a multitude? They
only can force me who obey a higher law than I. They force me
to become like themselves. I do not hear of *men* being *forced* to
live this way or that by masses of men. What sort of life were that

to live? When I meet a government, which says to me, "Your money or your life," why should I be in haste to give it my money? It may be in a great strait, and not know what to do: I cannot help that. It must help itself; do as I do. It is not worth the while the snivel about it. I am not responsible for the successful working of the machinery of society. I am not the son of the engineer. I perceive that, when an acorn and a chestnut fall side by side, the one does not remain inert to make way for the other, but both obey their own laws, and spring and grow and flourish as best they can, till one, perchance, overshadows and destroys the other. If a plant cannot live according to its nature, it dies; and so a man. . . .

The authority of government, even such as I am willing to submit to—for I will cheerfully obey those who know and can do better than I, and in many things even those who neither know nor can do so well—is still an impure one: to be strictly just, it must have the sanction and consent of the governed. It can have no pure right over my person and property but what I concede to it. The progress from an absolute to a limited monarchy, from a limited monarchy to a democracy, is a progress toward a true respect for the individual. Even the Chinese philosopher was wise enough to regard the individual as the basis of the empire. Is a democracy, such as we know it, the last improvement possible in government? Is it not possible to take a step further towards recognizing and organizing the rights of man? There will never be a really free and enlightened State, until the State comes to recognize the individual as a higher and independent power, from which all its own power and authority are derived, and treats him accordingly. I please myself with imagining a State at last which can afford to be just to all men, and to treat the individual with respect as a neighbor; which even would not think it inconsistent with its own repose, if a few were to live aloof from it, not meddling with it, nor embraced by it, who fulfilled all the duties of neighbors and fellow-men. A State which bore this kind of fruit, and suffered it to drop off as fast as it ripened, would prepare the way for a still more perfect and glorious State, which also I have imagined, but not yet anywhere seen.

12. LYSANDER SPOONER

Limitations Imposed Upon the Majority
(1852)

Lysander Spooner (1808-1887) was born in Athol, Massachusetts. He early showed his independence by beginning the practice of law before completing the three-year apprenticeship required of non-college graduates. A strong believer in the concept of natural law, he became an uncompromising foe of slavery and a staunch defender of individual rights and liberties. This philosophy led in 1844 to his founding of a private mail company to compete with the United States Post Office. Although the venture had some commercial success, the threat of government prosecution stopped its operations. Spooner believed that if trial by jury could be extended from criminal to civil cases, it would serve as an important bulwark of individual and minority rights.

The principal objection, that will be made to the doctrine of this essay, is, that under it, a jury would paralyze the power of the majority, and veto all legislation that was not in accordance with the will of the whole, or nearly the whole, people.

The answer to this objection is, that the limitation, which would be thus imposed upon the legislative power (whether that power be vested in the majority, or minority, of the people), is the crowning merit of the trial by jury. It has other merits; but, though important in themselves, they are utterly insignificant and worthless in comparison with this.

It is this power of vetoing all partial and oppressive legislation, and of restricting the government to the maintenance of such laws as the *whole,* or substantially the whole, people *are agreed in,* that makes the trial by jury "the palladium of liberty." Without this power it would never have deserved that name.

The will, or the pretended will, of the majority, is the last lurking place of tyranny at the present day. The dogma, that certain individuals and families have a divine appointment to govern the rest of mankind, is fast giving place to the one that the larger number have a right to govern the smaller; a dogma, which may, or may not, be less oppressive in its practical operation, but which certainly is no less false or tyrannical in principle, than the one it is so rapidly supplanting. Obviously there is nothing in the nature of majorities, that insures justice at their hands. They have the same passions as minorities, and they have no qualities whatever that should be expected to prevent them from practicing the same tyranny as minorities, if they think it will be for their interest to do so.

There is no particle of truth in the notion that the majority have a *right* to rule, or to exercise arbitrary power over, the minority, simply because the former are more numerous than the latter. Two men have no more natural right to rule one, than one has to rule two. Any single man, or any body of men, many or few, have a natural right to maintain justice for themselves, and for any others who may need their assistance, against the injustice of any and all other men, without regard to their numbers; and majorities have no right to do any more than this. The relative numbers of the opposing parties have nothing to do with the question of right. And no more tyrannical principle was ever avowed, than that the will of the majority ought to have the force of law, without regard to its justice; or, what is the same thing, that the will of the majority ought always to be presumed to be in accordance with justice. Such a doctrine is only another form of the doctrine that might makes right.

When *two* men meet *one* upon the highway, or in the wilderness, have they a right to dispose of his life, liberty, or property at their pleasure, simply because they are the more numerous party? Or is he bound to submit to lose his life, liberty, or property, if they demand it, merely because he is the less numerous party? Or, because they are more numerous than he, is he bound to presume that they are governed only by superior wisdom, and the principles of justice, and by no selfish passion that can lead them to do him a wrong? Yet this is the principle, which it is claimed, should govern men in all their civil relations to each other. Mankind fall in company with each other on the highway or in the wilderness of life, and it is claimed that the more numerous party, simply by virtue of their superior numbers, have the right arbitrarily to dispose of the life, liberty, and property of the minority; and that the minority are bound, by reason of their inferior numbers, to practice abject submission, and consent to hold their natural rights—any, all, or none, as the case may be—at the mere will and pleasure of the majority. . . .

Since, then, all questions as to the *rights* of the members of the political corporation, must be determined by members of the corporation itself, the trial by jury says that no man's *rights*—neither his right to his life, his liberty, nor his property—shall be determined by any such standard as the mere will and pleasure of majorities; but only by the unanimous verdict of a tribunal fairly representing the whole people—that is, a tribunal of twelve men, taken at random from the whole body, and ascertained to be as impartial as the nature of the case will admit, *and sworn to the observance of justice*. Such is the difference in the two kinds of corporations; and the custom of managing by majorities the mere discretionary matters of business corporations (the majority having no power to determine the *rights* of any member), furnishes no analogy to the practice, adopted by political corporations, of disposing of all the *rights* of their members by the arbitrary will of majorities.

But further. The doctrine that the majority have a *right* to rule, proceeds upon the principle that minorities have no *rights* in the government; for certainly the minority cannot be said to have any *rights* in a government, so long as the majority alone determine what their rights shall be. They hold everything, or nothing, as the case may be, at the mere will of the majority.

It is indispensable to a *"free* government" (in the political sense of that term), that the minority, the weaker party, have a veto upon the acts of the majority. Political liberty is liberty for the *weaker party* in a nation. It is only the weaker party that lose their liberties, when a government becomes oppressive. The stronger party, in all governments, are free by virtue of their superior strength. They never oppress themselves.

Legislation is the work of this stronger party; and if, in addition to the sole power of legislating, they have the sole power of determining what legislation shall be enforced, they have all power in their hands, and the weaker party are the subjects of an absolute government.

Unless the weaker party have a veto, either upon the making, or the enforcement of laws, they have no power whatever in the government, and can of course have no liberties except such as the stronger party, in their arbitrary discretion, see fit to permit them to enjoy.

In England and the United States, the trial by jury is the only institution that gives the weaker party any veto upon the power of the stronger. Consequently it is the only institution, that gives them any effective voice in the government, or any guaranty against oppression.

Suffrage, however free, is of no avail for this purpose; because the suffrage of the minority is overborne by the suffrage of the majority, and is thus rendered powerless for purposes of legislation. The responsibility of officers can be made of no avail, because they are responsible only to the majority. The minority, therefore, are wholly without rights in the government, wholly at the mercy of the majority, unless, through the trail by jury, they have a veto upon such legislation as they think unjust.

Government is established for the protection of the weak against the strong. This is the principal, if not the sole, motive for the establishment of all legitimate government. Laws, that are sufficient for the protection of the weaker party, are of course sufficient for the protection of the stronger party; because the strong can certainly need no more protection than the weak. It is, therefore, right that the weaker party should be represented in the tribunal which is finally to determine what legislation may be enforced; and that no legislation shall be enforced against their consent. They being presumed to be competent judges of what kind of legislation makes for their safety, and what for their injury, it must be presumed that any legislation, which *they* object to enforcing, tends to their oppression, and not to their security.

There is still another reason why the weaker party, or the minority, should have a veto upon all legislation which they disapprove. *That reason is, that that is the only means by which the government can be kept within the limits of the contract, compact, or constitution, by which the whole people agree to establish government.* If the majority were allowed to interpret the compact for themselves, and enforce it according to their own interpretation, they would, of course, make it authorize them to do whatever they wish to do.

The theory of free government is that it is formed by the voluntary contract of the people individually with each other. This is the theory (although it is not, as it ought to be, the fact) in all the governments in the United States, as also in the government of England. The theory assumes that each man, who is a party to the government, and contributes to its support, has individually and freely consented to it. Otherwise the government would have no right to tax him for its support—for taxation without consent is robbery. This theory, then, necessarily supposes that this government, which is formed by the free consent of all, has no powers except such as *all* the parties to it have individually agreed that it shall have; and especially that it has no power to pass any *laws,* except such as *all* the parties have agreed that it may pass.

This theory supposes that there may be certain laws that will be beneficial to *all*—so beneficial that *all* consent to be taxed for their maintenance. For the maintenance of these specific laws, in which all are interested, all associate. And they associate for the maintenance of those laws *only,* in which *all* are interested. It would be absurd to suppose that all would associate, and consent to be taxed, for purposes which were beneficial only to a part; and especially for purposes that were injurious to any. A government of the whole, therefore, can have no powers except such as *all* the parties consent that it may have. It can do nothing except what *all* have consented that it may do. And if any portion of the people—no matter how large their number, if it be less than the whole—desire a government for any purposes other than those that are common to all, and desired by all, they must form a separate association for those purposes. They have no right—by perverting this government of the whole, to the accomplishment of purposes desired only by a part—to compel any one to contribute to purposes that are either useless or injurious to himself.

Such being the principles on which the government is formed, the question arises, how shall this government, when formed, be kept within the limits of the contract by which it was established? How shall this government, instituted by the whole people, agreed to by the whole people, supported by the contributions of the whole people, be confined to the accomplishment of those purposes alone, which the whole people desire? How shall it be preserved from degenerating into a mere government for the benefit of a part only of those who established, and who support it? How shall it be prevented from even injuring a part of its own members, for the aggrandizement of the rest? Its laws must be (or at least now are), passed, and most of its other acts performed, by mere agents —agents chosen by a part of the people, and not by the whole. How can these agents be restrained from seeking their own interests, and the interests of those who elected them, at the expense of the rights of the remainder of the people, by the passage and enforcement of laws that shall be partial, unequal, and unjust in their operation? That is the great question. And the trial by jury answers it. And how does the trial by jury answer it? It answers it, as has already been shown throughout this volume, by saying that these mere agents and attorneys, who are chosen by a part only of the people, and are liable to be influenced by partial and unequal purposes, shall not have unlimited authority in the enactment and enforcement of laws; that they shall not exercise *all* the functions of government. It says that they shall never exercise that ultimate power of compelling obedience to the laws by punishing for disobedience, or of executing the laws against the person or property of any man, without first getting the consent of the people, through a tribunal that may fairly be presumed to represent the whole, or substantially the whole, people. It says that if the power to make laws, and the power also to enforce them, were committed to these agents, they would have all power—would be absolute masters of the people, and could deprive them of their rights at pleasure. It says, therefore, that the people themselves will hold a veto upon the enforcement of any and every law, which these agents may enact, and that whenever the occasion arises for them to give or withhold their consent—inasmuch as the whole people cannot assemble, or devote the time and attention necessary to the investigation of each case—twelve of their number shall be taken by lot, or otherwise at random, from the whole body; that they shall not be chosen by majorities (the same majorities that elected the agents who enacted the laws to be put in issue), nor by any interested or suspected party; that they shall not be appointed by, or be in any way dependent upon, those who enacted the law; that their opinions, whether for or against the law that is in issue, shall not be inquired of beforehand; and that if these twelve men give their consent to the enforcement of the law, their consent shall stand for the consent of the whole.

This is the mode, which the trial by jury provides, for keeping the government within the limits designed by the whole people, who have associated for its establishment. And it is the only mode, provided either by the English or American constitutions, for the accomplishment of that object.

But it will, perhaps, be said that if the minority can defeat the will of the majority, then the minority *rule* the majority. But this is not true in any unjust sense. The minority enact no laws of their own. They simply refuse their assent to such laws of the majority as they do not approve. The minority assume no authority over the majority; they simply defend themselves. They do not interfere with the right of the majority to seek their own happiness in their own way, so long as they (the majority) do not interfere with the minority. They claim simply not to be oppressed, and not to be compelled to assist in doing anything which they do not approve. They say to the majority, "We will unite with you, if you desire it, for the accomplishment of all those purposes, in which we have a common interest with you. You can certainly expect us to do nothing more. If you do not choose to associate with us on those terms, there must be two separate associations. You must associate for the accomplishment of your purposes; we for the accomplishment of ours."

In this case, the minority assume no authority over the majority; they simply refuse to surrender their own liberties into the hands of the majority. They propose a union; but decline submission. The majority are still at liberty to refuse the connection, and to seek their own happiness in their own way, except that they cannot be gratified in their desire to become absolute masters of the minority.

But, it may be asked, how can the minority be trusted to enforce even such legislation as is equal and just? The answer is, that they are as reliable for that purpose as are the majority; they are as much presumed to have associated, and are as likely to have associated, for that object, as are the majority; and they have as much interest in such legislation as have the majority. They have even more interest in it; for, being the weaker party, they must rely on it for their security—having no other security on which they can rely. Hence their consent to the establishment of government, and to the *taxation* required for its support, is *presumed* (although it ought not to be presumed), without any express consent being given. This presumption of their consent to be taxed for the maintenance of laws, would be absurd, or they could not themselves be trusted to act in good faith in enforcing those laws. And hence, they cannot be presumed to have consented to be taxed for the maintenance of any laws, except such as they are themselves ready to aid in enforcing. It is therefore unjust to tax them, unless they are eligible to seats in a jury, with power to judge of the justice of the laws. Taxing them for the support of the laws, on the assumption that they are in favor of the laws, and at the same time refusing them the right, as jurors, to judge of the justice of the laws, on the assumption that they are opposed to the laws, are flat contradictions.

But, it will be asked, what motive have the majority, when they have all power in their own hands, to submit their will to the veto of the minority?

One answer is, that they have the motive of justice. It would be *unjust* to compel the minority to contribute, by taxation, to the support of any laws which they did not approve.

Another answer is, that if the stronger party wish to use their power only for purposes of justice, they have no occasion to fear the veto of the weaker party; for the latter have as strong motives for the maintenance of *just* government, as have the former.

Another answer is, that if the stronger party use their power *unjustly,* they will hold it by an uncertain tenure, especially in a community where knowledge is diffused; for knowledge will enable the weaker party to make itself in time the stronger party. It also enables the weaker party, even while it remains the weaker party, perpetually to annoy, alarm, and injure their oppressors. Unjust power—or rather power that is *grossly* unjust, and that is known to be so by the minority—can be sustained only at the expense of standing armies, and all the other machinery of force; for the oppressed party are always ready to risk their lives for purposes of vengeance, and the acquisition of their rights, whenever there is any tolerable chance of success. Peace, safety, and quiet for all, can be enjoyed only under laws that obtain the consent of all. Hence tyrants frequently yield to the demands of justice from those weaker than themselves, as a means of buying peace and safety.

Still another answer is, that those who are in the majority on one law, will be in the minority on another. All, therefore, need the benefit of the veto, at some time or other, to protect themselves from injustice.

That the limits, within which legislation would, by this process, be confined, would be exceedingly narrow, in comparison with those it at present occupies, there can be no doubt. All monopolies, all special privileges, all sumptuary law, all restraints upon any traffic, bargain, or contract, that was naturally lawful, all restraints upon men's natural rights, the whole catalogue of *mala prohibita,* and all taxation to which the taxed parties had not individually, severally, and freely consented, would be at an end; because all such legislation implies a violation of the rights of a greater or less minority. This minority would disregard, trample upon, or resist, the execution of such legislation, and then throw themselves upon a jury of the whole people for justification and protection. In this way all legislation would be nullified, except the legislation of that general nature which impartially protected the rights, and subserved the interests, of all. The only legislation that could be sustained, would probably be such as tended directly to the maintenance of justice and liberty; such, for example, as should contribute to the enforcement of contracts, the protection of property, and the prevention and punishment of acts intrinsically criminal. In short, government in practice would be brought to the necessity of a strict adherence to natural law, and natural justice, instead of being, as it now is, a great battle, in which avarice and ambition are constantly fighting for and obtaining advantages over the natural rights of mankind.

13. CALEB SPRAGUE HENRY

The Historical Destination of the Human Race
(1855)

Caleb Sprague Henry (1804-1884), clergyman, edu-
cator, and author, was born in Rutland, Massachusetts.
After being graduated from Dartmouth College in
1825, he studied theology and was ordained to the
Congregational ministry. From 1838 to 1852 he
served as professor of moral philosophy and history
at New York University. Although apparently an in-
spiring teacher, he was more important as a magazine
editor and writer who covered a wide range of subjects. A leader of the peace movement, Henry, however, unlike most reformers, was enough of a pessi-
mist to question the reigning popular belief of the
age in the idea of progress.

How profoundly this idea of a perfect commonweath has stirred
the best and noblest minds in every age, from Plato to Milton and
Harrington, to Fenelon and St. Simon. It has inspired the song
of the poet, the thought of the sage, the prayer of the devout, the
hope of the believer, and the labors of the philanthropist, of statesmen and legislators, planters of colonies and founders of states. In
short, all human history reveals the power of this idea and this
impulse—and that in spite of the follies and crimes with which the
annals of the world are filled, often indeed precisely in and through
those follies and crimes, as mistakes and perversions of the true

idea, as blind workings of the impulse. All history is the history of human strivings after a better, higher, more perfect social state. Its actual realization in the world, in individuals and in society, in nations and states, and in their relations to each other, would be the regeneration of human society, the fraternization of the nations, and the pacification of the world. Wars and crimes would cease, and with the moral nearly all the physical evils of human life would disappear. It would be the inauguration of the Age of Reason, in the true and noble sense of those much abused words.

But is humanity destined ever to reach this perfection of the social state during the world's historical lifetime? The Age of Reason—will it ever actually arrive? The millennial reign of universal justice and love, brotherhood and peace, which every good heart that believes in a good God is so fain to cling to—will it ever be established on the earth? . . .

Again: does the actual history of mankind thus far warrant any confident prediction that human society will ever reach its normal possible perfection during the lifetime of the world? I exclude now all reference to whatever Divine ideas and interventions human history does or may hereafter disclose, or to any Divine purpose which may thereby be ultimately accomplished. I speak now only of the actual progress which the history of human effort to perfect itself in society discloses. And I say that after four thousand years of human strivings, humanity, neither as a whole, nor in any single state or nation, presents the spectacle of society advanced to a true rational state, nor to any such degrees of it as measurably to satisfy the demands of reason or the wishes of the heart, or to contain the certain promise of a better future. . . .

Consider this point. There is, I humbly think, a great liability to delusion, in much that is said nowadays about the marvellous progress of the age, and the glories of its civilization. Look at it, then, in its highest forms. Take London. Take Paris. Take our own New York. It is precisely to such places, and nowhere else, that you are to look, if you would see what the highest actual civilization is, and how much it has accomplished towards perfecting the social state. Look sharply, then, at the spectacle which this civilization presents. What do you there see? You see there the greatest concentration and the freest, most diversified play of human energies and activities of every kind. There the greatest wealth—the greatest abundance of the means of physical ease and comfort. There, too, the greatest social polish and the highest culture. There flourish philosophy, science, art, letters, industries. There noble virtues and much of the beautiful happiness of a pure and right life. Undoubtedly. But there, also, the greatest proportionable prevalence of vice and crime, and the misery of an evil life. There the greatest refinement of luxurious enjoyment, side by side with the greatest proportionable amount of want and destitution. There gorgeous equipages, with glittering appointments, soft rolling side by side with shivering, ill-clad beggars, whom civilized language, noticeably enough, terms *mendicants*. There gilded palaces, purple and fine linen and sumptuous fare, soft music, mirth and elegant revelry—and, not far off, starvation in rags, sunk and crowded down into damp cellars, or stowed and packed up under sharp-roofed garrets.

Here is civilization in its highest actual state. Here you see all and the utmost that the civilization of the age has done to perfect the social state. Look at the picture then. Does it present the type of humanity advanced to the perfection of the social state? Does it satisfy the demands of reason, or the wishes of the good heart? Is it a rational state of society? No, I answer. No. It is a thousand million miles away from it. And if such a civilization were spread all over the globe, the spectacle would be very far from satisfying the wise and good man, either in the contemplation of the present or in the prospect of the future. On the contrary, *the progressive development of such a civilization in the same line, would be the intensification of all the irrational aspects it now presents*—wealth more and more regarded as the great good and the limits to its desire and pursuit more and more extended, with a corresponding increase in the strength of the temptations to frauds, dishonesties and other wrongs and crimes peculiarly incident to such a state of society—and, with the increase of wealth, a greater and greater increase in the number, variety and ingenious refinements of luxurious enjoyment and gratifications of vanity and worldly pride —and, by the inevitable laws of such a civilization, all this tending, not to equalize among the laboring masses the conditions of comfort and welfare, but to make the poor poorer, and more poorly off in physical comforts, in the leisure and means for rational development and true domestic life, and so to increase the causes of degradation and the temptations to vice and crime.

Besides: the perfection of human society on the earth implies not only the advancement of individuals and communities, but also of nations and the community of nations, to a true rational life. It implies the pacification of the world, the union of the nations in a true brotherhood of justice, love, and peace. But if mere civilization does not and cannot make individual men in society live together as brethren, how is to effect the pacification of the world? The widest extension of commercial relations is no certain guaranty for the universal reign of peace, though it tends that way. But as in the past, so in the future, there is no security against collisions of interest; and ambition, pride and passion may still be stronger than the dictates of prudence and enlightened self-love. With all its progress, all its superiority, the civilization of our century—which flatters itself, as Carlyle says, that it is the nineteenth—has not protected the fairest, the most civilized portions of the world from the scourge of bloody and desolating wars

springing from oppositions of material interests or the mad ambition of sovereigns. During the early years of this period what
scenes of carnage and devastation, what millions of human lives
sacrificed on the battle field, what orphanage and heartbreaking
sorrow in millions of homes—all to gratify the boundless selfishness of the most heartless egotist the world ever saw!

Nor did the downfall of that great disturber of the world bring
permanent peace. Europe has since then been repeatedly the theatre
of bloody battles; while the late Mexican war has proved that the
civilization of the nineteenth century has been no more a security
for peace on this than on the other side of the Ocean. And we
have no reason to suppose it will be on either side a security in
the future more than in the past. I am not saying whether or not
these recent wars are just and necessary according to the common
way of judging. I am only urging the undeniable fact that civilization in itself is no guaranty for the abolition of the custom of war,
no security against the perpetual recurrence of the spectacle of
human beings coming together by thousands, and hundreds of
thousands, to butcher each other—a spectacle which I say is a
million miles away from being a rational spectacle, or a spectacle
compatible with the idea of human society even measurably advanced to a truly rational state. Not until wars cease will humanity
have advanced to the perfection of its social life. Not until then
the Age of Reason. Not until then the Millennium. This no world-
wide spread of our present nineteenth-century European and
American civilization, and no intensification of its present elements and powers in the future, can ever accomplish.

But the progress of Civil Liberty and the establishment of Free
Institutions, is much relied on as a ground of hope for the regeneration of society. It must be admitted that ideas of popular rights,
and the disposition to demand free institutions, are gaining prevalence in many parts of the old world. It may be that the despotic

governments of Europe are destined, at no distant day, to fall shattered to pieces, in the shock of ideas coming face to face, or to be gradually replaced by freer forms, through the transforming force of prevailing opinion. . . .

But what then? Suppose this accomplished—the preliminary conditions fulfilled, the requisite training gone through with, and the same degrees also of civilization attained as we have reached —and all the nations of the earth to be in the enjoyment of free governments, civil and political institutions modelled after the pattern of our own. What then? Would the moral evils peculiarly incident to a high artificial civilization, would the physical evils resulting from the inevitable working of its economical laws, be done away? No: no more then, than in our own country now. Would the world present the spectacle of humanity advanced to a true rational life? Would it contain the guaranties for the continual progress of humanity in the line of rational development? Would it even contain the securities for its own conservation? No: no more in the world at large, than in our own country now.

Besides: the tendency of democratic, as of all other power, is to absolutism. We see it in our land. But democratic absolutism is not necessarily any more rational or beneficent in its workings than monarchic or oligarchic absolutism. If not informed and actuated by wisdom and virtue, it is more dangerous and disastrous—of which truth history gives us more than one impressive demonstration. Let the spirit of a people become an exaggerated sense of rights without a corresponding sense of duties; let it challenge for mere will—the present will of self-willed majorities that legitimate supremacy which belongs to absolute right alone— and what are constitutions and compacts if they stand in the way? Paper and words to men who will neither read nor hear—especially in any conflict of ideas or interests, any struggle of parties or passions. That such is the tendency of democratic absolutism, of the supremacy of self-willed majorities, to override the checks of constitutions and compacts, of reason and moral right—it is impossible to deny. It may take long years before it becomes developed in any destructive way; but that in its unchecked working it leads on to anarchic convulsion, the subversion of rational freedom and the dissolution of the social bonds—it is equally impossible to deny.

And what are the checks that are to restrain the dangerous tendencies of democratic absolutism? Without enumerating those which may be conceived to lie in the modes in which, from the necessity of circumstances, the public will may be obliged to express and realize itself, I will say that there is one without which all other checks are inadequate, and that is the prevalence among the people of the spirit of unselfish patriotism, of justice and of love. This affords the only adequate conservative principle, the only certain guaranty for the beneficent working and permanent continuance of democratic institutions. . . .

Now if the picture of political corruption and violence—which I have rather referred to than sketched—be to any extent a true picture—and you know it is—I ask again: does it lie in the mere working of democratic institutions to create, or to cherish, or even to give fair play to the spirit of unselfish patriotism, justice, and love? And again I answer no. And if the evils we deplore have been greatly increasing for the last twenty-five years—and that they have cannot be denied—what guaranty for the future progress of our nation in public and private virtue can democratic institutions give? What guaranty can they give even for their own conservation and continuance? And therefore, in fine, what guaranty could they give, if spread all over the earth, for the social perfection of the human race, for the advancement of humanity to a true rational life, for the cure of the moral and physical evils of society, for the fraternization of men and nations, the universal reign of justice and of peace?

But again: the advancement of Science and the diffusion of Knowledge, are much looked to as the promise of a better future. No one can think more highly of these than I do as conditions and elements of the highest social state; but as they do not in themselves alone constitute it, so neither in their own efficacy nor in any efficacies which they necessarily imply, do they make it sure.

Much stress is laid upon the marvels of scientific discovery and their application to human uses, to which the last fifty years has given birth. The secrets of the Life of Nature are disclosed; the wonderful processes, conditions and laws of the growth and nutrition of vegetable life are so ascertained, that agriculture—the great art on which the physical life of humanity mainly rests—is coming to be the most scientific of all arts, supplying with the greatest certainty, exactitude, and economy, the conditions for the restoration of worn-out fertility, and the appropriate food and tillage for each several product, and thus multiplying a hundredfold the capabilities of human subsistence on the face of the earth, to which the earthly life of man is tied; the sun is made to copy as no artistic human eye and hand can portray; steam and lightning have annihilated space and time, and brought the ends of the world into contact—the world both of matter and of mind. These are indeed the marvels of the age. I stand in admiration, wonder, and awe, before them. And greater marvels still will doubtless be disclosed in the coming age.

But it should be remembered that all the dominion over nature which the human understanding gains should be subordinated to the control of reason, should be used for rational ends. . . .

And as to the general diffusion of knowledge—it must be remembered that knowledge is a power for evil as well as for good. Light in the head is not necessarily goodness in the heart. Men instructed with knowledge may be the wiser and the better for it, or they may be merely more sharp and knowing in evil. Scientific discoveries, the most useful and beneficent in their proper application, can be turned to account as instruments of crime. Knaves and rogues have seized on photography and made counterfeit bank notes, which the bank officers, whose names they bore, could not distinguish from those they signed. Anaesthetic agents, designed to relieve human pain, are employed by thieves and burglars, to put to sleep, or to deepen the slumbers of those they would plunder. It may indeed be said that science will ever find out, and general instruction diffuse the knowledge of new methods for protecting society against such evil uses of scientific discoveries. What sort of a race is this? Quite a forlorn hope for human progress—it seems to me. . . .

Unless, then, we give over in despair of a brighter future, where shall we turn to look for those corrective and saving powers? I know but one direction in which it remains to look. We have already looked everywhere else. Shall we then turn to CHRISTIANITY as the last hope for the social perfectionment of the human race? Shall we consider what and how much Christianity can effect— how and under what conditions—and what promise for the future is herein contained?

Here I see at once—as all must see—that the universal prevalence of Christianity as an *actuating principle* in the life of the world would be the advancement of the human race to the rational perfection of the social state. Let the life of humanity—of men and of nations, in their individual, social, and political relations, in their civilization, culture, science, and art—become permeated and actuated by the *moral spirit* of Christianity, and there would be nothing more for reason to demand or the heart to desire.

I see, too, that Christianity purports to embody the conditions and means of making its moral spirit a living principle in the life of humanity. In Christianity—not, indeed, considered merely as a body of doctrines and ethical precepts, and a visible institute of worship and moral discipline, but in Christianity considered as an historical organization of supernatural Divine powers—I see propounded the only adequate cure for the corruption of the human race.

14. BENJAMIN R. CURTIS

Executive Power
(1862)

Benjamin R. Curtis (1809-1874), a leading jurist of the Civil War era, was graduated from Harvard in 1829, second in his class. A successful, scholarly, and conservative lawyer, Curtis also won renown as one of the two United States Supreme Court Justices who dissented in the Dred Scott case. During the Civil War he bitterly criticized President Lincoln's use of the war power to suspend the writ of habeas corpus. Later, as one of Andrew Johnson's chief legal counsel, he made an outstanding defense of the President at the impeachment trial.

The war in which we are now engaged is a just and necessary war. It must be prosecuted with the whole force of this government till the military power of the South is broken, and they submit themselves to their duty to obey, and our right to have obeyed, the Constitution of the United States as "the supreme law of the land." But with what sense of right can we subdue them by arms to obey the Constitution as the supreme law of *their* part of the land, if we have ceased to obey it, or failed to preserve it, as the supreme law of *our* part of the land.

I am a member of no political party. Duties, inconsistent, in my opinion, with the preservation of any attachments to a political party, caused me to withdraw from all such connections, many years ago, and they have never been resumed. I have no occasion to listen to the exhortations, now so frequent, to divest myself of party ties, and disregard party objects, and act for my country. I have nothing but my country for which to act, in any public affair; and solely because I have that yet remaining, and know not but it may be possible, from my studies and reflections, to say something to my countrymen which may aid them to form right conclusions in these dark and dangerous times, I now, reluctantly, address them.

I do not propose to discuss the question whether the first of these proclamations [Emancipation Proclamation] of the President, if definitively adopted, can have any practical effect on the unhappy race of persons to whom it refers; nor what its practical consequences would be, upon them and upon the white population of the United States, if it should take effect; nor through what scenes of bloodshed, and worse than bloodshed, it may be, we should advance to those final conditions; nor even the lawfulness, in any Christian or civilized sense, of the use of such means to attain *any* end.

If the entire social condition of nine millions of people has, in the providence of God, been allowed to depend upon the executive decree of one man, it will be the most stupendous fact which the history of the race has exhibited. But, for myself, I do not yet perceive that this vast responsibility is placed upon the President of the United States. I do not yet see that it depends upon his executive decree, whether a servile war shall be invoked to help twenty millions of the white race to assert the rightful authority of the Constitution and laws of their country, over those who refuse to obey them. *But I do see that this proclamation asserts the power of the Executive to make such a decree.*

I do not yet perceive how it is that my neighbors and myself, residing remote from armies and their operations, and where all the laws of the land may be enforced by constitutional means, should be subjected to the possibility of military arrest and imprisonment, and trial before a military commission, and punishment at its discretion for offences unknown to the law; a possibility to be converted into a fact at the mere will of the President, or of some subordinate officer, clothed by him with this power. *But I do perceive that this executive power is asserted.*

I am quite aware, that in times of great public danger, unexpected perils, which the legislative power have failed to provide against, may imperatively demand instant and vigorous executive action, passing beyond the limits of the laws; and that, when the Executive has assumed the high responsibility of such a necessary exercise of mere power, he may justly look for indemnity to that department of the government which alone has the rightful authority to grant it—an indemnity which should be always sought and accorded *upon the clearest admission of legal wrong,* finding its excuse in the exceptional case which made that wrong absolutely necessary for the public safety.

But I find no resemblance between such exceptional cases and the substance of these proclamations and these orders. They do not relate to exceptional cases—they establish a system. They do not relate to some instant emergency—they cover an indefinite future. They do not seek for excuses—they assert powers and rights. They are general rules of action, applicable to the entire country, and to every person in it; or to great tracts of country and to the social condition of their people; and they are to be applied whenever and wherever and to whomsoever the President, or any subordinate officer whom he may employ, may choose to apply them.

Certainly these things are worthy of the most deliberate and searching examination.

Let us, then, analyze these proclamations and orders of the President; let us comprehend the nature and extent of the powers they assume. Above all, let us examine that portentous cloud of the military power of the President, which is supposed to have overcome us and the civil liberties of the country, pursuant to the will of the people, ordained in the Constitution *because we are in a state of war*.

And first, let us understand the nature and operation of the proclamation of emancipation, as it is termed; then, let us see the character and scope of the other proclamation, and the orders of the Secretary of War, designed to give it practical effect, and having done so, let us examine the asserted source of these powers.

The proclamation of emancipation, if taken to mean what in terms it asserts, is an executive decree, that on the first day of January next, all persons held as slaves, within such States or parts of States as shall then be designated, shall cease to be lawfully held to service, and may by their own efforts, and with the aid of the military power of the United States, vindicate their lawful right to their personal freedom.

The persons who are the subjects of this proclamation are held to service by the laws of the respective States in which they may reside, enacted by State authority, as clear and unquestionable, under our system of government, as any law passed by any State on any subject.

This proclamation, then, by an executive decree, proposes to repeal and annul valid State laws which regulate the domestic relations of their people. Such is the mode of operation of the decree.

The next observable characteristic is, that this executive decree holds out this proposed repeal of State laws as a threatened *penalty* for the continuance of a governing majority of the people of each State, or part of a State, in rebellion against the United States. So that the President hereby assumes to himself the power to denounce it as a punishment against the entire people of a State, that the valid laws of that State which regulate the domestic condition of its inhabitants, shall become null and void, at a certain future date, by reason of the criminal conduct of a governing majority of its people.

This penalty, however, it should be observed, is not to be inflicted on those persons who have been guilty of treason. The freedom of *their* slaves was already provided for by the act of Congress, recited in a subsequent part of the proclamation. It is not, therefore, as a punishment of guilty persons, that the Commander-in-chief decrees the freedom of slaves. It is upon the slaves of loyal persons, or of those who, from their tender years, or other disability, cannot be either disloyal or otherwise, that the proclamation is to operate, if at all; and it is to operate to set them free, in spite of the valid laws of their States, because a majority of the legal voters do not send representatives to Congress.

Now it is easy to understand how persons held to service under the laws of these States, and how the army and navy under the orders of the President, may overturn these valid laws of the States, just as it is easy to imagine that any law may be *violated by physical force*. But I do not understand it to be the purpose of the President to incite a part of the inhabitants of the United States to rise in insurrection against valid laws; but that by virtue of some power which he possesses, he proposes to annul those laws, so that they are no longer to have any operation.

The second proclamation, and the orders of the Secretary of War, which follow it, place every citizen of the United States under the direct military command and control of the President. They declare and define new offences, not known to any law of the United States. They subject all citizens to be imprisoned upon a military order, at the pleasure of the President, when, where, and so long as he, or whoever is acting for him, may choose. They hold the citizen to trial before a military commission appointed by the President, or his representative, for such acts or omissions as the President may think proper to decree to be offences; and they subject him to such punishment as such military commission may be pleased to inflict. They create new offices, in such number, and whose occupants are to receive such compensation, as the President may direct; and the holders of these offices, scattered through the States, but with one chief inquisitor at Washington, are to inspect and report upon the loyalty of the citizens, with a view to the above described proceedings against them, when deemed suitable by the central authority. . . .

When the Constitution says that the President shall be the commander-in-chief of the army and navy of the United States, and of the militia of the several States when called into the actual service of the United States, does it mean that he shall possess military power and command *over all citizens of the United States;* that, by military edicts, he may control all citizens, as if enlisted in the army or navy, or in the militia called into the actual service of the United States? Does it mean that he may make himself a legislator, and enact penal laws governing the citizens of the United States, and erect tribunals, and create offices to enforce his penal edicts upon citizens? Does it mean that he may, by a prospective executive decree, repeal and annul the laws of the several States, which respect subjects reserved by the Constitution for the exclusive action of the States and the people? The President is the commander-in-chief of the army and navy, not only by force of the Constitution, but under and subject to the Constitution, and to every restriction therein contained, and to every law enacted by its authority, as completely and clearly as the private in his ranks.

He is general-in-chief; but can a general-in-chief *disobey any law of his own country?* When he can, he superadds to his *rights* as commander the *powers* of a usurper; and that is military despotism. In the noise of arms have we become deaf to the warning voices of our fathers, to take care that the military shall always be subservient to the civil power? Instead of listening to these voices, some persons now seem to think that it is enough to silence objection, to say, true enough, there is no civil right to do this or that, but it is a military act. They seem to have forgotten that every military act is to be tested by the Constitution and laws of the country under whose authority it is done. And that under the Constitution and laws of the United States, no more than under the government of Great Britain, or under any free or any settled government, the mere authority to command an army, is not an authority to disobey the laws of the country.

The framers of the Constitution thought it wise that the powers of the commander-in-chief of the military forces of the United States should be placed in the hands of the chief civil magistrate. But the powers of commander-in-chief are in no degree enhanced or varied by being conferred upon the same officer who has important civil functions. If the Constitution had provided that a commander-in-chief should be appointed by Congress, his powers would have been the same as the military powers of the President now are. And what would be thought by the American people of an attempt by a general-in-chief, to legislate by his decrees, for the people and the States.

Besides, all the powers of the President are executive merely. He cannot make a law. He cannot repeal one. He can only execute the laws. He can neither make, nor suspend, nor alter them. He cannot even make an article of war. He may govern the army, either by general or special orders, but only in subordination to the Constitution and laws of the United States, and the articles of war enacted by the legislative power.

The time has certainly come when the people of the United States *must* understand, and *must* apply those great rules of civil liberty, which have been arrived at by the self-devoted efforts of thought and action of their ancestors, during seven hundred years of struggle against arbitrary power. If they fail to understand and apply them, if they fail to hold every branch of their government steadily to them, who can imagine what is to come out of this great and desperate struggle. The military power of eleven of these States being destroyed—what then? What is to be their condition? What is to be *our* condition?

Are the great principles of free government to be used and consumed as means of war? Are we not wise enough and strong enough to carry on this war to a successful military end without submitting to the loss of any one great principle of liberty? We are strong enough. *We are wise enough,* if the people and their servants will but understand and observe the just limits of military power.

What, then, are those limits? They are these. There is military law; there is martial law. *Military* law is that system of laws enacted by the legislative power for the government of the army and navy of the United States, and of the militia when called into the actual service of the United States. It has no control whatever over any person or any property of any citizen. It could not even apply to the teamsters of an army, save by force of express provisions of the laws of Congress, making such persons amenable thereto. The persons and the property of private citizens of the United States, are as absolutely exempted from the control of military law as they are exempted from the control of the laws of Great Britain.

But there is also *martial law*. What is this? It is the will of a military commander, operating without any restraint, save his judgment, upon the lives, upon the property, upon the entire social and individual condition of all over whom this law extends. But, under the Constitution of the United States, *over whom does such law extend?*

Will any one be bold enough to say, in view of the history of our ancestors and ourselves, that the President of the United States can extend such law as that over the entire country, or over any defined geographical part thereof, save in connection with some particular military operations which he is carrying on there? Since Charles I lost his head, there has been no king in England who could make such law, in that realm. And where is there to be found, in our history, or our constitutions, either State or national, any warrant for saying, that a President of the United States has been empowered by the Constitution to extend martial law over the whole country, and to subject thereby to his military power, every right of every citizen? He has no such authority.

In time of war, a military commander, whether he be the Commander-in-chief, or one of his subordinates, must possess and exercise powers both over the persons and the property of citizens which do not exist in time of peace. But he possesses and exercises such powers, *not in spite of the Constitution and laws of the United States, or in derogation from their authority, but in virtue thereof and in strict subordination thereto.* The general who moves his army over private property in the course of his operations in the field, or who impresses into the public service means of transportation, or subsistence, to enable him to act against the enemy, or who seizes persons within his lines as spies, or destroys supplies in immediate danger of falling into the hands of the enemy, uses authority unknown to the Constitution and laws of the United States in time of *peace;* but not unknown to that Constitution and those laws in time of *war.* The power to declare war, includes the power to use the customary and necessary means effectually to carry it on. As Congress may institute a state of war, it may legislate into existence and place under executive control the means for its prosecution. And, in time of war without any special legislation, not the Commander-in-chief only, but every commander of an expedition, or of a military post, is lawfully empowered by the

Constitution and laws of the United States to do whatever is necessary, and is sanctioned by the laws of war, to accomplish the lawful
objects of his command. But it is obvious that this implied authority must find early limits somewhere. If it were admitted that a
commanding general in the field might do whatever in his discretion might be necessary to subdue the enemy, he could levy contributions to pay his soldiers; he could force conscripts into his
service; he could drive out of the entire country all persons not
desirous to aid him—in short, he would be the absolute master of
the country for the time being.

No one has ever supposed—no one will now undertake to maintain—that the Commander-in-chief, in time of war, has any such
lawful authority as this.

What, then, is his authority over the persons and property of
citizens? I answer that, over all persons enlisted in his forces he
has military power and command; that over all persons and property *within the sphere of his actual operations in the field,* he may
lawfully exercise such restraint and control as the successful prosecution of his particular military enterprise may, in his honest
judgment, absolutely require; and upon such persons as have committed offences against any article of war, he may, through appropriate military tribunals, inflict the punishment prescribed by
law. *And there his lawful authority ends.*

The military power over citizens and their property is a power
to *act,* not a power to prescribe rules for *future* action. It springs
from present pressing emergencies, and is limited by them. It cannot assume the functions of the statesman or legislator, and make
provision for future or distant arrangements by which persons or
property may be made subservient to military uses. It is the physical force of an army in the field, and may control whatever is so
near as to be actually reached by that force, in order to remove obstructions to its exercise.

But when the military commander controls the persons or property of citizens, who are beyond the sphere of his actual operations in the field when he makes laws to govern their conduct, he becomes a legislator. Those laws may be made actually operative; obedience to them may be enforced by military power; their purpose and effect may be solely to recruit or support his armies, or to weaken the power of the enemy with whom he is contending. *But he is a legislator still;* and whether his edicts are clothed in the form of proclamations, or of military orders, by whatever name they may be called, they are laws. If he have the legislative power, conferred on him by the people, it is well. If not, he usurps it.

He has no more lawful authority to hold all the *citizens* of the entire country, outside of the sphere of his actual operations in the field, amenable to his military edicts, than he has to hold all the *property* of the country subject to his military requisitions. He is not the military commander of the *citizens* of the United States, but of its *soldiers*.

15. HENRY GEORGE

What the Railroad Will Bring Us
(1868)

Henry George (1839-1897) arrived in San Francisco
in 1858, an impoverished young man with little
education. Here he was able to observe at firsthand
the great extremes of wealth and poverty left in the
wake of the gold rush. Studying the social causes of
poverty, George came to believe that the trouble lay
in the ratio of population to land, and in the system
of taxes that allowed vast tracts to be held for purposes of speculation. His solution—the taxation of
the unearned increment in the price of land—became
famous with the publication in 1879 of his book
Progress and Poverty.

What is the railroad to do for *us?*—this railroad that we have
looked for, hoped for, prayed for so long?

Much as the matter has been thought about and talked about;
many as have been the speeches made and newspaper articles
written on the subject, there are probably but few of us who really
comprehend all it will do. We are so used to the California of the
stagecoach, widely separated from the rest of the world, that we
can hardly realize what the California of the railroad will be—the
California netted with iron tracks, and almost as near in point of
time to Chicago and St. Louis, as Virginia City was to San Francisco when the Washoe excitement first commenced, or as Red
Bluff is now.

The sharpest sense of Americans—the keen sense of gain, which certainly does not lose its keenness in our bracing air—is the first to realize what is coming with our railroad. All over the State, land is appreciating—fortunes are being made in a day by buying and parcelling out Spanish ranches; the Government surveyors and registrars are busy; speculators are grappling the public domain by the hundred of thousand of acres; while for miles in every direction around San Francisco, ground is being laid off into homestead lots. The spirit of speculation, doubles, trebles, quadruples the past growth of the city in its calculations, and then discounts the result, confident that there still remains a margin. And it is not far wrong. The new era will be one of great material prosperity, if material prosperity means more people, more houses, more farms and mines, more factories and ships. Calculations based upon the growth of San Francisco can hardly be wild. There are men now in their prime among us who will live to see this the second, perhaps the first city on the continent. This, which may sound like the sanguine utterance of California speculation, is simply a logical deduction from the past.

After the first impulse which settled California had subsided, there came a time of stagnation, if not of absolute decay. As the placers one after another were exhausted, the miners moved off; once populous districts were deserted, once flourishing mining towns fell into ruin, and it seemed to superficial observers as though the State had passed the acme of her prosperity. During this period quartz mining was being slowly developed, agriculture steadily increasing in importance, and manufactures gaining a foot-hold; but the progress of these industries was slow; they could not at once compensate for the exhaustion of the placer mines; and though San Francisco, drawing her support from the whole coast, continued to grow steadily if not rapidly, the aggregate population and wealth of the State diminished rather than increased. Through this period we have passed. Although the decay of portions of the mining regions still continues, there has been going on for some time a steady, rapid development of the State at large—felt principally in the agricultural counties and the metropolis, but which is now beginning to make itself felt from one end of the State to the other. To produce this, several causes have combined, but prominent among them must be reckoned the new force to which we principally and primarily look for the development of the future—railroads. This year—during which more has been done in railroad building and railroad projecting than in all previous years combined—the immediate and prospective influence of this new force, the great settler of States and builder up of cities, has first been powerfully felt. This year we have received the first great wave of the coming tide of immigration, the country has filled up more rapidly than for many years before, more new farms have been staked off and more land sold. And this year a spirit of sanguine enterprise has sprung from present prosperity. . . .

The new era into which our State is about entering—or, perhaps, to speak more correctly, has already entered—is without doubt an era of steady, rapid and substantial growth; of great addition to population and immense increase in the totals of the Assessor's lists. Yet we cannot hope to escape the great law of compensation which exacts some loss for every gain. And as there are but few of us who, could we retrace our lives, retaining the knowledge we have gained, would pass from childhood into youth, or from youth into manhood, with unmixed feelings, so we imagine that if the genius of California, whom we picture on the shield of our State, were really a sentient being, she would not look forward now entirely without regret. The California of the new era will be greater, richer, more powerful than the California of the past; but will she be still the same California whom her adopted children, gathered from all climes, love better than their own mother lands; from which all who have lived within her bounds are proud to hail; to which all who have known her long to return? She will have more people; but among those people will there be so large a proportion of full, true men? She will have more wealth; but will it be so evenly distributed? She will have more luxury and refinement and culture; but will she have such general comfort, so little squalor and misery; so little of the grinding, hopeless poverty that chills and cramps the souls of men, and converts them into brutes?

Amid all our rejoicing and all our gratulation let us see clearly whither we are tending. Increase in population and in wealth past a certain point means simply an approximation to the condition of older countries—the Eastern States and Europe. Would the average Californian prefer to "take his chances" in New York or Massachusetts, or in California as it is and has been? Is England, with her population of twenty millions to an area not more than one-third that of our State, and a wealth which per inhabitant is six or seven times that of California, a better country than California to live in? Probably, if one were born a duke or a factory lord, or to any place among the upper ten thousand; but if one were born among the lower millions—how then?

And so the California of the future—the California of the new era—will be a better country for some classes than the California of the present; and so too, it must be a worse country for others. Which of these classes will be the largest? Are there more mill owners or factory operatives in Lancastershire; more brown stone mansions, or tenement rooms in New York?

With the tendency of human nature to set the highest value on that which it has not, we have clamored for immigration, for population, as though that was the one sole good. But if this be so, how is it that the most populous countries in the world are the most miserable, most corrupt, most stagnant and hopeless? How is it that in populous and wealthy England there is so much more misery, vice and social disease than in her poor and sparsely populated colonies? If the large population is not a curse as well as a blessing, how was it that the black-death which swept off one-third of the population of England produced such a rise in the standard of wages and the standard of comfort among the people?

We want great cities, large factories, and mines worked cheaply, in this California of ours! Would we esteem ourselves gainers if New York, ruled and robbed by thieves, loafers and brothel-keepers; nursing a race of savages fiercer and meaner than any who ever shrieked a war-whoop on the plains; could be set down on our bay to-morrow? Would we be the gainers, if the cotton-mills of Massachusetts, with their thousands of little children who, official papers tell us, are being literally worked to death, could be transported to the banks of the American; or the file and pin factories of England, where young girls are treated worse than ever slaves on Southern plantations, be reared as by magic at Antioch? Or if among our mountains we could by wishing have the miners, men, women and children, who work the iron and coal mines of Belgium and France, where the condition of production is that the laborer shall have meat but once a week—would we wish them here?

Can we have one thing without the other? We might, perhaps. But does human nature differ in different longitudes? Do the laws of production and distribution, inexorable in their sphere as the law of gravitation in its, lose their power in a country where no rain falls in the summer time?

For years the high rate of interest and the high rate of wages prevailing in California have been special subjects for the lamentation of a certain school of local political economists, who could not see that high wages and high interest were indications that the natural wealth of the country was not yet monopolized, that great opportunities were open to all—who did not know that these were evidences of social health, and that it were as wise to lament them as for the maiden to wish to exchange the natural bloom on her cheek for the interesting pallor of the invalid?

But however this be, it is certain that the tendency of the new era—of the more dense population and more thorough development of the wealth of the State—will be to a reduction both of the rate of interest and the rate of wages, particularly the latter. This tendency may not, probably will not, be shown immediately; but it will be before long, and that powerfully, unless balanced and counteracted by other influences which we are not now considering, which do not yet appear, and which it is probable will not appear for some time yet.

The truth is, that the completion of the railroad and the consequent great increase of business and population, will not be a benefit to all of us, but only to a portion. As a general rule (liable of course to exceptions) those who *have,* it will make wealthier; for those who *have not,* it will make it more difficult to get. Those who have lands, mines, established businesses, special abilities of certain kinds, will become richer for it and find increased opportunities; those who have only their own labor will become poorer, and find it harder to get ahead—first, because it will take more capital to buy land or to get into business; and second, because as competition reduces the wages of labor, this capital will be harder for them to obtain.

What, for instance, does the rise in land mean? Several things, but certainly and prominently this; that it will be harder in future for a poor man to get a farm or a homestead lot. In some sections of the State, land which twelve months ago could have been had for a dollar an acre, cannot now be had for less than fifteen dollars. In other words, the settler who last year might have had at once a farm of his own, must now either go to work on wages for some one else, pay rent or buy on time; in either case being compelled to give to the capitalist a large proportion of the earnings which, had he arrived a year ago, he might have had all for himself. And as proprietorship is thus rendered more difficult and less profitable to the poor, more are forced into the labor market to compete with each other, and cut down the rate of wages—that is, to make the division of their joint production between labor and capital more in favor of capital and less in favor of labor.

And so in San Francisco the rise in building lots means that it will be harder for a poor man to get a house and lot for himself, and if he has none that he will have to use more of his earnings for rent; means a crowding of the poorer classes together; signifies courts, slums, tenement-houses, squalor and vice.

San Francisco has one great advantage—there is probably a larger proportion of her population owning homesteads and homestead lots than in any other city of the United States. The product of the rise of real estate will thus be more evenly distributed, and the social and political advantages of this diffused proprietorship cannot be overestimated. Nor can it be too much regretted that the princely domain which San Francisco inherited as the successor of the pueblo was not appropriated to furnishing free, or almost free, homesteads to actual settlers, instead of being allowed to pass into the hands of a few, to make more millionaires. Had the matter been taken up in time and in a proper spirit, this disposition might easily have been secured, and the great city of the future would have had a population bound to her by the strongest ties—a population better, freer, more virtuous, independent and public spirited than any great city the world has ever had.

To say that "Power is constantly stealing from the many to the few," is only to state in another form the law that wealth tends to concentration. In the new era into which the world has entered since the application of steam, this law is more potent than ever; in the new era into which California is entering, its operations will be more marked here than ever before. The locomotive is a great centralizer. It kills little towns and builds up great cities, and in the same way kills little businesses and builds up great ones. We have had comparatively but few rich men; no very rich ones, in the meaning "very rich" has in these times. But the process is going on. The great city that is to be will have its Astors, Vanderbilts, Stewarts and Spragues, and he who looks a few years ahead may even now read their names as he passes along Montgomery, California or Front streets. With the protection which property gets in modern times—with stocks, bonds, burglar-proof safes and police-men; with the railroad and the telegraph—after a man gets a cer-tain amount of money it is plain sailing, and he need take no risks. Astor said that to get his first thousand dollars was his great-est struggle; but when one gets a million, if he has ordinary prudence, how much he will have is only a question of life. Nor can we rely on the absence of laws of primogeniture and entail to dissipate these large fortunes so menacing to the general weal. Any large fortune will, of course, become dissipated in time, even in spite of laws of primogeniture and entail; but every aggregation of wealth implies and necessitates others, and so that the aggregations remain, it matters little in what particular hands. Stewart, in the natural course of things, will die before long, and being childless, his wealth will be dissipated, or at least go out of the dry goods business. But will this avail the smaller dealers whom he has crushed or is crushing now? Not at all. Some one else will step in, take his place in the trade, and run the great money-making machine which he has organized, or some other similar one. Stewart and other great houses have concentrated the business, and it will remain concentrated.

Nor is it worth while to shut our eyes to the effects of this concentration of wealth. One millionaire involves the existence of just so many proletarians. It is the great tree and the saplings over again. We need not look far from the palace to find the hovel. When people can charter special steamboats to take them to watering places, pay four thousand dollars for the summer rental of a cottage, build marble stables for their horses, and give dinner parties which cost by the thousand dollars a head, we may know that there are poor girls on the streets pondering between starvation and dishonor. When liveries appear, look out for bare-footed children. A few liveries are now to be seen on our streets; we think their appearance coincides in date with the establishment of the alms-house. They are few, plain and modest now; they will grow more numerous and gaudy—and then we will not wait long for the children—their corollaries.

But there is another side: we are to become a great, populous, wealthy community. And in such a community many good things are possible that are not possible in a community such as ours has been. There have been artists, scholars, and men of special knowledge and ability among us, who could and some of whom have since won distinction and wealth in older and larger cities, but who here could only make a living by digging sand, peddling vegetables, or washing dishes in restaurants. It will not be so in the San Francisco of the future. We shall keep such men with us, and reward them, instead of driving them away. We shall have our noble charities, great museums, libraries and universities; a class of men who have leisure for thought and culture; magnificent theatres and opera houses; parks and pleasure gardens.

We shall develop a literature of our own, issue books which

will be read wherever the English language is spoken, and maintain periodicals which will rank with those of the East and Europe. The *Bulletin, Times* and *Alta,* good as they are, must become, or must yield to, journals of the type of the New York *Herald* or the Chicago *Tribune.* The railroads which will carry the San Francisco newspapers over a wide extent of country the same day that they are issued, will place them on a par, or almost on a par in point of time, with journals printed in the interior, while their metropolitan circulation and business will enable them to publish more and later news than interior papers can.

The same law of concentration will work in other businesses in the same way. The railroads may benefit Sacramento and Stockton by making of them workshops, but no one will stop there to buy goods when he can go to San Francisco, make his choice from larger stocks, and return the same day.

But again comes the question: will this California of the future, with its facilities for travel and transportation; its huge metropolis and pleasant watering places; its noble literature and great newspapers; universities, libraries and museums; parks and operas; fleets of yachts and miles of villas, possess still the charm which makes Californians prefer their State, even as it is, to places where all these things are to be found?

What constitutes the peculiar charm of California, which all who have lived here long enough feel? Not the climate alone. Heresy though it may be to say so, there are climates as good; some that are better. Not merely that there is less social restraint, for there are parts of the Union—and parts from which tourists occasionally come to lecture us—where there is much less social restraint than in California. Not simply that the opportunities of making money have been better here; for the opportunities for making large fortunes have not been so good as in some other places, and there are many who have not made money here, who prefer this country to any other; many who after leaving us throw away certainty of profit to return and "take the chances" of California. It certainly is not in the growth of local attachment, for the Californian has even less local attachment than the average American, and will move about from one end of the State to the other with perfect indifference. It is not that we have the culture or the opportunities to gratify luxurious and cultivated tastes that older countries afford, and yet those who leave us on this account as a general thing come back again.

No: the potent charm of California, which all feel but few analyze, has been more in the character, habits and modes of thought of her people—called forth by the peculiar conditions of the young State—than in anything else. In California there has been a certain cosmopolitanism, a certain freedom and breadth of common thought and feeling, natural to a community made up from so many different sources, to which every man and woman had been transplanted—all travellers to some extent, and with native angularities of prejudice and habit more or less worn off. Then there has been a feeling of personal independence and equality, a general hopefulness and self-reliance, and a certain large-heartedness and open-handedness which were born of the comparative evenness with which property was distributed, the high standard of wages and of comfort, and the latent feeling of everyone that he might "make a strike," and certainly could not be kept down long.

While we have had no very rich class, we have had no really poor class. There have been enough "dead brokes," and how many Californians are there who have not gone through that experience; but there never was a better country to be "broken" in, and where almost every man, even the most successful, had been in the same position, it did not involve the humiliation and loss of hope which attaches to utter poverty in older and more settled communities.

In a country where all had started from the same level—where the banker had been a year or two before a journeyman carpenter, the merchant a foremast hand; the restaurant waiter had perhaps been educated for the bar or the church, and the laborer once counted his "pile," and where the wheel of fortune had been constantly revolving with a rapidity in other places unknown, social lines could not be sharply drawn, nor a reverse dispirit. There was something in the great possibilities of the country; in the feeling that it was one of immense latent wealth; which furnished a background of which a better filled and more thoroughly developed country is destitute, and which contributed not a little to the active, generous, independent social tone.

The characteristics of the principal business—mining—gave a color to all California thought and feeling. It fostered a reckless, generous, independent spirit, with a strong disposition to "take chances" and "trust to luck." Than the placer mining, no more independent business could be conceived. The miner working for himself, owned no master; worked when and only when he pleased; took out his earnings each day in the shining particles which depended for their value on no fluctuations of the market, but would pass current and supply all wants the world over. When his claim gave out, or for any reason he desired to move, he had but to shoulder his pick and move on. Mining of this kind developed its virtues as well as its vices. If it could have been united with ownership of land and the comforts and restraints of home, it would have given us a class of citizens of the utmost value to a republican state. But the "honest miner" of the placers has passed away in California. The Chinaman, the mill-owner and his laborers, the mine superintendent and his gang, are his successors.

This crowding of people into immense cities, this aggregation of wealth into large lumps, this marshalling of men into big gangs under the control of the great "captains of industry," does not

tend to foster personal independence—the basis of all virtues—
nor will it tend to preserve the characteristics which particularly
have made Californians proud of their State.

However, we shall have some real social gains, with some that
are only apparent. We shall have more of home influences, a
deeper religious sentiment, less of the unrest that is bred of an
adventurous and reckless life. We shall have fewer shooting and
stabbing affrays, but we will have probably something worse, from
which, thank God, we have hitherto been exempt—the low, brutal,
cowardly rowdyism of the great Eastern cities. We shall hear less
of highway robberies in the mountains, but more, perhaps, of
pick-pockets, burglars and sneak thieves.

That we can look forward to any political improvement is, to
say the least, doubtful. There is nothing in the changes which are
coming that of itself promises that. There will be a more permanent population, more who will look on California as their home;
but we would not aver that there will be a larger proportion of the
population who will take an intelligent interest in public affairs. In
San Francisco the political future is full of danger. As surely as
San Francisco is destined to become as large as New York, as certain as it is that her political condition is destined to become as bad
as that of New York, unless her citizens are aroused in time to
the necessity of preventive or rather palliative measures. And in
the growth of large corporations and other special interests is an
element of great danger. Of these great corporations and interests
we shall have many. Look, for instance, at the Central Pacific Railroad Company, as it will be, with a line running to Salt Lake, controlling more capital and employing more men than any of the
great Eastern railroads who manage legislatures as they manage
their workshops, and name governors, senators and judges almost
as they name their own engineers and clerks! Can we rely upon
sufficient intelligence, independence and virtue among the many to

resist the political effects of the concentration of great wealth in the hands of a few?

And this in general is the tendency of the time, and of the new era opening before us: to the great development of wealth; to concentration; to the differentiation of classes; to less personal independence among the many and the greater power of the few. We shall lose much which gave a charm to California life; much that was valuable in the character of our people, while we will also wear off defects, and gain some things that we lacked.

With our gains and our losses will come new duties and new responsibilities. Connected more closely with the rest of the nation, we will feel more quickly and keenly all that affects it. We will have to deal, in time, with all the social problems that are forcing themselves on older communities (like the riddles of a Sphinx, which not to answer is death), with one of them, the labor question, rendered peculiarly complex by our proximity to Asia. Public spirit, public virtue, the high resolve of men and women who are capable of feeling the "enthusiasm of humanity," will be needed in the future more than ever.

A great change is coming over our State. We should not prevent it if we could, and could not if we would, but we can view it in all its bearings—look at the dark as well as the bright side, and endeavor to hasten that which is good and retard or prevent that which is bad. A great State is forming; let us see to it that its foundations are laid firm and true.

And as California becomes populous and rich, let us not forget that the character of a people counts for more than their numbers; that the distribution of wealth is even a more important matter than its production. Let us not imagine ourselves in a fools' paradise, where the golden apples will drop into our mouths; let us not think that after the stormy seas and head gales of all the ages, *our* ship has at last struck the trade winds of time. The future of our

State, of our nation, of our race, looks fair and bright; perhaps the future looked so to the philosophers who once sat in the porches of Athens—to the unremembered men who raised the cities whose ruins lie south of us. Our modern civilization strikes broad and deep and looks high. So did the tower which men once built almost unto Heaven.

16. WILLIAM GRAHAM SUMNER

The Case of the Forgotten Man Farther Considered
(1883)

William Graham Sumner (1840-1910), usually regarded as an unyielding conservative, was in many
ways more an old-fashioned liberal and staunch individualist. An erudite scholar in a number of subjects and a highly popular professor at Yale from
1872, Sumner did most of his later writing in sociology, publishing his important *Folkways* in 1907.
Despite his pessimistic belief that the future was
largely determined by the mores and social customs
of the past, he took an active role in behalf of free
trade, academic freedom, and anti-imperialism. At the
same time his criticisms of socialism and social legislation won him the approval of conservatives.

There is a beautiful notion afloat in our literature and in the minds
of our people that men are born to certain "natural rights." If
that were true, there would be something on earth which was got
for nothing, and this world would not be the place it is at all. The
fact is, that there is no right whatever inherited by man which has
not an equivalent and corresponding duty by the side of it, as the
price of it. The rights, advantages, capital, knowledge, and all
other goods which we inherit from past generations have been
won by the struggles and sufferings of past generations; and the
fact that the race lives, though men die, and that the race can by

163

heredity accumulate within some cycle its victories over Nature, is one of the facts which make civilization possible. The struggles of the race as a whole produce the possessions of the race as a whole. Something for nothing is not to be found on earth.

If there were such things as natural rights, the question would arise, Against whom are they good? Who has the corresponding obligation to satisfy these rights? There can be no rights against Nature, except to get out of her whatever we can, which is only the fact of the struggle for existence stated over again. The common assertion is, that the rights are good against society; that is, that society is bound to obtain and secure them for the persons interested. Society, however, is only the persons interested plus some other persons; and as the persons interested have by the hypothesis failed to win the rights, we come to this, that natural rights are the claims which certain persons have by prerogative against some other persons. Such is the actual interpretation in practice of natural rights—claims which some people have by prerogative on other people.

This theory is a very far-reaching one, and of course it is adequate to furnish a foundation for a whole social philosophy. In its widest extension it comes to mean that if any man finds himself uncomfortable in this world, it must be somebody else's fault, and that somebody is bound to come and make him comfortable. Now, the people who are most uncomfortable in this world (for if we should tell all our troubles it would not be found to be a very comfortable world for anybody) are those who have neglected their duties, and consequently have failed to get their rights. The people who can be called upon to serve the uncomfortable must be those who have done their duty, as the world goes, tolerably well. Consequently the doctrine which we are discussing turns out to be in practice only a scheme for making injustice prevail in human society by reversing the distribution of rewards and punishments between those who have done their duty and those who have not.

We are constantly preached at by our public teachers, as if respectable people were to blame because some people are not respectable—as if the man who has done his duty in his own sphere was responsible in some way for another man who has not done his duty in his sphere. There are relations of employer and employee which need to be regulated by compromise and treaty. There are sanitary precautions which need to be taken in factories and houses. There are precautions against fire which are necessary. There is care needed that children be not employed too young, and that they have an education. There is care needed that banks, insurance companies, and railroads be well managed, and that officers do not abuse their trusts. There is a duty in each case on the interested parties to defend their own interest. The penalty of neglect is suffering. The system of providing for these things by boards and inspectors throws the cost of it, not on the interested parties, but on the tax-payers. Some of them, no doubt, are the interested parties, and they may consider that they are exercising the proper care by paying taxes to support an inspector. If so, they only get their fair deserts when the railroad inspector finds out that a bridge is not safe after it is broken down, or when the bank examiner comes in to find out why a bank failed after the cashier has stolen all the funds. The real victim is the Forgotten Man again—the man who has watched his own investments, made his own machinery safe, attended to his own plumbing, and educated his own children, and who, just when he wants to enjoy the fruits of his care, is told that it is his duty to go and take care of some of his negligent neighbors, or, if he does not go, to pay an inspector to go. No doubt it is often in his interest to go or to send, rather than to have the matter neglected, on account of his own connection with the thing neglected, and his own secondary peril; but the point now is, that if preaching and philosophizing can do any good in the premises, it is all wrong to preach to the Forgotten Man that it is his duty to go and remedy other people's neglect. It is not his duty. It is a harsh and unjust burden which is laid upon him, and it is only the more unjust because no one thinks of him when laying the burden so that it falls on him. The exhortations ought to be expended on the negligent—that they take care of themselves.

It is an especially vicious extension of the false doctrine above mentioned that criminals have some sort of a right against or claim on society. Many reformatory plans are based on a doctrine of this kind when they are urged upon the public conscience. A criminal is a man who, instead of working with and for the society, has turned against it, and become destructive and injurious. His punishment means that society rules him out of its membership, and separates him from its association, by execution or imprisonment, according to the gravity of his offense. He has no claims against society at all. What shall be done with him is a question of expediency to be settled in view of the interests of society—that is, of the non-criminals. The French writers of the school of '48 used to represent the badness of the bad men as the fault of "society." As the object of this statement was to show that the badness of the bad men was not the fault of the bad men, and as society contains only good men and bad men, it followed that the badness of the bad men was the fault of the good men. On that theory, of course the good men owed a great deal to the bad men who were in prison and at the galleys on their account. If we do not admit that theory, it behooves us to remember that any claim which we allow to the criminal against the "State" is only so much burden laid upon those who have never cost the State anything for discipline or correction. The punishments of society are just like those of God and Nature—they are warnings to the wrong-doer to reform himself.

When public offices are to be filled numerous candidates at once appear. Some are urged on the ground that they are poor, or cannot earn a living, or want support while getting an education, or have female relatives dependent on them, or are in poor health, or belong in a particular district, or are related to certain persons, or have done meritorious service in some other line of work than that which they apply to do. The abuses of the public service are to be condemned on account of the harm to the public interest, but there is an incidental injustice of the same general character with that which we are discussing. If an office is granted by favoritism or for any personal reason to A, it cannot be given to B. If an office is filled by a person who is unfit for it, he always keeps out somebody somewhere who is fit for it; that is, the social injustice has a victim in an unknown person—the Forgotten Man—and he is some person who has no political influence, and who has known no way in which to secure the chances of life except to deserve them. He is passed by for the noisy, pushing, importunate, and incompetent.

I have said something disparagingly in a previous chapter about the popular rage against combined capital, corporations, corners, selling futures, etc., etc. The popular rage is not without reason, but it is sadly misdirected and the real things which deserve attack are thriving all the time. The greatest social evil with which we have to contend is jobbery. Whatever there is in legislative charters, watering stocks, etc., etc., which is objectionable, comes under the head of jobbery. Jobbery is any scheme which aims to gain, not by the legitimate fruits of industry and enterprise, but by extorting from somebody a part of his product under guise of some pretended industrial undertaking. Of course it is only a modification when the undertaking in question has some legitimate character, but the occasion is used to graft upon it devices for obtaining what has not been earned. Jobbery is the vice of plutocracy, and it is the especial form under which plutocracy corrupts a democratic and republican form of government. The United States is deeply afflicted with it, and the problem of civil liberty here is to conquer it. It affects everything which we really need to have done to such an extent that we have to do without public objects which we need through fear of jobbery. Our public buildings are jobs— not always, but often. They are not needed, or are costly beyond all necessity or even decent luxury. Internal improvements are jobs. They are not made because they are needed to meet needs which have been experienced. They are made to serve private ends, often incidentally the political interests of the persons who vote the appropriations. Pensions have become jobs. In England pensions used to be given to aristocrats, because aristocrats had political influence, in order to corrupt them. Here pensions are given to the great democratic mass, because they have political power, to corrupt them. Instead of going out where there is plenty of land and making a farm there, some people go down under the Mississippi River to make a farm, and then they want to tax all the people in the United States to make dikes to keep the river off their farms. The California gold-miners have washed out gold, and have washed the dirt down into the rivers and on the farms below. They want the Federal Government to now clean out the rivers and restore the farms. The silver-miners found their product declining in value, and they got the Federal Government to go into the market and buy what the public did not want, in order to sustain (as they hoped) the price of silver. The Federal Government is called upon to buy or hire unsalable ships, to build canals which will not pay, to furnish capital for all sorts of experiments, and to provide capital for enterprises of which private individuals will win the profits. All this is called "developing our resources," but it is, in truth, the great plan of all living on each other.

The greatest job of all is a protective tariff. It includes the biggest log-rolling and the widest corruption of economic and political ideas. It was said that there would be a rebellion if the taxes were not taken off whiskey and tobacco, which taxes were paid into the public Treasury. Just then the importations of Sumatra tobacco became important enough to affect the market. The Connecticut tobacco-growers at once called for an import duty on tobacco which would keep up the price of their product. So it appears that if the tax on tobacco is paid to the Federal Treasury there will be a rebellion, but if it is paid to the Connecticut tobacco-raisers there will be no rebellion at all. The farmers have long paid tribute to the manufacturers; now the manufacturing and other laborers are to pay tribute to the farmers. The system is made more comprehensive and complete, and we all are living on each other more than ever.

Now, the plan of plundering each other produces nothing. It only wastes. All the material over which the protected interests wrangle and grab must be got from somebody outside of their circle. The talk is all about the American laborer and American industry, but in every case in which there is not an actual production of wealth by industry there are two laborers and two industries to be considered—the one who gets and the one who gives. Every protected industry has to plead, as the major premise of its argument, that any industry which does not pay *ought* to be carried on at the expense of the consumers of the product, and, as its minor premise, that the industry in question does not pay; that is, that it cannot reproduce a capital equal in value to that which it consumes plus the current rate of profit. Hence every such industry must be a parasite on some other industry. What is the other industry? Who is the other man? This, the real question, is always overlooked.

In all jobbery the case is the same. There is a victim somewhere who is paying for it all. The doors of waste and extravagance stand open, and there seems to be a general agreement to squander and spend. It all belongs to somebody. There is somebody who had to contribute it, and who will have to find more. Nothing is ever said about him. Attention is all absorbed by the clamorous interests, the importunate petitioners, the plausible schemers, the pitiless bores. Now, who is the victim? He is the Forgotten Man. If we go to find him, we shall find him hard at work tilling the soil to get out of it the fund for all the jobbery, the object of all the plunder, the cost of all the economic quackery, and the pay of all the politicians and statesmen who have sacrificed his interests to his enemies. We shall find him an honest, sober, industrious citizen, unknown outside his little circle, paying his debts and his taxes, supporting the church and the school, reading his party newspaper, and cheering for his pet politician. . . .

The Forgotten Man is not a pauper. It belongs to his character to save something. Hence he is a capitalist, though never a great one. He is a "poor" man in the popular sense of the word, but not in a correct sense. In fact, one of the most constant and trustworthy signs that the Forgotten Man is in danger of a new assault is, that "the poor man" is brought into the discussion. Since the Forgotten Man has some capital, any one who cares for his interest will try to make capital secure by securing the inviolability of contracts, the stability of currency, and the firmness of credit. Any one, therefore, who cares for the Forgotten Man will be sure to be considered a friend of the capitalist and an enemy of the poor man.

It is the Forgotten Man who is threatened by every extension of the paternal theory of government. It is he who must work and pay. When, therefore, the statesmen and social philosophers sit down to think what the State can do or ought to do, they really mean to decide what the Forgotten Man shall do. What the

Forgotten Man wants, therefore, is a fuller realization of constitutional liberty. He is suffering from the fact that there are yet mixed in our institutions mediaeval theories of protection, regulation, and authority, and modern theories of independence and individual liberty and responsibility. The consequence of this mixed state of things is, that those who are clever enough to get into control use the paternal theory by which to measure their own rights—that is, they assume privileges; and they use the theory of liberty to measure their own duties—that is, when it comes to the duties, they want to be "let alone." The Forgotten Man never gets into control. He has to pay both ways. His rights are measured to him by the theory of liberty—that is, he has only such as he can conquer; his duties are measured to him on the paternal theory —that is, he must discharge all which are laid upon him, as is the fortune of parents. In a paternal relation there are always two parties, a father and a child; and when we use the paternal relation metaphorically, it is of the first importance to know who is to be father and who is to be child. The *role* of parent falls always to the Forgotten Man. What he wants, therefore, is that ambiguities in our institutions be cleared up, and that liberty be more fully realized.

It behooves any economist or social philosopher, whatever be the grade of his orthodoxy, who proposes to enlarge the sphere of the "State," or to take any steps whatever having in view the welfare of any class whatever, to pursue the analysis of the social effects of his proposition until he finds that other group whose interests must be curtailed or whose energies must be placed under contribution by the course of action which he proposes; and he cannot maintain his proposition until he has demonstrated that it will be more advantageous, *both quantitatively and qualitatively,* to those who must bear the weight of it than complete non-interference by the State with the relations of the parties in question.

17. WILLIAM GRAHAM SUMNER

The Conquest of the United States by Spain
(1899)

William Graham Sumner's individualism was broad
enough to cover the preceding selection as well as the
following biting satire on the Spanish-American War
and imperialism, which he delivered as the Phi Beta
Kappa address at Yale University in 1899.

During the last year the public has been familiarized with de-
scriptions of Spain and of Spanish methods of doing things until
the name of Spain has become a symbol for a certain well-defined
set of notions and policies. On the other hand, the name of the
United States has always been, for all of us, a symbol for a state
of things, a set of ideas and traditions, a group of views about
social and political affairs. Spain was the first, for a long time the
greatest, of the modern imperialist states. The United States, by
its historical origin, its traditions and its principles, is the chief
representative of the revolt and reaction against that kind of a
state. I intend to show that, by the line of action now proposed
to us, which we call expansion and imperialism, we are throwing
away some of the most important elements of the American symbol, and are adopting some of the most important elements of
the Spanish symbol. We have beaten Spain in a military conflict,
but we are submitting to be conquered by her on the field of
ideas and policies. Expansionism and imperialism are nothing but

the old philosophies of national prosperity which have brought Spain to where she now is. Those philosophies appeal to national vanity and national cupidity. They are seductive, especially upon the first view and the most superficial judgment, and therefore it cannot be denied that they are very strong for popular effect. They are delusions, and they will lead us to ruin unless we are hard-headed enough to resist them. In any case, the year 1898 is a great landmark in the history of the United States. The consequences will not be all good or all bad, for such is not the nature of societal influences. They are always mixed of good and ill, and so it will be in this case. Fifty years from now, the historian, looking back to 1898, will no doubt see, in the course which things will have taken, consequences of the proceedings of that year, and of this present one, which will not all be bad, but you will observe that that is not a justification for a happy-go-lucky policy; that does not affect our duty today in all that we do to seek wisdom and prudence, and to determine our actions by the best judgment which we can form. . . .

We talk about "liberty" all the time in a glib and easy way, as if liberty was a thing that men could have if they want it, and to any extent to which they want it. It is certain that a very large part of human liberty consists simply in the choice either to do a thing or to let it alone. If we decide to do it, a whole series of consequences is entailed upon us in regard to which it is exceedingly difficult, or impossible, for us to exercise any liberty at all. The proof of this from the case before us is so clear and easy that I need spend no words upon it. Here, then, you have the reason why it is a rule of sound statesmanship not to embark on an adventurous policy. A statesman could not be expected to know in advance that we should come out of the war with the Philippines on our hands, but it belongs to his education to warn him that a policy of adventure and of gratuitous enterprise would be sure to entail embarrassments of some kind. What comes to us in the evolution of our own life and interests, that we must meet; what we go to seek which lies beyond that domain, is a waste of our energy and a compromise of our liberty and welfare. If this is not sound doctrine, then the historical and social sciences have nothing to teach us which is worth any trouble.

There is another observation, however, about the war which is of far greater importance; that is, that it was a gross violation of self-government. We boast that we are a self-governing people, and in this respect, particularly, we compare ourselves with pride with older nations. . . . If we Americans believe in self-government, why do we let it slip away from us? Why do we barter it away for military glory as Spain did?

There is not a civilized nation which does not talk about its civilizing mission just as grandly as we do. The English, who really have more to boast of in this respect than anybody else, talk least about it, but the Phariseeism with which they correct and instruct other people has made them hated all over the globe. The French believe themselves the guardians of the highest and purest culture, and that the eyes of all mankind are fixed on Paris, from whence they expect oracles of thought and taste. The Germans regard themselves as charged with a mission, especially to us Americans, to save us from egoism and materialism. The Russians, in their books and newspapers, talk about the civilizing mission of Russia, in language that might be translated from some of the finest paragraphs in our imperialistic newspapers. The first principle of Mohammedanism is that we Christians are dogs and infidels, fit only to be enslaved or butchered by Moslems. It is a corollary that, wherever Mohammedanism extends, it carries, in the belief of its votaries, the highest blessings, and that the whole human race would be enormously elevated if Mohammedanism should supplant Christianity everywhere. To come last to Spain, the Spaniards have, for centuries, considered themselves the most zealous and self-sacrificing Christians, especially charged by the Almighty, on this account, to spread true religion and civilization over the globe. They think themselves free and noble, leaders in refinement and the sentiments of personal honor, and they despise us as sordid money-grabbers and heretics. I could bring you passages from peninsular authors of the first rank about the grand role of Spain and Portugal in spreading freedom and truth. Serpa Pinto, the distinguished Portuguese explorer of Africa, speaks of Portugal as the freest country in the world, and he says that it has extended to all its African possessions the blessing of the institutions which it enjoys at home. Now each nation laughs at all the others when it observes these manifestations of national vanity. You may rely upon it that they are all ridiculous by virtue of these pretensions, including ourselves. The point is that each of them repudiates the standards of the others, and the outlying nations, which are to be civilized, hate all the standards of civilized men. We assume that what we like and practise, and what we think better, must come as a welcome blessing to Spanish-Americans and Filipinos. This is grossly and obviously untrue. They hate our ways. They are hostile to our ideas. Our religion, language, institutions, and manners offend them. They like their own ways, and if we appear amongst them as rulers, there will be social discord on all the great departments of social interest. The most important thing which we shall inherit from the Spaniards will be the task of suppressing rebellions. If the United States takes out of the hands of Spain her mission, on the ground that Spain is not executing it well, and if this nation, in its turn, attempts to be schoolmistress to others, it will shrivel up into the same vanity and self-conceit of which Spain now presents an example. To read our current literature one would think that we were already well on the way to it. Now, the great reason why all these enterprises, which begin by saying to somebody else: We know what is good for you, better than you know yourself, and we are going to make you do it—are false and wrong, is that they violate liberty; or, to turn the same statement into other words: the reason why liberty, of which we Americans talk so much, is a good thing, is, that it means leaving people to live out their own lives in their own way, while we do the same. If we believe in liberty, as an American principle, why do we not stand by it? Why are we going to throw it away to enter upon a Spanish policy of dominion and regulation? . . .

Another phenomenon which deserves earnest attention from the student of contemporaneous history and of the trend of political institutions, is the failure of the masses of our people to perceive *the inevitable effect of imperialism on democracy*. On the twenty-ninth of last November the Prime Minister of France was quoted in a cable despatch as follows: "For twenty-eight years we have lived under a contradiction. The army and democracy subsist side by side. The maintenance of the traditions of the army is a menace to liberty, yet they assure the safety of the country and its most sacred duties."

That antagonism of democracy and militarism is now coming to a crisis in France, and militarism is sure to win, because the French people would make any other sacrifice rather than diminish their military strength. In Germany the attempt has been going on for thirty years to establish constitutional government with parliamentary institutions. The parts of the German system are at war with each other. The emperor constantly interferes with the operation of the system, and utters declarations which are entirely personal. He is not responsible, and cannot be answered or criticised. The situation is not so delicate as in France, but it is exceedingly unstable. All the desire of the Germans for self-government and civil liberty runs out into socialism, and socialism is repressed by force or by trickery. The conservative classes of the country acquiesce in the situation, while they deplore it. The reason is because the Emperor is the war-lord. His power and authority are essential to the military strength of the state in face of its neigh- bors. That is the preponderating consideration to which everything else has to yield, and the consequence of it is that there is today scarcely an institution in Germany except the army.

Everywhere you go on the Continent of Europe at this hour you see the conflict between militarism and industrialism. You see the expansion of industrial power pushed forward by the energy, hope, and thrift of men, and you see the development arrested, diverted, crippled, and defeated by measures which are dictated by military considerations. At the same time the press is loaded down with discussions about political economy, political philosophy, and social policy. They are discussing poverty, labor, socialism, charity, re- form, and social ideals, and are boasting of enlightenment and progress, at the same time that the things which are done are dictated not by these considerations, but by military interest. It is militarism which is eating up all the products of science and art, defeating the energy of the population, and wasting its sav- ings. It is militarism which forbids the people to give their atten- tion to the problems of their own welfare, and to give their strength to the education and comfort of their children. It is militarism which is combating the grand efforts of science and art to ameliorate the struggle for existence.

The American people believe that they have a free country, and we are treated to grandiloquent speeches about our Flag and our reputation for freedom and enlightenment. The common opin- ion is that we have these things because we have chosen and adopted them, because they are in the Declaration of Independence and the Constitution. We suppose, therefore, that we are sure to keep them, and that the follies of other people are things which we can hear about with complacency. People say that this country is like no other, that its prosperity proves its exceptionality, and so on. These are popular errors which in time will meet with harsh correction. The United States is in a protected situation. It is easy to have equality where land is abundant, and where the population is small. It is easy to have prosperity where a few men have a great continent to exploit. It is easy to have liberty when you have no dangerous neighbors, and when the struggle for existence is easy. There are no severe penalties, under such circumstances, for political mistakes. Democracy is not then a thing to be nursed and defended, as it is in an old country like France. It is rooted and founded in the economic circumstances of the country. The orators and constitution-makers do not make democracy. They are made by it. This protected position, however, is sure to pass away. As the country fills up with population, and the task of getting a living out of the ground becomes more difficult, the struggle for existence will become harder, and the competition of life more severe. Then liberty and democracy will cost something if they are to be maintained.

Now what will hasten the day when our present advantages will wear out, and when we shall come down to the conditions of the older and densely populated nations? The answer is: war, debt, taxation, diplomacy, a grand governmental system, pomp, glory, a big army and navy, lavish expenditures, political jobbery—in a word, imperialism. In the old days the democratic masses of this country, who knew little about our modern doctrines of social philosophy, had a sound instinct on these matters, and it is no small ground of political disquietude to see it decline. They resisted every appeal to their vanity in the way of pomp and glory which they knew must be paid for. They dreaded a public debt and a standing army. They were narrow-minded and went too far with these notions, but they were at least right, if they wanted to strengthen democracy.

The great foe of democracy now and in the near future is plutocracy. Every year that passes brings out this antagonism more distinctly. It is to be the social war of the twentieth century. In that war militarism, expansion, and imperialism will all favor plutocracy. In the first place, war and expansion will favor jobbery, both in the dependencies and at home. In the second place, they will take away the attention of the people from what the plutocrats are doing. In the third place, they will cause large expenditures of the people's money, the return for which will not go into the Treasury, but into the hands of the few schemers. In the fourth place, they will call for a large public debt and taxes, and these things especially tend to make men unequal because any social burdens bear more heavily on the weak than on the strong, and so make the weak weaker and the strong stronger. Therefore expansion and imperialism are a grand onslaught on democracy.

The point which I have tried to make in this lecture is that expansion and imperialism are at war with the best traditions, principles, and interests of the American people, and that they will plunge us into a network of difficult problems and political perils, which we might have avoided, while they offer us no corresponding advantage in return.

Of course "principles," phrases, and catchwords are always invented to bolster up any policy which anybody wants to recommend. So in this case. The people who have led us on to shut ourselves in, and who now want us to break out, warn us against the terrors of "isolation." Our ancestors all came here to isolate themselves from the social burdens and inherited errors of the Old World. When the others are all over ears in trouble, who would not be isolated in freedom from care? When the others are crushed under the burden of militarism, who would not be isolated in peace and industry? When the others are all struggling under debt and taxes, who would not be isolated in the enjoyment of his own earnings for the benefit of his own family? When the rest are all in a quiver of anxiety, lest at a day's notice they may be involved in a social cataclysm, who would not be isolated out of reach of the disaster? What we are doing is that we are abandoning this blessed isolation to run after a share in the trouble.

The expansionists answer our remonstrances on behalf of the great American principles by saying that times have changed, and that we have outlived the fathers of the Republic and their doctrines. As far as the authority of the great men is concerned, that may well be sacrificed without regret. Authority of persons and names is a dangerous thing. Let us get at the truth and the right. I, for my part, am also afraid of the great principles, and I would make no fight on their behalf. In the ten years before the Revolution our ancestors invented a fine lot of "principles" which they thought would help their case. They repudiated many of them as soon as they got their independence, and the rest of them have since made us a great deal of trouble. I have examined them all critically, and there is not one of them which I consider sound, as it is popularly understood. I have been denounced as a political heretic on this account by people who now repudiate them all in a sentence. But this only clears the ground for the real point. There is a consistency of character for a nation as well as for a man. A man who changes his principles from week to week is destitute of character and deserves no confidence. The great men of this nation were such because they embodied and expressed the opinion and sentiments of the nation in their time. Their names are something more than clubs with which to knock an opponent down when it suits one's purpose, but to be thrown away with contempt when they happen to be on the other side. So of the great principles; whether some of us are skeptical about their entire validity, and want to define and limit them somewhat, is of little importance. If the nation has accepted them, sworn by them, founded its legislation on them, imbedded them in the decisions of its courts, and then if it throws them away at six months' warning, you may depend upon it that that nation will suffer in its moral and political rectitude a shock of the severest kind. . . .

All the validity that the great principles ever had they have now. Anybody who ever candidly studied them and accepted them for no more than they were really worth can stand by them now as well as ever. The time when a maxim or principle is worth something is when you are tempted to violate it.

Another answer which the imperialists make is that Americans can do anything. They say that they do not shrink from responsibilities. They are willing to run into a hole, trusting to luck and cleverness to get out. There are some things the Americans cannot do. Americans cannot make 2 and $2=5$. You may answer that that is an arithmetical impossibility, and is not in the range of our subject. Very well: Americans cannot collect $2 a gallon tax on whiskey. They tried it for many years and failed. That is an economic or political impossibility, the roots of which are in human nature. It is as absolute an impossibility on this domain as the former on the domain of mathematics. So far as yet appears, Americans cannot govern a city of 100,000 inhabitants so as to get comfort and convenience in it at a low cost and without jobbery. The fire department of this city is now demoralized by political jobbery. Spain and all her possessions are not worth as much to you and me as the efficiency of the fire department of New Haven. The Americans in Connecticut cannot abolish the rotten borough system. The English abolished their rotten borough system seventy years ago, in spite of nobles and landlords. We cannot abolish ours in spite of the small towns. Americans cannot reform the pension list. Its abuses are rooted in the methods of democratic self-government, and no one dares to touch them. It is very doubtful indeed if Americans can keep up an army of 100,000 men in time of peace. Where can 100,000 men be found in this country who are willing to spend their lives as soldiers? or, if they are found, what pay will it require to induce them to take this career? Americans cannot disentangle their currency from the confusion into which it was thrown by the Civil War, and they cannot put their currency on a simple, sure, and sound basis which would give stability to the business of the country. This is a political impossibility. Americans cannot assure the suffrage to Negroes throughout the United States. They have tried it for thirty years, and now, contemporaneously with this war with Spain, it has been finally demonstrated that it is a failure. Inasmuch as the Negro is now out of fashion, no further attempt to accomplish this purpose will be made. It is an impossibility on account of the complexity of our system of State and Federal government. If I had time to do so, I could go back over the history of Negro suffrage and show you how curbstone arguments, exactly analogous to the arguments about expansion, were used to favor it, and how objections were thrust aside in this same blustering and senseless manner in which objections to imperialism are met. The ballot, we were told, was an educator, and would solve all difficulties in its own path as by magic. Worse still: Americans cannot assure life, liberty, and the pursuit of happiness to Negroes inside of the United States. When the Negro postmaster's house was set on fire in the night in South Carolina, and not only he, but his wife and children were murdered as they came out, and when, moreover, this incident passed without legal investigation or punishment, it was a bad omen for the extension of liberty, etc., to Malays and Tagals by simply setting over them the American Flag. Upon a little serious examination, the off-hand disposal of an important question of policy, by the declaration that Americans can do anything, proves to be only a silly piece of bombast, and, upon a little reflection, we find that our hands are quite full at home of problems by the solution of which the peace and happiness of the American people could be greatly increased. The laws of nature and of human nature are just as valid for Americans as for anybody else, and if we commit acts, we shall have to take consequences, just like other people. Therefore, prudence demands that we look ahead to see what we are about to do, and that we gauge the means at our disposal, if we do not want to bring calamity on ourselves and our children. We see that the peculiarities of our system of government set limitations on us. We cannot do things which a great centralized monarchy could do. The very blessings and special advantages which we enjoy, as compared with others, bring disabilities with them. That is the great fundamental cause of what I have tried to show throughout this lecture, that we cannot govern dependencies consistently with our political system, and that, if we try it, the state which our fathers founded will suffer a reaction which will transform it into another empire just after the fashion of all the old ones. That is what imperialism means. That is what it will be, and the democratic republic, which has been, will stand in history as a mere transition form like the colonial organization of earlier days.

And yet this scheme of a republic which our fathers formed was a glorious dream which demands more than a word of respect and affection before it passes away. Indeed, it is not fair to call it a dream or even an ideal. It was a possibility which was within our reach if we had been wise enough to grasp and hold it. It was favored by our comparative isolation, or, at least, by our distance from other strong states. The men who came here were able to throw off all the trammels of tradition and established doctrine. They went out into a wilderness, it is true, but they took with them all the art, science, and literature which, up to that time, civilization had produced. They could not, it is true, strip their minds of the ideas which they had inherited, but, in time, as they lived on in the New World, they sifted and selected these ideas, retaining what they chose. Of the Old World institutions, also, they selected and adopted what they chose, and threw aside the rest. It was a grand opportunity to be thus able to strip off all the follies and errors which they had inherited, so far as they chose to do so. They had unlimited land with no feudal restrictions to hinder them in the use of it. Their idea was that they would never allow any of the social and political abuses of the Old World to grow up here. There should be no manors, no barons, no ranks, no prelates, no idle classes, no paupers, no disinherited ones, except the vicious. There were to be no armies except a militia, which would have no functions but those of police. They would have no court and no pomp; no orders, or ribbons, or decorations, or titles. They would have no public debt. They repudiated with scorn the notion that a public debt is a public blessing. If debt was incurred in war it was to be paid in peace and not entailed on posterity. There was to be no grand diplomacy, because they intended to mind their own business, and not be involved in any of the intrigues to which European statesmen were accustomed. There was to be no balance of power and no "reason of state" to cost the life and happiness of citizens. The only part of the Monroe Doctrine which is valid was their determination that the social and political systems of Europe should not be extended over any part of the American Continent, lest people who were weaker than we should lose the opportunity which the new continent gave them to escape from those systems if they wanted to. Our fathers would have an economical government, even if grand people called it a parsimonious one, and taxes should be no greater than were absolutely necessary to pay for such a government. The citizen was to keep all the rest of his earnings, and use them as he thought best for the happiness of himself and his family. The citizen was, above all, to be ensured peace and quiet while he pursued his honest industry and obeyed the laws. No adventurous policies of conquest or ambition, such as, in their belief, kings and nobles had forced, for their own advantage, on European states, would ever be undertaken by a free democratic republic. Therefore the citizen here would never be forced to leave his family, or to give his sons to shed blood for glory, and to leave widows and orphans in misery for nothing. Justice and law were to reign in the midst of simplicity, and a government which had little to do was to offer little field for ambition. In a society where industry, frugality, and prudence were honored, it was believed that the vices of wealth would never flourish.

We know that these beliefs, hopes, and intentions have been only partially fulfilled. We know that, as time has gone on, and we have grown numerous and rich, some of these things have proved impossible ideals, incompatible with a large and flourishing society, but it is by virtue of this conception of a commonwealth that the United States has stood for something unique and grand in the history of mankind, and that its people have been happy. It is by virtue of these ideals that we have been "isolated," isolated in a position which the other nations of the earth have observed in silent envy, and yet there are people who are boasting of their patriotism, because they say that we have taken our place now amongst the nations of the earth by virtue of this war. My patriotism is of the kind which is outraged by the notion that the United States never was a great nation until in a petty three months' campaign it knocked to pieces a poor, decrepit, bankrupt old state like Spain. To hold such an opinion as that is to abandon all American standards, to put shame and scorn on all that our ancestors tried to build up here, and to go over to the standards of which Spain is a representative.

18. ROBERT G. INGERSOLL

What Is Religion?
(1899)

Robert G. Ingersoll (1833-1899) was born in Dresden, New York, but moved as a young man to Illinois.
Largely self-educated and a successful lawyer, Ingersoll was also a highly skilled speaker and debater.
After service in the Union Army during the Civil
War, he became a stalwart nationalist and Republican.
This political conservatism was in curious contrast
with his firm agnostic convictions and enthusiasm for
the Darwinian theory of evolution. Determined to
enlighten the world concerning "some mistakes of
Moses," his sincerity and charm won Ingersoll large
popular audiences despite the radical unconventional
nature of his religious ideas.

Religion has been tried, and in all countries, in all times, has failed.

Religion has never made man merciful.

Remember the Inquisition.

What effect did religion have on slavery?

What effect upon Libby, Saulsbury and Andersonville?

Religion has always been the enemy of science, of investigation
and thought.

Religion has never made man free.

It has never made man moral, temperate, industrious and honest.

Are Christians more temperate, nearer virtuous, nearer honest
than savages?

Among savages do we not find that their vices and cruelties are the fruits of their superstitions?

To those who believe in the Uniformity of Nature, religion is impossible.

Can we affect the nature and qualities of substance by prayer? Can we hasten or delay the tides by worship? Can we change winds by sacrifice? Will kneelings give us wealth? Can we cure disease by supplication? Can we add to our knowledge by ceremony? Can we receive virtue or honor as alms?

Are not the facts in the mental world just as stubborn—just as necessarily produced—as the facts in the material world? Is not what we call mind just as natural as what we call body?

Religion rests on the idea that Nature has a master and that this master will listen to prayer; that this master punishes and rewards; that he loves praise and flattery and hates the brave and free.

Has man obtained any help from heaven?

If we have a theory, we must have facts for the foundation. We must have corner-stones. We must not build on guesses, fancies, analogies or inferences. The structure must have a basement. If we build, we must begin at the bottom.

I have a theory and I have four corner-stones.

The first stone is that matter—substance—cannot be destroyed, cannot be annihilated.

The second stone is that force cannot be destroyed, cannot be annihilated.

The third stone is that matter and force cannot exist apart—no matter without force—no force without matter.

The fourth stone is that that which cannot be destroyed could not have been created; that the indestructible is the uncreateable.

If these corner-stones are facts, it follows as a necessity that matter and force are from and to eternity; that they can neither be increased nor diminished.

It follows that nothing has been or can be created; that there never has been or can be a creator.

It follows that there could not have been any intelligence, any design back of matter and force.

There is no intelligence without force. There is no force without matter. Consequently there could not by any possibility have been any intelligence, any force, back of matter.

It therefore follows that the supernatural does not and cannot exist. If these four corner-stones are facts, Nature has no master. If matter and force are from and to eternity, it follows as a necessity that no God exists; that no God created or governs the universe; that no God exists who answers prayer; no God who succors the oppressed; no God who pities the sufferings of innocence; no God who cares for the slaves with scarred flesh, the mothers robbed of their babes; no God who rescues the tortured, and no God that saves a martyr from the flames. In other words it proves that man has never received any help from heaven; that all sacrifices have been in vain, and that all prayers have died unanswered in the heedless air. I do not pretend to know. I say what I think.

If matter and force have existed from eternity, it then follows that all that has been possible has happened, all that is possible is happening, and all that will be possible will happen.

In the universe there is no chance, no caprice. Every event has parents.

That which has not happened, could not. The present is the necessary product of all the past, the necessary cause of all the future.

In the infinite chain there is, and there can be, no broken, no missing link. The form and motion of every star, the climate of every world, all forms of vegetable and animal life, all instinct, intelligence and conscience, all assertions and denials, all vices and virtues, all thoughts and dreams, all hopes and fears, are necessities. Not one of the countless things and relations in the universe could have been different.

If matter and force are from eternity, then we can say that man had no intelligent creator, that man was not a special creation.

We now know, if we know anything, that Jehovah, the divine potter, did not mix and mould clay into the forms of men and women, and then breathe the breath of life into these forms.

We now know that our first parents were not foreigners. We know that they were natives of this world, produced here, and that their life did not come from the breath of any god. We now know, if we know anything, that the universe is natural, and that men and women have been naturally produced. We now know our ancestors, our pedigree. We have the family tree.

We have all the links of the chain, twenty-six links inclusive from moner to man.

We did not get our information from inspired books. We have fossil facts and living forms.

From the simplest creatures, from blind sensation, from organism, from one vague want, to a single cell with a nucleus, to a hollow ball filled with fluid, to a cup with double walls, to a flat worm, to a something that begins to breathe, to an organism that has a spinal chord, to a link between the invertebrate to the vertebrate, to one that has a cranium—a house for a brain—to one with fins, still onward to one with fore and hinder fins, to the reptile mammalia, to the marsupials, to the lemures, dwellers in trees, to the simiae, to the pithecanthropi, and lastly, to man.

We know the paths that life has traveled. We know the footsteps of advance. They have been traced. The last link has been found. For this we are indebted, more than to all others, to the greatest of biologists, Ernst Haeckel.

We now believe that the universe is natural and we deny the existence of the supernatural.

For thousands of years men and women have been trying to reform the world. They have created gods and devils, heavens and hells; they have written sacred books, performed miracles, built cathedrals and dungeons; they have crowned and uncrowned kings and queens; they have tortured and imprisoned, flayed alive and burned; they have preached and prayed; they have tried promises and threats; they have coaxed and persuaded; they have preached and taught, and in countless ways have endeavored to make people honest, temperate, industrious and virtuous; they have built hospitals and asylums, universities and schools, and seem to have done their very best to make mankind better and happier, and yet they have not succeeded.

Why have the reformers failed? I will tell them why.

Ignorance, poverty, and vice are populating the world. The gutter is a nursery. People unable even to support themselves fill the tenements, the huts and hovels with children. They depend on the Lord, on luck and charity. They are not intelligent enough to think about consequences or to feel responsibility. At the same time they do not want children, because a child is a curse, a curse to them and to itself. The babe is not welcome, because it is a burden. These unwelcome children fill the jails and prisons, the asylums and hospitals, and they crowd the scaffolds. A few are rescued by chance or charity, but the great majority are failures. They become vicious, ferocious. They live by fraud and violence, and bequeath their vices to their children.

Against this inundation of vice the forces of reform are helpless, and charity itself becomes an unconscious promoter of crime.

Failure seems to be the trademark of Nature. Why? Nature

has no design, no intelligence. Nature produces without purpose, sustains without intention and destroys without thought. Man has a little intelligence, and he should use it. Intelligence is the only lever capable of raising mankind.

The real question is, can we prevent the ignorant, the poor, the vicious, from filling the world with their children?

Can we prevent this Missouri of ignorance and vice from emptying into the Mississippi of civilization?

Must the world forever remain the victim of ignorant passion? Can the world be civilized to that degree that consequences will be taken into consideration by all?

Why should men and women have children that they cannot take care of, children that are burdens and curses? Why? Because they have more passion than intelligence, more passion than conscience, more passion than reason.

You cannot reform these people with tracts and talk. You cannot reform these people with preach and creed. Passion is, and always has been, deaf. These weapons of reform are substantially useless. Criminals, tramps, beggars and failures are increasing every day. The prisons, jails, poor-houses and asylums are crowded. Religion is helpless. Law can punish, but it can neither reform criminals nor prevent crime. The tide of vice is rising. The war that is now being waged against the forces of evil is as hopeless as the battle of the fireflies against the darkness of night.

There is but one hope. Ignorance, poverty, and vice must stop populating the world. This cannot be done by moral suasion. This cannot be done by talk or example. This cannot be done by religion or by law, by priest or by hangman. This cannot be done by force, physical or moral.

To accomplish this there is but one way. Science must make woman the owner, the mistress of herself. Science, the only possible saviour of mankind, must put it in the power of woman to decide for herself whether she will or will not become a mother.

This is the solution of the whole question. This frees woman. The babes that are then born will be welcome. They will be clasped with glad hands to happy breasts. They will fill homes with light and joy.

Men and women who believe that slaves are purer, truer, than the free, who believe that fear is a safer guide than knowledge, that only those are really good who obey the commands of others, and that ignorance is the soil in which the perfect, perfumed flower of virtue grows, will with protesting hands hide their shocked faces.

Men and women who think that light is the enemy of virtue, that purity dwells in darkness, that it is dangerous for human beings to know themselves and the facts in Nature that affect their well being, will be horrified at the thought of making intelligence the master of passion.

But I look forward to the time when men and women by reason of their knowledge of consequences, of the morality born of intelligence, will refuse to perpetuate disease and pain, will refuse to fill the world with failures.

When that time comes the prison walls will fall, the dungeons will be flooded with light, and the shadow of the scaffold will cease to curse the earth. Poverty and crime will be childless. The withered hands of want will not be stretched for alms. They will be dust. The whole world will be intelligent, virtuous and free.

Religion can never reform mankind because religion is slavery.

It is far better to be free, to leave the forts and barricades of fear, to stand erect and face the future with a smile.

It is far better to give yourself sometimes to negligence, to drift with wave and tide, with the blind force of the world, to think and dream, to forget the chains and limitations of the breathing life, to forget purpose and object, to lounge in the picture gallery of the brain, to feel once more the clasps and kisses of the past, to bring life's morning back, to see again the forms and faces of the dead, to paint fair pictures for the coming years, to forget all gods, their promises and threats, to feel within your veins life's joyous stream and hear the martial music, the rhythmic beating of your fearless heart.

And then to rouse yourself to do all useful things, to reach with thought and deed the ideal in your brain, to give your fancies wing, that they, like chemist bees, may find art's nectar in the weeds of common things, to look with trained and steady eyes for facts, to find the subtle threads that join the distant with the now, to increase knowledge, to take burdens from the weak, to develop the brain, to defend the right, to make a palace for the soul.

This is real religion. This is real worship.

19. W. E. B. DU BOIS

The Souls of Black Folk
(1903)

William Edward Burghardt Du Bois (1868-1963) was born in Great Barrington, Massachusetts. After studying at Fisk University, he went on to receive the Ph. D. degree at Harvard for his dissertation *The Suppression of the African Slave-Trade.* Although possessed of a scholarly interest in history and sociology, which he taught at Atlanta University, Du Bois was more concerned with advancing the cause of equal rights for Negroes. In 1909 he helped organize the National Association for the Advancement of Colored People, and from 1910 to 1932 he was editor of *Crisis,* its official publication.

Between me and the other world there is ever an unasked question: unasked by some through feelings of delicacy; by others through the difficulty of framing it. All, nevertheless, flutter around it. They approach me in a half-hesitant sort of way, eye me curiously or compassionately, and then, instead of saying directly, How does it feel to be a problem? they say, I know an excellent colored man in my town; or, I fought at Mechanicsville; or, Do not these Southern outrages make your blood boil? At these I smile, or am interested, or reduce the boiling to a simmer, as the occasion may require. To the real question, How does it feel to be a problem? I answer seldom a word.

And yet, being a problem is a strange experience—peculiar even for one who has never been anything else, save perhaps in babyhood and in Europe. It is in the early days of rollicking boyhood that the revelation first bursts upon one, all in a day, as it were. I remember well when the shadow swept across me. I was a little thing, away up in the hills of New England, where the dark Housatonic winds between Hoosac and Taghkanic to the sea. In a wee wooden schoolhouse, something put it into the boys' and girls' heads to buy gorgeous visiting-cards—ten cents a package —and exchange. The exchange was merry, till one girl, a tall newcomer, refused my card—refused it peremptorily, with a glance. Then it dawned upon me with a certain suddenness that I was different from the others; or like, mayhap, in heart and life and longing, but shut out from their world by a vast veil. I had thereafter no desire to tear down that veil, to creep through; I held all beyond it in common contempt, and lived above it in a region of blue sky and great wandering shadows. That sky was bluest when I could beat my mates at examination-time, or beat them at a foot-race, or even beat their stringy heads. Alas, with the years all this fine contempt began to fade; for the worlds I longed for, and all their dazzling opportunities, were theirs, not mine. But they should not keep these prizes, I said; some, all, I would wrest from them. Just how I would do it I could never decide: by reading law, by healing the sick, by telling the wonderful tales that swam in my head—some way. With other black boys the strife was not so fiercely sunny: their youth shrunk into tasteless sycophancy, or into silent hatred of the pale world about them and mocking distrust of everything white; or wasted itself in a bitter cry, Why did God make me an outcast and a stranger in mine own house? The shades of the prison-house closed round about us all: walls strait and stubborn to the whitest, but relentlessly narrow, tall, and unscaleable to sons of night who must plod darkly on in resignation, or beat unavailing palms against the stone, or steadily, half hopelessly, watch the streak of blue above.

After the Egyptian and Indian, the Greek and Roman, the Teuton and Mongolian, the Negro is a sort of seventh son, born with a veil, and gifted with second-sight in this American world —a world which yields him no true self-consciousness, but only lets him see himself through the revelation of the other world. It is a peculiar sensation, this double-consciousness, this sense of always looking at one's self through the eyes of others, of measuring one's soul by the tape of a world that looks on in amused contempt and pity. One ever feels his two-ness—an American, a Negro; two souls, two thoughts, two unreconciled strivings; two warring ideals in one dark body, whose dogged strength alone keeps it from being torn asunder.

The history of the American Negro is the history of this strife —this longing to attain self-conscious manhood, to merge his double self into a better and truer self. In this merging, he wishes neither of the older selves to be lost. He would not Africanize America, for America has too much to teach the world and Africa. He would not bleach his Negro soul in a flood of white Americanism, for he knows that Negro blood has a message for the world. He simply wishes to make it possible for a man to be both a Negro and an American, without being cursed and spat upon by his fellows, without having the doors of Opportunity closed roughly in his face.

This, then, is the end of his striving: to be a co-worker in the kingdom of culture, to escape both death and isolation, to husband and use his best powers and his latent genius. These powers of body and mind have in the past been strangely wasted, dispersed, or forgotten. The shadow of a mighty Negro past flits through the tale of Ethiopia the Shadowy and of Egypt the Sphinx. Throughout history, the powers of single black men flash here and there like falling stars, and die sometimes before the world has rightly gauged their brightness. Here in America, in the few days since Emancipation, the black man's turning hither and thither in hesitant and doubtful striving has often made his very strength to lose effectiveness, to seem like absence of power, like weakness. And yet it is not weakness—it is the contradiction of double aims. The double-aimed struggle of the black artisan—on the one hand to escape white contempt for a nation of mere hewers of wood and drawers of water, and on the other hand to plough and nail and dig for a poverty-stricken horde—could only result in making him a poor craftsman, for he had but half a heart in either cause. By the poverty and ignorance of his people, the Negro minister or doctor was tempted toward quackery and demagogy; and by the criticism of the other world, toward ideals that made him ashamed of his lowly tasks. The would-be black *savant* was confronted by the paradox that the knowledge his people needed was a twice-told tale to his white neighbors, while the knowledge which would teach the white world was Greek to his own flesh and blood. The innate love of harmony and beauty that set the ruder souls of his people a-dancing and a-singing raised but confusion and doubt in the soul of the black artist; for the beauty revealed to him was the soul-beauty of a race which his larger audience despised, and he could not articulate the message of another people. This waste of double aims, this seeking to satisfy two unreconciled ideals, has wrought sad havoc with the courage and faith and deeds of ten thousand thousand people —has sent them often wooing false gods and invoking false means of salvation, and at times has even seemed about to make them ashamed of themselves.

Away back in the days of bondage they thought to see in one divine event the end of all doubt and disappointment; few men

ever worshipped Freedom with half such unquestioning faith as
did the American Negro for two centuries. To him, so far as he
thought and dreamed, slavery was indeed the sum of all vil-
lainies, the cause of all sorrow, the root of all prejudice; Emancipation was the key to a promised land of sweeter beauty than
ever stretched before the eyes of wearied Israelites. In song and
exhortation swelled one refrain—Liberty; in his tears and curses
the God he implored had Freedom in his right hand. At last it
came—suddenly, fearfully, like a dream. With one wild carnival
of blood and passion came the message in his own plaintive
cadences:—

> Shout, O children!
> Shout, you're free!
> For God has bought your liberty!

Years have passed away since then—ten, twenty, forty; forty
years of national life, forty years of renewal and development
—and yet the swarthy spectre sits in its accustomed seat at the
Nation's feast. In vain do we cry to this our vastest social problem:—

> Take any shape but that, and my firm nerves
> Shall never tremble!

The Nation has not yet found peace from its sins; the freedman
has not yet found in freedom his promised land. Whatever of
good may have come in these years of change, the shadow of a
deep disappointment rests upon the Negro people—a disappointment all the more bitter because the unattained ideal was unbounded save by the simple ignorance of a lowly people.

The first decade was merely a prolongation of the vain search
for freedom, the boon that seemed ever barely to elude their
grasp, like a tantalizing will-o'-the-wisp, maddening and mislead-
ing the headless host. The holocaust of war, the terrors of the

Ku-Klux Klan, the lies of carpet-baggers, the disorganization of industry, and the contradictory advice of friends and foes, left the bewildered serf with no new watchword beyond the old cry for freedom. As the time flew, however, he began to grasp a new idea. The ideal of liberty demanded for its attainment powerful means, and these the Fifteenth Amendment gave him. The ballot, which before he had looked upon as a visible sign of freedom, he now regarded as the chief means of gaining and perfecting the liberty with which war had partially endowed him. And why not? Had not votes made war and emancipated millions? Had not votes enfranchised the freedmen? Was anything impossible to a power that had done all this? A million black men started with renewed zeal to vote themselves into the kingdom. So the decade flew away, the revolution of 1876 came, and left the half-free serf weary, wondering, but still inspired. Slowly but steadily, in the following years, a new vision began gradually to replace the dream of political power—a powerful movement, the rise of another ideal to guide the unguided, another pillar of fire by night after a clouded day. It was the ideal of "book-learning"; the curiosity, born of compulsory ignorance, to know and test the power of the cabalistic letters of the white man, the longing to know. Here at last seemed to have been discovered the mountain path to Canaan; longer than the highway of Emancipation and law, steep and rugged, but straight, leading to heights high enough to overlook life.

Up the new path the advance guard toiled, slowly, heavily, doggedly; only those who have watched and guided the faltering feet, the misty minds, the dull understandings, of the dark pupils of these schools know how faithfully, how piteously, this people strove to learn. It was weary work. The cold statistician wrote down the inches of progress here and there, noted also where here and there a foot had slipped or some one had fallen. To the tired climbers, the horizon was ever dark, the mists were often cold, the Canaan was always dim and far away. If, however, the vistas disclosed as yet no goal, no resting-place, little but flattery and criticism, the journey at least gave leisure for reflection and self-examination; it changed the child of Emancipation to the youth with dawning self-consciousness, self-realization, self-respect. In those sombre forests of his striving his own soul rose before him, and he saw himself, darkly as through a veil; and yet he saw in himself some faint revelation of his power, of his mission. He began to have a dim feeling that, to attain his place in the world, he must be himself, and not another. For the first time he sought to analyze the burden he bore upon his back, that dead-weight of social degradation partially masked behind a half-named Negro problem. He felt his poverty; without a cent, without a home, without land, tools, or savings, he had entered into competition with rich, landed, skilled neighbors. To be a poor man is hard, but to be a poor race in a land of dollars is the very bottom of hardships. He felt the weight of his ignorance—not simply of letters, but of life, of business, of the humanities; the accumulated sloth and shirking and awkwardness of decades and centuries shackled his hands and feet. Nor was his burden all poverty and ignorance. The red stain of bastardy, which two centuries of systematic legal defilement of Negro women had stamped upon his race, meant not only the loss of ancient African chastity, but also the hereditary weight of a mass of corruption from white adulterers, threatening almost the obliteration of the Negro home.

A people thus handicapped ought not to be asked to race with the world, but rather allowed to give all its time and thought to its own social problems. But alas! while sociologists gleefully count his bastards and his prostitutes, the very soul of the toiling, sweating black man is darkened by the shadow of a vast despair. Men call the shadow prejudice, and learnedly explain it as the

natural defense of culture against barbarism, learning against
ignorance, purity against crime, the "higher" against the "lower"
races. To which the Negro cries Amen! and swears that to so
much of this strange prejudice as is founded on just homage to
civilization, culture, righteousness, and progress, he humbly bows
and meekly does obeisance. But before that nameless prejudice
that leaps beyond all this he stands helpless, dismayed, and well-
nigh speechless; before that personal disrespect and mockery, the
ridicule and systematic humiliation, the distortion of fact and
wanton license of fancy, the cynical ignoring of the better and
the boisterous welcoming of the worse, the all-pervading desire
to inculcate disdain for everything black, from Toussaint to the
devil—before this there rises a sickening despair that would dis-
arm and discourage any nation save that black host to whom "dis-
couragement" is an unwritten word.

But the facing of so vast a prejudice could not but bring the
inevitable self-questioning, self-disparagement, and lowering of
ideals which ever accompany repression and breed in an atmosphere
of contempt and hate. Whisperings and portents came borne upon
the four winds: Lo! we are diseased and dying, cried the dark
hosts; we cannot write, our voting is vain; what need of education,
since we must always cook and serve? And the Nation echoed
and enforced this self-criticism, saying: Be content to be servants,
and nothing more; what need of higher culture for half-men?
Away with the black man's ballot, by force or fraud—and behold
the suicide of a race! Nevertheless, out of the evil came something
of good—the more careful adjustment of education to real life,
the clearer perception of the Negroes' social responsibilities, and
the sobering realization of the meaning of progress.

So dawned the time of *Sturm und Drang:* storm and stress
today rocks our little boat on the mad waters of the world-sea;
there is within and without the sound of conflict, the burning of

body and rending of soul; inspiration strives with doubt, and faith with vain questionings. The bright ideals of the past— physical freedom, political power, the training of brains and the training of hands—all these in turn have waxed and waned, until even the last grows dim and overcast. Are they all wrong, all false? No, not that, but each alone was over-simple and incomplete, the dreams of a credulous race-childhood, or the fond imaginings of the other world which does not know and does not want to know our power. To be really true, all these ideals must be melted and welded into one. The training of the schools we need today more than ever—the training of deft hands, quick eyes and ears, and above all the broader, deeper, higher culture of gifted minds and pure hearts. The power of the ballot we need in sheer self-defense—else what shall save us from a second slavery? Freedom, too, the long-sought, we still seek—the freedom of life and limb, the freedom to work and think, the freedom to love and aspire. Work, culture, liberty—all these we need, not singly but together, not successively but together, each growing and aiding each, and all striving toward that vaster ideal that swims before the Negro people, the ideal of human brotherhood, gained through the unifying ideal of Race; the ideal of fostering and developing the traits and talents of the Negro, not in opposition to or contempt for other races, but rather in large conformity to the greater ideals of the American Republic, in order that some day on American soil two world-races may give each to each those characteristics both so sadly lack. We the darker ones come even now not altogether empty-handed: there are today no truer exponents of the pure human spirit of the Declaration of Independence than the American Negroes; there is no true American music but the wild sweet melodies of the Negro slave; the American fairy tales and folk-lore are Indian and African; and, all in all, we black men seem the sole oasis of simple faith and reverence in a dusty desert of dollars and smartness. Will America be poorer if she replace her brutal dyspeptic blundering with light-hearted but determined Negro humility? or her coarse and cruel wit with loving jovial good-humor? or her vulgar music with the soul of the Sorrow Songs?

Merely a concrete test of the underlying principles of the great Republic is the Negro Problem, and the spiritual striving of the freedmen's sons is the travail of souls whose burden is almost beyond the measure of their strength, but who bear it in the name of an historic race, in the name of this the land of their fathers' fathers, and in the name of human opportunity.

20. WASHINGTON GLADDEN

Shall Ill-Gotten Gains Be Sought for Christian Purposes?
(1905)

Washington Gladden (1836-1918), a leader in the
Social Gospel movement of the late nineteenth century, was born in Pottsgrove, Pennsylvania, and graduated from Williams College. From 1882 until his
death he was the respected pastor of the First Congregational Church in Columbus, Ohio. Although
generally conciliatory and moderate in his writings
and sermons, Gladden seriously questioned the ethical standards of big business and the compatibility of
luxurious expenditures of wealth with Christian principles. In 1905, accordingly, he voiced strong objection to the way in which the American Board of
Commissioners for Foreign Missions was engaged in
soliciting contributions of "tainted" money.

The right and duty of making discrimination among those who are
invited to contribute to its treasury will not, I dare say, be disputed
on this floor. The line is drawn, and will be drawn. The only question is where it shall be drawn.

The Committee say that "investigation by the executive officers
to determine the sources from which gifts come is neither justifi-
able nor practical." However this may be it is certainly competent
and wise for them to make some inquiry respecting the character
and reputation of the persons to whom *they apply* for assistance.

This is the simple, practical question to which the whole of Principle One and Principle Two must be reduced, and the answer is so obvious that I will not waste a word in arguing it.

Using the discretion which they must use in soliciting donations, there are one or two simple rules by which they should be guided.

In the first place, as we have already seen, they must not seek the co-operation in their work of persons whose gains have been and are being made by scandalous immoralities. About this there is no dispute.

In the second place, they must not invite gifts from persons who are conspicuous enemies of society.

It is a bitter truth that such a class exists among us, and that the nation is now confronting, with anxiety and fear, the problem of restraining its depredations. The class is composed of persons who have rapidly acquired enormous wealth. The number of these persons is not large, but the power which they have acquired is prodigious. No such aggregations of wealth have ever been known.

The existence of such fortunes is prima facie evidence of social injustice. I think that a man may, by means fairly legitimate, accumulate a considerable fortune, but no man can possibly render to society a kind and amount of service which shall entitle him, within a generation, to heap up for himself a fortune of a thousand million or five hundred millions of dollars. The existence of such fortunes is an enormous peril to a democratic state; they could never have been accumulated, in a democracy, without a great deal of social and political rottenness; and the men who have taken advantage of such conditions, or have, perhaps, helped to create them, in the building of their fortunes, are entitled to be regarded as the most dangerous enemies of society.

These colossal gains have, in all cases, been made by practices which are glaringly unjust and iniquitous. By obtaining control of the public highways and levying tribute on the traffic of competitors, and taxing the necessaries of life for the millions; by cor-

ruptly controlling legislatures and city councils and thus obtaining
franchises and contracts, by which they are able to extort from the
people exorbitant compensation for public service rendered; by
enormous inflations of capital, and the dishonest manipulation of
the stock and grain markets and by the exploitation of trust funds
for private gain, these great accumulations have been made. Most
of these practices are flagrantly illegal, those which are not covered
by explicit legislation are none the less unjust and oppressive.

The true character of these giant combinations, these grasping
monopolies is now pretty well understood by the people at large.
It is evident that they must be sharply restrained or our liberties
will soon disappear. It is evident that they have narrowed the
bounds of individual initiative—that is industrial freedom—and
have shut the gates of opportunity upon millions; that they have
greatly intensified the strife of classes; above all that they have
done more than all other causes put together to corrupt and de-
bauch our govenments, municipal, state and national. The vital
relation between big business and political corruption has been
brought to light most vividly within the past six months. And the
deadly damage that has been done to the nation in dulling the
sense of business honor and intensifying the passion of avarice no
statistics can ever show.

Against these merciless and portentous powers the conscience of
the nation is now pretty well aroused; our President has spoken,
again and again, with clearness and emphasis; our ex-President,
Mr. Cleveland, has borne strong testimony; the government of the
nation and the governments of some of the states are exerting their
powers to restrain and punish these transgressors; quite a number
of them are now under indictment for crime and many others are
dreading it; it begins to be pretty plain that this is not a windmill
that we are attacking but a strong and dangerous foe to the national life.

What, now, should be the attitude of the church toward men

who stand in this relation to the commonwealth? I think that the church cannot afford to cultivate their friendship or seek their co-operation in its work. They may be courteous and cultivated gentlemen, estimable husbands and fathers and constant attendants upon church and prayer-meeting, but if their business methods involve a peril to public morality and threaten the public welfare the church must not invite their co-operation in its work.

It must not do so because such solicitation involves an endorsement of them which it has no right to give. If the acceptance of a voluntary gift implies no recognition of the giver, the solicitation of a gift puts the matter upon a different rooting. The man himself has a right to infer and the public has a right to draw the same inference, that the church values his friendship and does not disapprove his conduct. No other interpretation can be put upon such an action. The Committee affirms in Principle Three that "by the acceptance of gifts the officers and members (of the Board) are not stopped from criticizing the business methods" of donors. Will they say that they would feel entirely free to criticize the business methods of a donor whose gifts they have diligently solicited for the space of two years? I will do them the credit of not imputing to them any such conduct. I know that they do not intend to forfeit the respect of gentlemen. It is the simple historical fact that the business methods of such givers are not criticized by those who have solicited their bounty. When an instance of such criticism is produced we may admit the validity of this contention.

The Church is not wise to solicit the gifts of multi-millionaires because in this quest its own power is apt to be paralyzed and its natural resources dried up. Nothing is more fatal than the habit of dependence on such sources. Even when there is no moral question raised, the exploiting of big donations lessens the interest of the multitude of small givers on whom the work must mainly rest. . . .

We know what our tasks are, and what are the difficulties before us. We are trying to bridge the chasm that divides the great masses of the working people of this country from the church. It is the one urgent business of the Christian church today. We know that the churches, in the view of these people, are in altogether too close relations with the predatory wealth. If we cannot correct this impression we cannot win these people.

"For years," says a professor in one of our leading New England colleges, "I have been seeing more of the wage-earning people of New England. Their alienation from the church is a fact with us. . . . They are watching to see what decision is to be made of this question of tainted money. If the resolution which you have framed as an offset to the statement issued by the Prudential Committee is rejected, in substance or form, at Seattle, we must expect, in this part of the country, to see the working-men turn their backs upon our churches."

Not upon our churches alone. Such action will affect not merely the Congregational churches. It will be laid up against all the churches. It will be regarded as indicating the attitude which the Christian Church of this country has taken upon this question. And it will send a chill through the frame of every working-man who reads it and widen and deepen the chasm between the church and the entire class of wage-workers. The task of every man who is trying to close up that chasm, and to convince the working people that the church of today is the church of Him who came to preach the gospel to the poor, will be made more arduous, and hope will die in his heart.

Don't tell me I am making too much of a small matter. I know what I am talking about. I have been on the firing-line in this warfare for a good many years, and I know how the battle is going. The appalling thing about it all is that so many of those who ought to be our leaders know so little and seem to care so little. But I implore you, as one whose experience is entitled to some credit, that you will not, by your action here today, put any more obstacles in the way of those who seek to make the Congregational Church the church of the common people.

I think I have given adequate reasons why the missionary society of the Congregational churches should not cultivate the friendship and co-operation of men who represent the aggregations of predatory wealth which now threaten the life of this Republic. It may be asked who these men are. It is not necessary to name them. There are not many of them. It will not be difficult for the officers of the society to learn their names by a little inquiry among their neighbors. With such a caution as the resolution which I am advocating contains, I am willing to leave the matter to the discretion of the Committee.

But I shall be asked whether all rich men are not under the same condemnation. I answer no. There are multitudes of them who are governed by no such purposes. There are thousands and tens of thousands of men in large and active business whose methods are in the main honorable and fair.

It may be true, I think it is true, that there have been evil tendencies among them. Some of them have been sometimes tempted to imitate the schemes of the rebate robbers, and the frenzied financiers; and the church may be partly to blame for this, for the churches and the colleges have been giving their certificates of character to the worst of these offenders, and it could hardly be wondered at if ambitious men sometimes assumed that their methods were laudable and exemplary. We owe to our active business men sounder ethical instruction—not such as is expressed in the moral indifferentism respecting the sources of gifts in the statement of principles before us. . . .

21. ROBERT M. LA FOLLETTE

Speech on the Declaration of War Against Germany
(1917)

Robert M. La Follette (1855-1925), after an early career as a lawyer and conservative Republican Congressman in the 1880's, returned to politics in 1901 as the reform governor of his native Wisconsin. In 1906 he resigned the governorship to become United States Senator, a position which he retained until his death. Widely denounced by hysterical patriots for his opposition to American entry into the First World War, La Follette held to his isolationist convictions and voted against America joining the League of Nations. In 1924 he ran for President on the Progressive Party ticket.

Mr. President, I had supposed until recently that it was the duty of Senators and Representatives in Congress to vote and act according to their convictions on all public matters that came before them for consideration and decision.

Quite another doctrine has recently been promulgated by certain newspapers, which unfortunately seems to have found considerable support elsewhere, and that is the doctrine of "standing back of the President," without inquiring whether the President is right or wrong. For myself I have never subscribed to that doctrine and never shall. I shall support the President in the measures he proposes when I believe them to be right. I shall oppose measures proposed by the President when I believe them to be wrong. The fact that the matter which the President submits for consideration is of the grestest importance is only an additional reason why we should be sure that we are right and not to be swerved from that conviction or intimidated in its expression by any influence of power whatsoever. If it is important for us to speak and vote our convictions in matters of internal policy, though we may unfortunately be in disagreement with the President, it is infinitely more important for us to speak and vote our convictions when the question is one of peace or war, certain to involve the lives and fortunes of many of our people and, it may be, the destiny of all of them and of the civilized world as well. If, unhappily, on such momentous questions the most patient research and conscientious consideration we could give to them leave us in disagreement with the President, I know of no course to take except to oppose, regretfully but not the less firmly, the demands of the Executive.

On the second of this month the President addressed a communication to the Senate and House in which he advised that the Congress declare war against Germany and that this Government "assert all its powers and employ all its resources to bring the Government of the German Empire to terms and end the war."

On February 26, 1917, the President addressed the Senate and the House upon the conditions existing between this Government and the German Empire, and at that time said, "I am not now proposing or contemplating war or any steps that need lead to it. . . . I request that you will authorize me to supply our merchant ships with defensive arms, should that become necessary, and with the means of using them" against what he characterized as the unlawful attacks of German submarines.

A bill was introduced, and it was attempted to rush it through the closing hours of the last session of Congress, to give the President the powers requested, namely, to arm our merchant ships, and to place upon them guns and gunners from our Navy, to be used against German submarines, and to employ such other instrumentalities and methods as might in his judgment and discretion seem necessary and adequate to protect such vessels. That measure did not pass.

It is common knowledge that the President, acting without authority from Congress, did arm our merchant ships with guns and gunners from our Navy, and sent them into the prohibited "war zone." At the time the President addressed us on the second of April there was absolutely no change in the conditions between this Government and Germany. The effect of arming merchant ships had not been tested as a defensive measure. Late press reports indicate, however, that the *Aztec,* a United States armed merchantman, has been sunk in the prohibited zone, whether with mines or a torpedo, I believe, has not been established, so the responsibility for this sinking can not, so far as I know at this time, be placed.

When the request was made by the President on February twenty-sixth for authority to arm merchant ships, the granting of such authority was opposed by certain Members of the House and by certain Senators, of which I was one. I made at that time a careful investigation of the subject, and became convinced that arming our merchant ships was wholly futile and its only purpose and effect would be to lure our merchantmen to danger, and probably result in the destruction of the vessels and in the loss of the lives of those on board. The representatives of the President on this floor then having that bill in charge saw fit, by methods I do not care to characterize, to prevent my speaking upon the measure and giving to the Senate and to the country such information as I had upon the subject.

Under the circumstances, I did the only thing that seemed practical to me, and that was to give such publicity as I was able through the press to the fact that the proposition to arm merchant ships would be wholly futile, and could only result in loss of the lives and property of our own people, without accomplishing the results intended. I regret to say that the President, according to statements in the public press purporting to emanate from him, and which have never been denied, saw fit to characterize as "willful" the conduct of the Senators who, in obedience to their consciences and their oaths of office, opposed the armed-ship bill, and to charge that in so doing they were not representing the people by whose suffrages they are here. I know of no graver charge that could be made against the official conduct of any Member of this body than that his official action was the result of a "willful"—that is, an unreasoned and perverse—purpose.

Mr. President, many of my colleagues on both sides of this floor have from day to day offered for publication in the RECORD messages and letters received from their constituents. I have received some 15,000 letters and telegrams. They have come from 44 States in the Union. They have been assorted according to whether they speak in criticism or commendation of my course in opposing war.

Assorting the 15,000 letters and telegrams by States in that way, nine out of ten are an unqualified indorsement of my course in opposing war with Germany on the issue presented. . . .

Mr. President, let me make another suggestion. It is this: That a minority in one Congress—mayhap a small minority in one Congress—protesting, exercising the rights which the Constitution confers upon a minority, may really be representing the majority opinion of the country, and if, exercising the right that the Constitution gives them, they succeed in defeating for the time being the will of the majority, they are but carrying out what was in the mind of the framers of the Constitution; that you may have from time to time in a legislative body a majority in numbers that really does not represent the principle of democracy; and that if the question could be deferred and carried to the people it would be

found that a minority was the real representative of the public
opinion. So, Mr. President, it was that they wrote into the Constitution that a President—that one man—may put his judgment
against the will of a majority not only in one branch of the Congress but in both branches of the Congress; that he may defeat the
measure that they have agreed upon and may set his one single
judgment above the majority judgment of the Congress. That
seems, when you look at it nakedly, to be in violation of the principle that the majority shall rule; and so it is. Why is that power
given? It is one of the checks provided by the wisdom of the
fathers to prevent the majority from abusing the power that they
chance to have, when they do not reflect the real judgment, the
opinion, the will of the majority of the people that constitute the
sovereign power of the democracy. . . .

We need not disturb ourselves because of what a minority may
do. There is always lodged, and always will be, thank the God
above us, power in the people supreme. Sometimes it sleeps, sometimes it seems the sleep of death; but, sir, the sovereign power of
the people never dies. It may be suppressed for a time, it may be
misled, be fooled, silenced. I think, Mr. President, that it is being
denied expression now. I think there will come a day when it will
have expression.

The poor, sir, who are the ones called upon to rot in the
trenches, have no organized power, have no press to voice their
will upon this question of peace or war; but, oh, Mr. President, at
some time they will be heard. I hope and I believe they will be
heard in an orderly and a peaceful way. I think they may be heard
from before long. I think, sir, if we take this step, when the people
today who are staggering under the burden of supporting families
at the present prices of the necessaries of life find those prices
multiplied, when they are raised a hundred per cent, or 200 per
cent, as they will be quickly, aye, sir, when beyond that those who

pay taxes come to have their taxes doubled and again doubled to pay the interest on the nontaxable bonds held by Morgan and his combinations, which have been issued to meet this war, there will come an awakening; they will have their day and they will be heard. It will be as certain and as inevitable as the return of the tides, and as resistless, too.

I promise my colleagues that I will not be tempted again to turn aside from the thread of my discussion as I have outlined it here, and I will hasten with all possible speed.

Now that the President has in his message to us of April second admitted the very charge against the armed-ship bill which we made, I trust that he is fully convinced that the conduct of the Senators on the occasion in question was not unreasoned and obstinate, but that it was inspired by quite as high purposes and motives as can inspire the action of any public official.

I would not, however, have made this personal reference did not the question it suggests go to the very heart of the matter now under consideration. If the President was wrong when he proposed arming the ships; if that policy was, as he now says, "certain to draw us into the war without either the rights or the effectiveness of belligerents," is it so certain he is right now when he demands an unqualified declaration of war against Germany? If those Members of Congress who were supporting the President then were wrong, as it appears from the President's statement now they were, should not that fact prompt them to inquire carefully whether they are right in supporting the proposed declaration of war? If the armed-ship bill involved a course of action that was hasty and ill advised, may it not well be that this proposed declaration of war, which is being so hotly pressed, is also ill advised? . . .

The President in his message of April second says:

"The present German warfare against commerce is a warfare against mankind. It is a war against all nations."

Again referring to Germany's warfare he says:

"There has been no discrimination. The challenge is to all mankind."

Is it not a little peculiar that if Germany's warfare is against all nations the United States is the only nation that regards it necessary to declare war on that account? If it is true, as the President says, that "there has been no discrimination," that Germany has treated every neutral as she has treated us, is it not peculiar that no other of the great nations of the earth seem to regard Germany's conduct in this war as a cause for entering into it? Are we the only nation jealous of our rights? Are we the only nation insisting upon the protection of our citizens? Does not the strict neutrality maintained on the part of all the other nations of the earth suggest that possibly there is a reason for their action, and that that reason is that Germany's conduct under the circumstances does not merit from any nation which is determined to preserve its neutrality a declaration of war?

Norway, Sweden, the Netherlands, Switzerland, Denmark, Spain, and all the great Republics of South America are quite as interested in this subject as we are, and yet they have refused to join with us in a combination against Germany. I venture to suggest also that the nations named, and probably others, have a somewhat better right to be heard than we, for by refusing to sell war materiel and munitions to any of the belligerents they have placed themselves in a position where the suspicion which attaches to us of a desire for war profits can not attach to them.

On August 4, 1914, the Republic of Brazil declared the exportation of war materiel from Brazilian ports to any of these powers at war to be strictly forbidden, whether such exports be under the Brazilian flag or that of any other country.

In that connection I note the following dispatch from Buenos Aires, appearing in the Washington papers of yesterday:

> "President Wilson's war address was received here with interest, but no particular enthusiasm. . . . Government officials and politicians have adopted a cold shoulder toward the United States policy—an attitude apparently based on apprehension lest South American interests suffer."

The newspaper *Razon*'s view was illustrative of this. "Does not the United States consider this an opportune time to consolidate the imperialistic policy everywhere north of Panama?" it said.

This is the question that neutral nations the world over are asking. Are we seizing upon this war to consolidate and extend an imperialistic policy? We complain also because Mexico has turned the cold shoulder to us, and are wont to look for sinister reasons for her attitude. Is it any wonder that she should also turn the cold shoulder when she sees us unite with Great Britain, an empire founded upon her conquests and subjugation of weaker nations. There is no doubt that the sympathy of Norway, Sweden, and other countries close to the scene of war is already with Germany. It is apparent that they view with alarm the entrance into the European struggle of the stranger from across the sea. It is suggested by some that our entrance into the war will shorten it. It is my firm belief, based upon such information as I have, that our entrance into the war will not only prolong it, but that it will vastly extend its area by drawing in other nations. . . .

Just a word of comment more upon one of the points in the President's address. He says that this is a war "for the things which we have always carried nearest to our hearts—for democracy, for the right of those who submit to authority to have a voice in their own government." In many places throughout the address is this exalted sentiment given expression.

It is a sentiment peculiarly calculated to appeal to American hearts and, when accompanied by acts consistent with it, is certain to receive our support; but in this same connection, and strangely enough, the President says that we have become convinced that the German Government as it now exists—"Prussian autocracy" he calls it—can never again maintain friendly relations with us. His expression is that "Prussian autocracy was not and could never be our friend," and repeatedly throughout the address the suggestion is made that if the German people would overturn their Government it would probably be the way to peace. So true is this that the dispatches from London all hailed the message of the President as sounding the death knell of Germany's Government.

But the President proposes alliance with Great Britain, which, however liberty-loving its people, is a hereditary monarchy, with a hereditary ruler, with a hereditary House of Lords, with a hereditary landed system, with a limited and restricted suffrage for one class and a multiplied suffrage power for another, and with grinding industrial conditions for all the wage-workers. The President has not suggested that we make our support of Great Britain conditional to her granting home rule to Ireland, or Egypt, or India. We rejoice in the establishment of a democracy in Russia, but it will hardly be contended that if Russia was still an autocratic Government, we would not be asked to enter this alliance with her just the same. Italy and the lesser powers of Europe, Japan in the Orient; in fact, all of the countries with whom we are to enter into alliance, except France and newly revolutionized Russia, are still of the old order—and it will be generally conceded that no one of them has done as much for its people in the solution of municipal problems and in securing social and industrial reforms as Germany.

Is it not a remarkable democracy which leagues itself with allies already far overmatching in strength the German nation and holds out to such beleaguered nation the hope of peace only at the price of giving up their Government? I am not talking now of the merits or demerits of any government, but I am speaking of a profession of democracy that is linked in action with the most brutal and domineering use of autocratic power. Are the people of this country being so well represented in this war movement that we need to go abroad to give other people control of their governments? Will the President and the supporters of this war bill submit it to a vote of the people before the declaration of war goes into effect? Until we are willing to do that, it illy becomes us to offer as an excuse for our entry into the war the unsupported claim that this war was forced upon the German people by their Government "without their previous knowledge or approval."

Who has registered the knowledge or approval of the American people of the course this Congress is called upon to take in declaring war upon Germany? Submit the question to the people, you who support it. You who support it dare not do it, for you know that by a vote of more than ten to one the American people as a body would register their declaration against it.

In the sense that this war is being forced upon our people without their knowing why and without their approval, and that wars are usually forced upon all peoples in the same way, there is some truth in the statement; but I venture to say that the response which the German people have made to the demands of this war shows that it has a degree of popular support which the war upon which we are entering has not and never will have among our people. The espionage bills, the conscription bills, and other forcible military measures which we understand are being ground out of the war machine in this country is the complete proof that those responsible for this war fear that it has no popular support and that armies sufficient to satisfy the demand of the entente allies can not be recruited by voluntary enlistments. . . .

Jefferson asserted that we could not permit one warring nation to curtail our neutral rights if we were not ready to allow her enemy the same privileges, and that any other course entailed the sacrifice of our neutrality.

That is the sensible, that is the logical position. No neutrality could ever have commanded respect if it was not based on that equitable and just proposition; and we from early in the war threw our neutrality to the winds by permitting England to make a mockery of it to her advantage against her chief enemy. Then we expect to say to that enemy, "You have got to respect my rights as a neutral." What is the answer? I say Germany has been patient with us. Standing strictly on her rights, her answer would be, "Maintain your neutrality; treat those other Governments warring against me as you treat me if you want your neutral rights respected."

I say again that when two nations are at war any neutral nation, in order to preserve its character as a neutral nation, must exact the same conduct from both warring nations; both must equally obey the principles of international law. If a neutral nation fails in that, then its rights upon the high seas—to adopt the President's phrase—are relative and not absolute. There can be no greater violation of our neutrality than the requirement that one of two belligerents shall adhere to the settled principles of law and that the other shall have the advantage of not doing so. The respect that German naval authorities were required to pay to the rights of our people upon the high seas would depend upon the question whether we had exacted the same rights from Germany's enemies. If we had not done so we lost our character as a neutral nation, and our people unfortunately had lost the protection that belongs to neutrals. . . .

Had the plain principle of international law announced by Jefferson been followed by us, we would not be called on today to declare war upon any of the belligerents. The failure to treat the belligerent nations of Europe alike, the failure to reject the unlawful "war zones" of both Germany and Great Britain, is wholly accountable for our present dilemma. We should not seek to hide our blunder behind the smoke of battle, to inflame the mind of our people by half truths into the frenzy of war in order that they may never appreciate the real cause of it until it is too late. I do not believe that our national honor is served by such a course. The right way is the honorable way.

One alternative is to admit our initial blunder to enforce our rights against Great Britain as we have enforced our rights against Germany; demand that both those nations shall respect our neutral rights upon the high seas to the letter; and give notice that we will enforce those rights from that time forth against both belligerents and then live up to that notice.

The other alternative is to withdraw our commerce from both. The mere suggestion that food supplies would be withheld from both sides impartially would compel belligerents to observe the principle of freedom of the seas for neutral commerce.

22. RANDOLPH BOURNE

The War and the Intellectuals
(1917)

Randolph Bourne (1886-1918) was born in Bloom-
field, New Jersey. A brilliant student at Columbia
University, he came under the influence of John
Dewey and soon began to write the critical articles on
education and political philosophy which he contributed to the *Atlantic Monthly* and the *New Republic*.
The coming of the First World War worked a change
in Bourne. Although as a hunchback he was exempt
from service, unlike his mentor Professor Dewey, he
took a stand in complete opposition to America's
role in the war. Bourne died a month after the Armi-
stice, but his bitter wartime essays became an important part of the postwar literature of disillusionment.

To those of us who still retain an irreconcilable animus against
war, it has been a bitter experience to see the unanimity with
which the American intellectuals have thrown their support to
the use of war-technique in the crisis in which America found
herself. Socialists, college professors, publicists, new-republicans,
practitioners of literature, have vied with each other in confirming
with their intellectual faith the collapse of neutrality and the
riveting of the war-mind on a hundred million more of the world's
people. And the intellectuals are not content with confirming our
belligerent gesture. They are now complacently asserting that it

was they who effectively willed it, against the hesitation and dim perceptions of the American democratic masses. A war made deliberately by the intellectuals! A calm moral verdict, arrived at after a penetrating study of inexorable facts! Sluggish masses, too remote from the world-conflict to be stirred, too lacking in intellect to perceive their danger! An alert intellectual class, saving the people in spite of themselves, biding their time with Fabian strategy until the nation could be moved into war without serious resistance! An intellectual class, gently guiding a nation through sheer force of ideas into what the other nations entered only through predatory craft or popular hysteria or militarist madness! A war free from any taint of self-seeking, a war that will secure the triumph of democracy and internationalize the world! This is the picture which the more self-conscious intellectuals have formed of themselves, and which they are slowly impressing upon a population which is being led no man knows whither by an indubitably intellectualized President. And they are right, in that the war certainly did not spring from either the ideals or the prejudices, from the national ambitions or hysterias, of the American people, however acquiescent the masses prove to be, and however clearly the intellectuals prove their putative intuition.

Those intellectuals who have felt themselves totally out of sympathy with this drag toward war will seek some explanation for this joyful leadership. They will want to understand this willingness of the American intellect to open the sluices and flood us with the sewage of the war-spirit. We cannot forget the virtuous horror and stupefaction which filled our college professors when they read the famous manifesto of their ninety-three German colleagues in defense of their war. To the American academic mind of 1914 defense of war was inconceivable. From Bernhardi it recoiled as from a blasphemy, little dreaming that two years later would find it creating its own cleanly reasons for imposing military service on the country and for talking of the rough rude currents of health and regeneration that war would send through the American body politic. They would have thought anyone mad who talked of shipping American men by the hundreds of thousands—conscripts —to die on the fields of France. Such a spiritual change seems catastrophic when we shoot our minds back to those days when neutrality was a proud thing. But the intellectual progress has been so gradual that the country retains little sense of the irony. The war sentiment, begun so gradually but so perseveringly by the preparedness advocates who came from the ranks of big business, caught hold of one after another of the intellectual groups. With the aid of Roosevelt, the murmurs became a monotonous chant, and finally a chorus so mighty that to be out of it was at first to be disreputable and finally almost obscene. And slowly a strident rant was worked up against Germany which compared very credit-ably with the German fulminations against the greedy power of England. The nerve of the war-feeling centered, of course, in the richer and older classes of the Atlantic seaboard, and was keenest where there were French or English business and particularly social connections. The sentiment then spread over the country as a class-phenomenon, touching everywhere those upper-class ele-ments in each section who identified themselves with this Eastern ruling group. It must never be forgotten that in every community it was the least liberal and least democratic elements among whom the preparedness and later the war sentiment was found. The farmers were apathetic, the small business men and working-men are still apathetic towards the war. The election was a vote of con-fidence of these latter classes in a President who would keep the faith of neutrality. The intellectuals, in other words, have identi-fied themselves with the least democratic forces in American life. They have assumed the leadership for war of those very classes whom the American democracy has been immemorially fighting.

Only in a world where irony was dead could an intellectual class enter war at the head of such illiberal cohorts in the avowed cause of world-liberalism and world-democracy. No one is left to point out the undemocratic nature of this war-liberalism. In a time of faith, skepticism is the most intolerable of all insults.

Our intellectual class might have been occupied, during the last two years of war, in studying and clarifying the ideals and aspirations of the American democracy, in discovering a true Americanism which would not have been merely nebulous but might have federated the different ethnic groups and traditions. They might have spent the time in endeavoring to clear the public mind of the cant of war, to get rid of old mystical notions that clog our thinking. We might have used the time for a great wave of education, for setting our house in spiritual order. We could at least have set the problem before ourselves. If our intellectuals were going to lead the administration, they might conceivably have tried to find some way of securing peace by making neutrality effective. They might have turned their intellectual energy not to the problem of jockeying the nation into war, but to the problem of using our vast neutral power to attain democratic ends for the rest of the world and ourselves without the use of the malevolent technique of war. They might have failed. The point is that they scarcely tried. The time was spent not in clarification and education, but in a mulling over of nebulous ideals of democracy and liberalism and civilization which had never meant anything fruitful to those ruling classes who now so glibly used them, and in giving free rein to the elementary instinct of self-defense. The whole era has been spiritually wasted. The outstanding feature has been not its Americanism but its intense colonialism. The offense of our intellectuals was not so much that they were colonial—for what could we expect of a nation composed of so many national elements?—but that it was so one-sidedly and partisanly colonial. The official, reputable expression of the intellectual class has been that of the English colonial. Certain portions of it have been even more loyalist than the King, more British even than Australia. Other colonial attitudes have been vulgar. The colonialism of the other American stocks was denied a hearing from the start. America might have been made a meeting-ground for the different national attitudes. An intellectual class, cultural colonists of the different European nations, might have threshed out the issues here as they could not be threshed out in Europe. Instead of this, the English colonials in university and press took command at the start, and we became an intellectual Hungary where thought was subject to an effective process of Magyarization. The reputable opinion of the American intellectuals became more and more either what could be read pleasantly in London, or what was written in an earnest effort to put Englishmen straight on their war-aims and war-technique. This Magyarization of thought produced as a counter-reaction a peculiarly offensive and inept German apologetic, and the two partisans divided the field between them. The great masses, the other ethnic groups, were inarticulate. American public opinion was almost as little prepared for war in 1917 as it was in 1914. . . .

The American's training was such as to make the fact of war almost incredible. Both in his reading of history and in his lack of economic perspective he was badly prepared for it. He had to explain to himself something which was too colossal for the modern mind, which outran any language or terms which we had to interpret it in. He had to expand his sympathies to the breaking-point, while pulling the past and present into some sort of interpretative order. The intellectuals in the fighting countries had only to rationalize and justify what their country was already doing. Their task was easy. A neutral, however, had really to search out the truth. Perhaps perspective was too much to ask of any mind. Certainly the older colonials among our college professors let their prejudices at once dictate their thought. They have been comfortable ever since. The war has taught them nothing and will teach them nothing. And they have had the satisfaction, under the rigor of events, of seeing prejudice submerge the intellects of their younger colleagues. And they have lived to see almost their entire class, pacifists and democrats too, join them as apologists for the "gigantic irrelevance" of war.

We have had to watch, therefore, in this country the same process which so shocked us abroad—the coalescence of the intellectual classes in support of the military programme. In this country, indeed, the socialist intellectuals did not even have the grace of their German brothers to wait for the declaration of war before they broke for cover. And when they declared for war they showed how thin was the intellectual veneer of their socialism. For they called us in terms that might have emanated from any bourgeois journal to defend democracy and civilization, just as if it was not exactly against those very bourgeois democracies and capitalist civilizations that socialists had been fighting for decades. But so subtle is the spiritual chemistry of the "inside" that all this intellectual cohesion—herd-instinct become herd-intellect—which seemed abroad so hysterical and so servile, comes to us here in highly rational terms. We go to war to save the world from subjugation! But the German intellectuals went to war to save their culture from barbarization! And the French went to war to save their beautiful France! And the English to save international honor! And Russia, most altruistic and self-sacrificing of all, to save a small State from destruction! Whence is our miraculous intuition of our moral spotlessness? Whence our confidence that history will not unravel huge economic and imperialist forces upon which our rationalizations float like bubbles? The Jew often marvels that his race alone should have been chosen as the true people of the cosmic God. Are not our intellectuals equally fatuous when they tell us that our war of all wars is stainless and thrillingly achieving for good?

An intellectual class that was wholly rational would have called insistently for peace and not for war. For months the crying need has been for a negotiated peace, in order to avoid the ruin of a deadlock. Would not the same amount of resolute statesmanship thrown into intervention have secured a peace that would have been a subjugation for neither side? Was the terrific bargaining power of a great neutral ever really used? Our war followed, as all wars follow, a monstrous failure of diplomacy. Shamefacedness should now be our intellectuals' attitude, because the American play for peace was made so little more than a polite play. The intellectuals have still to explain why, willing as they now are to use force to continue the war to absolute exhaustion, they were not willing to use force to coerce the world to a speedy peace.

Their forward vision is no more convincing than their past rationality. We go to war now to internationalize the world! But surely their League to Enforce Peace is only a palpable apocalyptic myth, like the syndicalists' myth of the "general strike." It is not a rational programme so much as a glowing symbol for the purpose of focusing belief, of setting enthusiasm on fire for international order. As far as it does this it has pragmatic value, but as far as it provides a certain radiant mirage of idealism for this war and for a world-order founded on mutual fear, it is dangerous and obnoxious. Idealism should be kept for what is ideal. It is depressing to think that the prospect of a world so strong that none dare challenge it should be the immediate ideal of the American intellectual. If the League is only a makeshift, a coalition into which we enter to restore order, then it is only a description of existing fact, and the idea should be treated as such. But if it is an actually prospective outcome of the settlement, the keystone of American policy, it is neither realizable nor desirable. For the programme of

such a League contains no provision for dynamic national growth
or for international economic justice. In a world which requires
recognition of economic internationalism far more than of political internationalism, an idea is reactionary which proposes to
petrify and federate the nations as political and economic units.
Such a scheme for international order is a dubious justification for
American policy. And if American policy had been sincere in its
belief that our participation would achieve international beatitude,
would we not have made our entrance into the war conditional
upon a solemn general agreement to respect in the final settlement
these principles of international order? Could we have afforded, if
our war was to end war by the establishment of a league of honor,
to risk the defeat of our vision and our betrayal in the settlement?
Yet we are in the war, and no such solemn agreement was made,
nor has it ever been suggested.

The case of the intellectuals seems, therefore, only very spe-
ciously rational. They could have used their energy to force a just
peace or at least to devise other means than war for carrying
through American policy. They could have used their intellectual
energy to ensure that our participation in the war meant the international order which they wish. Intellect was not so used. It was
used to lead an apathetic nation into an irresponsible war, without
guarantees from those belligerents whose cause we were saving.
The American intellectual, therefore, has been rational neither in
his hindsight nor his foresight. . . .

The task of making our own country detailedly fit for peace was
abandoned in favor of a feverish concern for the management of
the war, advice to the fighting governments on all matters, military,
social and political, and a gradual working up of the conviction
that we were ordained as a nation to lead all erring brothers
towards the light of liberty and democracy. . . .

At last action, irresponsibility, the end of anxious and torturing attempts to reconcile peace-ideals with the drag of the world towards Hell. An end to the pain of trying to adjust the facts to what they ought to be! Let us consecrate the facts as ideal! Let us join the greased slide towards war! The momentum increased. Hesitations, ironies, consciences, considerations—all were drowned in the elemental blare of doing something aggressive, colossal. The new-found Sabbath "peacefulness of being at war"! The thankfulness with which so many intellectuals lay down and floated with the current betrays the hesitation and suspense through which they had been. The American university is a brisk and happy place these days. Simple, unquestioning action has superseded the knots of thought. The thinker dances with reality.

With how many of the acceptors of war has it been mostly a dread of intellectual suspense? It is a mistake to suppose that intellectuality necessarily makes for suspended judgments. The intellect craves certitude. It takes effort to keep it supple and pliable. In a time of danger and disaster we jump desperately for some dogma to cling to. The time comes, if we try to hold out, when our nerves are sick with fatigue, and we seize in a great healing wave of release some doctrine that can be immediately translated into action. Neutrality meant suspense, and so it became the object of loathing to frayed nerves. The vital myth of the League of Peace provides a dogma to jump to. With war the world becomes motor again and speculation is brushed aside like cobwebs. The blessed emotion of self-defense intervenes too, which focused millions in Europe. A few keep up a critical pose after war is begun, but since they usually advise action which is in one-to-one correspondence with what the mass is already doing, their criticism is little more than a rationalization of the common emotional drive.

The results of war on the intellectual class are already apparent. Their thought becomes little more than a description and justification of what is going on. They turn upon any rash one who continues idly to speculate. Once the war is on, the conviction spreads that individual thought is helpless, that the only way one can count is as a cog in the great wheel. There is no good holding back. We are told to dry our unnoticed and ineffective tears and plunge into the great work. Not only is every one forced into line, but the new certitude becomes idealized. It is a noble realism which opposes itself to futile obstruction and the cowardly refusal to face facts. This realistic boast is so loud and sonorous that one wonders whether realism is always a stern and intelligent grappling with realities. May it not be sometimes a mere surrender to the actual, an abdication of the ideal through a sheer fatigue from intellectual suspense? The pacifist is roundly scolded for refusing to face the facts, and for retiring into his own world of sentimental desire. But is the realist, who refuses to challenge or criticize facts, entitled to any more credit than that which comes from following the line of least resistance? The realist thinks he at least can control events by linking himself to the forces that are moving. Perhaps he can. But if it is a question of controlling war, it is difficult to see how the child on the back of a mad elephant is to be any more effective in stopping the beast than is the child who tries to stop him from the ground. The ex-humanitarian, turned realist, sneers at the snobbish neutrality, colossal conceit, crooked thinking, dazed sensibilities, of those who are still unable to find any balm of consolation for this war. We manufacture consolations here in America while there are probably not a dozen men fighting in Europe who did not long ago give up every reason for their being there except that nobody knew how to get them away.

But the intellectuals whom the crisis has crystallized into an acceptance of war have put themselves into a terrifyingly strategic position. It is only on the craft, in the stream, they say, that one has any chance of controlling the current forces for liberal purposes. If we obstruct, we surrender all power for influence. If we responsibly approve, we then retain our power for guiding. We will be listened to as responsible thinkers, while those who obstructed the coming of war have committed intellectual suicide and shall be cast into outer darkness. Criticism by the ruling powers will only be accepted from those intellectuals who are in sympathy with the general tendency of the war. Well, it is true that they may guide, but if their stream leads to disaster and the frustration of national life, is their guiding any more than a preference whether they shall go over the right-hand or the left-hand side of the precipice? Meanwhile, however, there is comfort on board. Be with us, they call, or be negligible, irrelevant. Dissenters are already excommunicated. Irreconcilable radicals, wringing their hands among the debris, become the most despicable and impotent of men. There seems no choice for the intellectual but to join the mass of acceptance. But again the terrible dilemma arises—either support what is going on, in which case you count for nothing because you are swallowed in the mass and great incalculable forces bear you on; or remain aloof, passively resistant, in which case you count for nothing because you are outside the machinery of reality.

Is there no place left, then, for the intellectual who cannot yet crystallize, who does not dread suspense, and is not yet drugged with fatigue? The American intellectuals, in their preoccupation with reality, seem to have forgotten that the real enemy is War rather than Imperial Germany. There is work to be done to prevent this war of ours from passing into popular mythology as a holy crusade. What shall we do with leaders who tell us that we go to war in moral spotlessness, or who make "democracy" synonymous with a republican form of government? There is work to be done in still shouting that all the revolutionary by-products will not justify the war, or make war anything else than the most noxious complex of all the evils that afflict men. There must be some to find no consolation whatever, and some to sneer at those who buy the cheap emotion of sacrifice. There must be some irreconcilables left who will not even accept the war with walrus tears. There must be some to call unceasingly for peace, and some to insist that the terms of settlement shall be not only liberal but democratic. There must be some intellectuals who are not willing to use the old discredited counters again and to support a peace which would leave all the old inflammable materials of armament lying about the world. There must still be opposition to any contemplated "liberal" world-order founded on military coalitions. The "irreconcilable" need not be disloyal. He need not even be "impossibilist." His apathy towards war should take the form of a heightened energy and enthusiasm for the education, the art, the interpretation that make for life in the midst of the world of death. The intellectual who retains his animus against war will push out more boldly than ever to make his case solid against it. The old ideals crumble; new ideals must be forged. His mind will continue to roam widely and ceaselessly. The thing he will fear most is premature crystallization. If the American intellectual class rivets itself to a "liberal" philosophy that perpetuates the old errors, there will then be need for "democrats" whose task will be to divide, confuse, disturb, keep the intellectual waters constantly in motion to prevent any such ice from ever forming.

23. OLIVER WENDELL HOLMES

Abrams *Versus* United States
(1919)

> Oliver Wendell Holmes (1841-1935), rooted by
> birth in the New England Puritan tradition and influ-
> enced as a young man by the romantic nationalism of
> the Civil War, had a profound effect upon American
> history. His *Common Law,* published in 1881, was
> a pioneer effort to stress the pragmatic empirical as-
> pects of the law. Over the next half-century as a
> justice, first on the bench of the Massachusetts Su-
> preme Court, and then, after 1902, in the United
> States Supreme Court, Holmes in his decisions and
> dissenting opinions gave important support to the
> cause of social justice and individual freedom.

This indictment is founded wholly upon the publication of two
leaflets which I shall describe in a moment. The first count
charges a conspiracy pending the war with Germany to publish
abusive language about the form of government of the United
States, laying the preparation and publishing of the first leaflet as
overt acts. The second count charges a conspiracy pending the war
to publish language intended to bring the form of government into
contempt, laying the preparation and publishing of the two leaflets
as overt acts. The third count alleges a conspiracy to encourage resistance to the United States in the same war and to attempt to
effectuate the purpose by publishing the same leaflets. The fourth

count lays a conspiracy to incite curtailment of production of things necessary to the prosecution of the war and to attempt to accomplish it by publishing the second leaflet to which I have referred.

The first of these leaflets says that the President's cowardly silence about the intervention in Russia reveals the hypocrisy of the plutocratic gang in Washington. It intimates that "German militarism combined with allied capitalism to crush the Russian revolution"—goes on that the tyrants of the world fight each other until they see a common enemy—working-class enlightenment, when they combine to crush it; and that now militarism and capitalism combined, though not openly, to crush the Russian revolution. It says that there is only one enemy of the workers of the world and that is capitalism; that it is a crime for workers of America, &c., to fight the workers' republic of Russia, and ends "Awake! Awake, you Workers of the World! Revolutionists." A note adds "It is absurd to call us pro-German. We hate and despise German militarism more than do you hypocritical tyrants. We have more reasons for denouncing German militarism than has the coward of the White House."

The other leaflet, headed "Workers—Wake Up," with abusive language says that America together with the Allies will march for Russia to help the Czecho-Slovaks in their struggle against the Bolsheviki, and that this time the hypocrites shall not fool the Russian emigrants and friends of Russia in America. It tells the Russian emigrants that they now must spit in the face of the false military propaganda by which their sympathy and help to the prosecution of the war have been called forth and says that with the money they have lent or are going to lend "they will make bullets not only for the Germans but also for the Workers Soviets of Russia," and further, "Workers in the ammunition factories, you are producing bullets, bayonets, cannon, to murder not only the Germans, but also your dearest, best, who are in Russia and are fighting for freedom." It then appeals to the same Russian emi-grants at some length not to consent to the "inquisitionary expedi-tion to Russia," and says that the destruction of the Russian revolu-tion is "the politics of the march to Russia." The leaflet winds up by saying "Workers, our reply to this barbaric intervention has to be a general strike!" and after a few words on the spirit of revolu-tion, exhortations not to be afraid, and some usual tall talk ends, "Woe unto those who will be in the way of progress. Let solidarity live! The Rebels."

No argument seems to me necessary to show that these pronun-ciamentos in no way attack the form of government of the United States, or that they do not support either of the first two counts. What little I have to say about the third count may be postponed until I have considered the fourth. With regard to that it seems too plain to be denied that the suggestion to workers in the ammuni-tion factories that they are producing bullets to murder their dear-est, and the further advocacy of a general strike, both in the second leaflet, do urge curtailment of production of things necessary to the prosecution of the war within the meaning of the Act of May 16, 1918, c. 75, 40 Stat. 553, amending Sec. 3 of the earlier Act of 1917. But to make the conduct criminal that statute requires that it should be "with intent by such curtailment to cripple or hin-der the United States in the prosecution of the war." It seems to me that no such intent is proved.

I am aware of course that the word intent as vaguely used in ordinary legal discussion means no more than knowledge at the time of the act that the consequences said to be intended will ensue. Even less than that will satisfy the general principle of civil and criminal liability. A man may have to pay damages, may be sent to prison, at common law might be hanged, if at the time of his act he knew facts from which common experience showed that the consequences would follow, whether he individually could foresee them or not. But, when words are used exactly, a deed is not done with intent to produce a consequence unless that consequence is the aim of the deed. It may be obvious, and obvious to the actor, that the consequence will follow, and he may be liable for it even if he regrets it, but he does not do the act with intent to produce it unless the aim to produce it is the proximate motive of the specific act, although there may be some deeper motive behind.

It seems to me that this statute must be taken to use its words in a strict and accurate sense. They would be absurd in any other. A patriot might think that we were wasting money on aeroplanes, or making more cannon of a certain kind than we needed, and might advocate curtailment with success, yet even if it turned out that the curtailment hindered and was thought by other minds to have been obviously likely to hinder the United States in the prosecution of the war, no one would hold such conduct a crime. I admit that my illustration does not answer all that might be said but it is enough to show what I think and to let me pass to a more important aspect of the case. I refer to the First Amendment to the Constitution that Congress shall make no law abridging the freedom of speech.

I never have seen any reason to doubt that the questions of law that alone were before this Court in the cases of *Schenck, Frohwerk* and *Debs,* 249 U. S. 47, 204, 211, were rightly decided. I do not doubt for a moment that by the same reasoning that would justify punishing persuasion to murder, the United States constitutionally may punish speech that produces or is intended to produce a clear and imminent danger that it will bring about forthwith certain substantive evils that the United States constitutionally may seek to prevent. The power undoubtedly is greater in time of war than in time of peace because war opens dangers that do not exist at other times.

But as against dangers peculiar to war, as against others, the principle of the right to free speech is always the same. It is only the present danger of immediate evil or an intent to bring it about that warrants Congress in setting a limit to the expression of opinion where private rights are not concerned. Congress certainly cannot forbid all effort to change the mind of the country. Now nobody can suppose that the surreptitious publishing of a silly leaflet by an unknown man, without more, would present any immediate danger that its opinions would hinder the success of the government arms or have any appreciable tendency to do so. Publishing those opinions for the very purpose of obstructing however, might indicate a greater danger and at any rate would have the quality of an attempt. So I assume that the second leaflet if published for the purposes alleged in the fourth count might be punishable. But it seems pretty clear to me that nothing less than that would bring these papers within the scope of this law. An actual intent in the sense that I have explained is necessary to constitute an attempt, where a further act of the same individual is required to complete the substantive crime, for reasons given in *Swift & Co. v. United States,* 196 U.S. 375, 396. It is necessary where the success of the attempt depends upon others because if that intent is not present the actor's aim may be accomplished without bringing about the evils sought to be checked. An intent to prevent interference with the revolution in Russia might have been satisfied without any hindrance to carrying on the war in which we were engaged.

I do not see how anyone can find the intent required by the statute in any of the defendants' words. The second leaflet is the only one that affords even a foundation for the charge, and there, without invoking the hatred of German militarism expressed in the former one, it is evident from the beginning to the end that the only object of the paper is to help Russia and stop American intervention there against the popular government—not to impede the United States in the war that it was carrying on. To say that two phrases taken literally might import a suggestion of conduct that would have interference with the war as an indirect and probably undesired effect seems to me by no means enough to show an attempt to produce that effect.

I return for a moment to the third count. That charges an intent to provoke resistance to the United States in its war with Germany. Taking the clause in the statute that deals with that in connection with the other elaborate provisions of the Act, I think that resistance to the United States means some forcible act of opposition to some proceeding of the United States in pursuance of the war. I think the intent must be the specific intent that I have described and for the reasons that I have given I think that no such intent was proved or existed in fact. I also think that there is no hint at resistance to the United States as I construe the phrase.

In this case sentences of twenty years' imprisonment have been imposed for the publishing of two leaflets that I believe the defendants had as much right to publish as the Government has to publish the Constitution of the United States now vainly invoked by them. Even if I am technically wrong and enough can be squeezed from these poor and puny anonymities to turn the color of legal litmus paper; I will add, even if what I think the necessary intent were shown; the most nominal punishment seems to me all that possibly could be inflicted, unless the defendants are to be made to suffer not for what the indictment alleges but for the creed that they avow—a creed that I believe to be the creed of ignorance and immaturity when honestly held, as I see no reason to doubt that it was held here, but which, although made the subject of examination at the trial, no one has a right even to consider in dealing with the charges before the Court.

Persecution for the expression of opinions seems to me perfectly logical. If you have no doubt of your premises or your power and want a certain result with all your heart you naturally express your wishes in law and sweep away all opposition. To allow opposition by speech seems to indicate that you think the speech impotent, as when a man says that he has squared the circle, or that you do not care whole-heartedly for the result, or that you doubt either your power or your premises. But when men have realized that time has upset many fighting faiths, they may come to believe even more than they believe the very foundations of their own conduct that the ultimate good desired is better reached by free trade in ideas—that the best test of truth is the power of the thought to get itself accepted in the competition of the market, and that truth is the only ground upon which their wishes safely can be carried out. That at any rate is the theory of our Constitution. It is an experiment, as all life is an experiment. Every year if not every day we have to wager our salvation upon some prophecy based upon imperfect knowledge. While that experiment is part of our system I think that we should be eternally vigilant against attempts to check the expression of opinions that we loathe and believe to be fraught with death, unless they so imminently threaten immediate interference with the lawful and pressing purposes of the law that an immediate check is required to save the country. I wholly disagree with the argument of the Government that the First Amendment left the common law as to seditious libel in force. History seems to me against the notion. I had conceived that the United States through many years had shown its repentance for the Sedition Act of 1798, by repaying fines that it imposed. Only the emergency that makes it immediately dangerous to leave the correction of evil counsels to time warrants making any exception to the sweeping command, "Congress shall make no law . . . abridging the freedom of speech." Of course I am speaking only of expressions of opinion and exhortations, which were all that were uttered here, but I regret that I cannot put into more impressive words my belief that in their conviction upon this indictment the defendants were deprived of their rights under the Constitution of the United States.

24. ANDRÉ SIEGFRIED

Puritan Resistance to Freedom of Thought
(1927)

André Siegfried (1875-1959), French scholar and author, was born at Le Havre and educated at the Sorbonne. Long a professor of economics and a member of the French Academy, he was also an economic advisor of the French government. Among the many foreign critics of American life after the First World War, Siegfried was perhaps the most thoughtful and the most severe.

The future of American civilization would work out quite differently if the Lutheran or the Catholic conception of the state were to become more powerful than the Calvinist. The recent revival of Calvinism is a sign of its struggle to retain supremacy in order to safeguard the national customs from foreign influence. Countless crusades of every description are undertaken to convert the unbeliever and impose by force the conditions of life advocated by the majority. The minority, they say, have no right to complain, for it is being done for their good. In anything that touches the life of the community, the American is in reality a sort of "collectivist." He is as intolerant as a convert, especially since in religious matters he is an absolutist.

The opposition to this program comes either from scattered groups or from the business interests that are unable to fall in with the plans of the moralists, for business will not agree unless it either profits by these campaigns or guides them.

The Lutheran is out of sympathy partly owing to his hereditary respect for the State, and partly because he is determined to keep his German customs. The Catholic, and even at times the Anglican ritualist, is indignant that the State should submit to the dictates of individual consciences instead of to the Church, for both prefer ecclesiastical authority and family traditions. The Irish colonies of the great cities have imported an original viewpoint of their own with regards to methods of government, and their half-Catholic, half-cynical outlook has become Americanized. The English idea of government by disinterested gentlemen devoting themselves to the general good, which existed in America before the wave of Irish immigration of 1840, has not been entirely stamped out. The Irish newcomers, however, looked upon the state as the property of the people and especially as a means of obtaining the greatest possible advantages for themselves and their friends. A clash was inevitable between the ideals of the Puritan democracy and that extraordinary potpourri of farce, intrigue, hurly-burly, and whimsicality that goes to make up Irish politics, and which we must admit has, with all its faults, saved America from becoming as dreary as a prayer-meeting!

The reformers have had to reckon with still another power. In America as elsewhere business competition follows the natural laws of the struggle for existence. It does not conform to the standards of brotherly love, and all the "service" in the world cannot change it. Therefore nothing can be done against the wishes of the manufacturing interests, especially since they have been amalgamated and disciplined by the evolution of modern industry. When the religious elite wish to modify the national customs or preserve those that are dying out, they are accordingly careful not to antagonize the business world. Whenever the self-interest of the capitalist coincides with the idealism of the apostle, the "urge" for moral uplift becomes irresistible; for in America the wealthy are Christians, and nothing forbids Christians to be wealthy. In such an alliance lies the vital force of this community. Though it receives its inspiration from Puritan mysticism, it really expresses itself in material wealth, and it is not at all concerned with the liberty of the individual.

It is essential to realize that the liberalism of the eighteenth-century philosophers counts for little among these social forces. It is sometimes held that American political thought is based on the Constitution, which was largely drawn up by Jefferson and is very French in its disregard of religion. In actual fact, however, as may be seen by the renaissance of Puritanism and the extraordinary irruption of the Ku-Klux Klan, the political thought of the Protestant masses is very different from that of Franklin, Paine, Jefferson, or Washington. Instead of going back to these great liberals who were so close to secular thought, we must turn rather to the narrow fervor of the Cromwellian Roundheads, who were totally opposed to such ideas. If we overlook this, we are bound to be shocked when we find in America certain intolerant aspects of Protestantism which in Western Europe are now supposed to belong to the past.

It is generally believed that the First Amendment to the American Constitution in 1791 assured complete religious equality, and the Americans were free to choose God, Jehovah, or Buddha as they pleased, or even to maintain that there was no God at all. This, however, is not the case, though it is true that there is no established church. It is nevertheless understood that America is a Christian nation and that Protestantism is the national religion. This distinction seems perfectly plausible to the Protestants, for though their idea of a church is attenuated, their religious zeal is vigorous in the extreme. A Catholic who is not used to separating religion from the Church is apt to find the distinction too subtle. President Wilson in 1917 had printed on the title page of the New Testament that was distributed to the soldiers, "The Bible is the word of God. I request you to read it," and the public did not feel that he had exceeded in the least his role as head of a Christian government.

In many States of the Union, Protestantism was the established religion in the eighteenth century; for in those days a nation without a religion was an anomaly. Jews, atheists, and in certain cases even Catholics did not enjoy the full rights of citizenship. Under these conditions the First Amendment did not really secularize the State, but aimed more at holding the balance between the numerous Protestant sects. What the American liberals desired both at that time and since was to divorce the State from the churches, but not to separate it from the Christian religion, and certainly not from Protestantism. The official indifference to religious matters which characterizes French secular thought seems scandalous even today to most Americans.

Even after a century of progress, laws protecting religion still exist in many States. To work on Sunday is everywhere an offence, and the unfortunate Jew, after having observed Saturday as his own Sabbath, is obliged by the Christians to respect the next day as well. In North Carolina the law forbids the sale of gasoline during church hours. In Maryland it is a crime to utter impious words about our Lord. In New Hampshire it is heresy to deny the existence of God. In several States—Maryland, Arkansas, and South Carolina—Jews have not, for a long time, been accorded the same legal status as Christians. In Massachusetts in 1921 a Finnish lecturer who had mocked the Bible was condemned as follows under the Blasphemy Act:

> The religion of Christ is the prevailing religion of this country and this State. . . . Congress and the State legislature open their

sessions with prayer addressed to the God of the Christian religion. . . . Shall we say that any word or deed which would expose the God of the Christian religion or the holy scriptures to
contempt and ridicule would be protected by a constitutional religious freedom? We register a most emphatic negative.

It is wrong, therefore, to speak of religious liberty or equality
as traditionally American.

Christianity in its Protestant form is so closely woven into the
whole fabric of society that it is impossible to conceive of a separa-
tion, even suppose it were desired. The recent passage of a law in
the State of Tennessee, forbidding the teaching of evolution in
the public schools, and the famous trial which resulted in 1925
from the violation of this law are not isolated and interesting facts,
but are quite in line with the traditions of secular legislation. The
intolerance thus denoted is not simply a relic of the past, but a reflection of present-day sentiments and of a type of nationalism
that cannot distinguish between patriotism and religion. . . .

If it can be made a crime today to teach evolution in the public
schools, why should such an interdiction not be extended to private
institutions tomorrow? Will not the very existence of free schools
be threatened by sectarian majorities intent on moral unity and
impatient of any deviation from it? A law in the State of Oregon,
passed in 1922 but later declared unconstitutional by the Supreme
Court, shows the menace clearly. It also exposes the existence at
the other end of the country of the same intolerance as in Tennessee. Oregon represents the centre of Anglo-Saxon Puritanism in
the Northwest. In contrast to the persistent Liberalism of the
exotic and charming San Francisco, the nationalism of Portland
and Los Angeles is very extreme. The revivals of Billy Sunday, the
evangelist, not to mention Prohibition, find a fertile soil in both
cities. Two Puritan migrations from the Mississippi valley made
for these points, one in the second half of the nineteenth century

going to Oregon, and one in the beginning of the twentieth century toward Southern California. Though in appearance more modern than the people of the Alleghanies, we find here the same bias, the same fears, and the same religious intolerance.

By popular initiative Oregon passed a law in 1922 declaring that all children between the ages of eight and thirteen years had to be educated in the public schools, although it meant the suppression of private elementary education. The inspiration of this measure appears to be astonishingly like those of the anti-evolutionists of Tennessee. In Oregon they wish to use the public schools, which are controlled by the Protestant majority, to protect from Catholic, Jewish, and even Lutheran influence that portion of the younger generation which for religious or ethnic reasons has not been assimilated with sufficient rapidity. A pamphlet published at the time of the vote by the initiators of this law gives their reasons without beating about the bush:

> Our public schools . . . are the creators of true citizens by common education, which teaches those ideals and standards upon which our government rests. Our nation supports the public school for the sole purpose of self-preservation. The assimilation and education of our foreign-born citizens in the principles of our government, the hopes and inspiration of our people, are best secured by and through attendance of all children in our public schools. We must now halt those coming to our country from forming groups, establishing schools, and thereby bringing up their children in an environment often antagonistic to the principles of our government. Mix the children of the foreign-born with the native-born, and the rich with the poor. Mix those with prejudices in the public school melting pot for a few years while their minds are plastic, and finally bring out the finished product—a true American.

This is the classic argument against allowing two types of youth to develop. It is with growing impatience that the true Americans tolerate the separate point of view that is being systematically encouraged by the Catholic Church, through the family and its own schools. Ranged against this determination to remain distinct though loyal is the full force of the free-masons, the Protestant masses, and the Ku-Klux Klan. If it were not for out-of-date constitutions upheld by the authority of the Courts, the organized majority would have demonstrated ere now as it did in Tennessee that unity comes before liberty.

The anti-liberal legislation of Oregon, Tennessee, and Mississippi is at once less dangerous legally and more dangerous actually than it appears at first sight to be. These bigoted outbursts are still scattered, and if it is finally decided that they are unconstitutional they will not survive, although of course similar laws may be enacted elsewhere, and judges under the pressure of public opinion may further weaken their timid resistance to such innovations. The real peril is that instruction of every kind will be constantly under suspicious supervision. It would not be so bad if education were superintended by professional inspectors whose competence and impartiality were assured. The supervision is more likely to be exercised by a hysterical public, extraordinarily lacking in critical sense, and always likely to be inflamed by some eloquent evangelist.

In the Fundamentalist States and in all the Protestant States generally, the schoolmaster is given very little rope, and even the universities do not escape pressure. In the case of State universities supported by public funds, the budget is at the mercy of the legislature; that is to say, of universal suffrage; and any unorthodox course of lectures runs the danger of being suppressed. In the independent universities there are always the trustees to be considered, and although these controllers of the purse-strings are generally well disposed, they have no marked leaning toward extreme ideas.

Under these conditions a liberally-minded professor who is anxious to teach what he believes to be the truth runs the risk of raising a scandal either in the local press or in the university itself, and so losing his appointment. In 1924, to take one example out of hundreds, the professor of biology at the University of Minnesota discussed the Fundamentalist theory of creation in his class and refuted it. The effect was immediate. Mr. Bryan hurried to the scene, and before a vast assembly of over 8,000 people in the largest auditorium in Minneapolis, he fulminated against the iniquitous doctrines of evolution and the godless professor who taught them. The newspapers, knowing their public, reproduced his speech *in extenso,* and so spread the message from one end of the country to the other. With the danger of such a campaign of indignation always imminent, the professors' hands are bound. They soon realize, not only from the atmosphere in which they live, but also from their immediate chiefs, that they are expected to be as conventional as possible. A good professor in the West or the South does not flaunt his independence of thought, and utters nothing that might offend the susceptibilities of the trustees of the university, the important manufacturers and bankers of the town, the ministers of the leading denominations, or the local Congressman.

Of course this may only be a passing phase in the history of the United States, but there is no doubt that at the present time the great Protestant majority is clinging to the old, old belief that has been disputed by philosophers throughout the ages, namely, that there is only one social truth, and unless every one accepts it the unity of the nation is imperilled. We thus have the extraordinary paradox of the descendants of English and Scotch Nonconformists being changed into the narrowest of conformists, and the United States becoming a country where a man runs the risk of not being allowed to express himself freely. In a word, a transformation of the rights of the individual is taking place under our very eyes. The principles of the freedom of speech, of the press, and of association, the inviolability of the individual and of the home, the right to be judged by a jury according to regular procedure, are all solemnly guaranteed by the Constitution, and were handed down to America as part of the sacred heritage of British freedom. Now, however, a new doctrine, vigorous but undefined, is trying to undermine them by teaching that the rights of the community are almost unlimited, if it is defending itself against alien ideas, or against a germ of dissolution threatening its integrity. For the past thirty years, and especially since the War, it is not only the liberty of speech and the press that has been dangerously censored, but even the liberty to unite and the elementary rights of the citizens against an arbitrary police.

The American Constitution still survives, however, without essential alteration, and its revered text upholds in writing the rights of the individual against the State. We must admit that the present tendency of public opinion is out of harmony with it on many points; for, aroused by the menace of foreign ideas, the people are preoccupied with the problem of assimilation and moral standardization. The letter of the law which restrains them was written at an earlier date, and it is doubtful whether the Constitution would be drawn up in the same spirit if it had to be done over again today. Jefferson, that great liberal aristocrat whose vague theism has since been denounced as atheistic by generations of rural ministers, is less popular in the West at present that the Fundamentalist demagogue of Dayton. If any relic of the Jeffersonian tradition still survives, it is to be found, strange to relate, in the democratic centres of the great Eastern cities, for ethnic or religious minorities are always in favor of liberty although they may be without doctrinal convictions. But what are we to think of a country of British origin where liberalism has to seek its champions among foreigners and Catholics? The reason is clear enough. In its pursuit of wealth and power, America has abandoned the ideal of liberty to follow that of prosperity.

25. RALPH BORSODI

This Ugly Civilization
(1929)

Ralph Borsodi (1888-   ), economist and author, was born in New York City. Privately educated, he became a leading critic of industrialism and of the way in which it made men dependent on the factory and the machine. He advanced his own theories for a return to a decentralized individualistic pattern of life in his School of Living at Suffern, New York.

This is an ugly civilization.

It is a civilization of noise, smoke, smells, and crowds—of people content to live amidst the throbbing of its machines; the smoke and smells of its factories; the crowds and the discomforts of the cities of which it proudly boasts.

The places in which the people work are noisy. The factories are filled with the recurring, though not the rhythmic, noises of machines and the crash and clatter incidental to their operation. The offices, too, are noisy with the rat-tat-tat of typewriters, the ringing of telephones, the grinding of adding machines. The streets on which the people move about, and around which they work and play, resound with the unending clatter of traffic—the roar of motors, the squeaks of brakes, the shrieks of sirens, and the banging of street cars. And even the homes in which they are supposed to rest are noisy because they are not only packed close together but built tier on tier so that the pianos, phonographs, and radios in them blare incongruously above, below, and on all sides of them.

The people of this factory-dominated civilization accept its noisiness. For noise is the audible evidence of their prowess; the inescapable accompaniment of their civilization's progress. The greater the noise, the greater the civilization.

The people of Pittsburgh, a city of more than half a million souls, live in a cloud of soot. Soot shuts out the sun by day; the moon and stars by night. Soot blackens Pittsburgh's churches and courthouses; its humble dwellings and towering office buildings. It creeps and sifts into Pittsburgh's homes. It smuts the walls, the draperies, the rugs, the furnishings in Pittsburgh's homes. In Pittsburgh people accept a sooty civilization because soot makes Pittsburgh great.

The people of Chicago, a city of over three million souls, live under an encircling and overpowering smell. At breakfast, at luncheon, at dinner: while working and playing; awake and asleep; Chicago's millions inhale penetrating smells from the mountains of dung and offal in its great stockyards. The greater the smells the stockyards make, the greater their contributions to Chicago. In Chicago people accept a smelly civilization because smells make Chicago great.

The people of New York, a city of over six million souls, shuttle back and forth morning and night between their flats at one end and their jobs at the other end of a series of long underground tubes. Twice each work day throughout their lives New Yorkers push and are pushed into their noisy, sweaty, obscenely crowded subways, elevated railroads, street cars and busses. In New York people accept a civilization of crowded homes, crowded streets, crowded stores, crowded offices, crowded theatres because crowds make New York great.

Pittsburgh is not our only sooty factory city; Chicago is not our only smelly stockyards town; New York is not our only crowded metropolis. The cities of the country differ from one another only in degrees of sootiness, smelliness, noisiness and crowdedness. What is most discouraging, those not so sooty as Pittsburgh, nor so smelly as Chicago, nor so crowded as New York, aspire to equal these three shining jewels of our civilization in the very things that make for ugliness.

Travel on the Erie Railroad from New York to Buffalo and you will see how this civilization scars what should be one of the most beautiful regions of the world. The train moves through a country-side that is one unending delight—a succession of hills and valleys, fields and streams of entrancing loveliness. From the time it leaves the factory-dotted area of northern New Jersey, which the sprawl-ing cities of Jersey City, Passaic and Paterson make hideous, it travels through a region that should inspire all of those who dwell in it to the building of beautiful places in which to work and play.

Instead, the cities and towns are eyesores, especially those that contain factories, and most of them do; made more hideous be-cause of the contrast between the dingy places built by men and the natural beauty around them. What the factory has left undone to mar the country seems to have been done by the signs and bill-boards advertising factory products; by the huddle of stores and warehouses in which factory products are distributed; by the drab, box-like houses in which dwell the makers of factory products. Between the factory itself and these by-products of a factory-dominated countryside all has been done that could be done to make the country ugly.

Above all, this civilization is ugly because of the subtle hypocrisy with which it persuades the people to engage in the factory production of creature comforts while imposing conditions which destroy their capacity for enjoying them. With one hand it gives comforts—with the other hand it takes comfort itself away.

The servitude to the factory which it enforces uniformly upon all men harnesses skilled workers and creative individuals in a repetitive treadmill which makes each muscle in their bodies, every drop of blood in their veins, the very fibres of their being, cry out in a voiceless agony that they are being made to murder time—the irreplaceable stuff of which life itself is composed.

For America is a respecter of things only, and time—why, time is only something to be killed, or butchered into things which can be bought and sold.

Wherever the factory dominates, there you will find the factory-generated waste of human life and natural resources, and the noise, soot, smell and crowds of industrialized America.

For the misdirection of human energy which destroys beauty is neither exclusively American nor exclusively modern. Ugliness has existed in all ages and is to be found among all the peoples of the earth. The tragic universality of the "misfortune" to which Friedrich Nietzsche calls attention in *Thus Spake Zarathustra* has made ugliness the common curse of mankind. Says Nietzsche: "There is no sorer misfortune in all human destiny, than when the mighty of the earth are not also the first men."

For "the mighty of the earth," when bereft of wisdom, have to devote themselves ruthlessly to perpetuating their own might. This is the genesis of the interminable warfare waged by predatory quantity-minded men upon the quality-minded men who seek to make the world a more beautiful place in which to live.

Substitute "church" for "factory" and the argument of this book applies equally well to the situation of mankind when Voltaire waged his war with *"l'Infame."* Hypatia the Church tore to pieces. Bruno it burned at the stake. Copernicus and Galileo it terrorized into temporary silence. What the Church did when it had full sway to the quality-minded individuals who sought to make the world a more intelligent place was similar in essence, although far worse in kind, to that which the factory does today.

Substitute "slavery" for "factory" and the argument applies equally to that period of history when mankind accepted the idea that heredity and power gave to limited numbers of men the right to enslave others. Nothing in all history is more vile than the institution which permitted a "noble" Roman to cripple Epictetus, because he owned him! What slavery did when it flourished to the quality-minded individuals, both slave and free, who sought to make life more beautiful, was no different in essence from that which the factory does today.

Substitute "absolutism" for "factory" and the argument applies equally to every period and every place in which kings, princes and nobles wielded absolute powers. What absolutism did wherever it had sway to quality-minded individuals was similar in essence to what the factory does today.

The civilization dominated by the Church, by slavery and by absolutism were each in their way ugly. But the superstitions, cruelties, and injustices which marred them were the symptoms and not the true causes of the perhaps incurable disease from which all of them suffered.

The institutions which dominated those civilizations, just as the factory dominates ours, expressed the activities of acquisitive, predatory, ruthless, quantity-minded types of men. Because these powerful but inferior types impose their wills upon superior types of men, the individuals who mitigate the tragedy of life—those who have contributed all the beauty to be found amidst the wealth of folly and waste in the world—are penalized and handicapped in their work.

Under penalty of all that is dear to men—work, comfort, fellowship, even life itself—they are forced to subscribe to the false facts, false hopes, false fears, false tastes of the conventions of their times. The penalties for failure to conform have varied from burnings-at-the-stake, the favorite method when the Church dominated civilization, to starvation-into-accepting-a-place-in-the factory system, the favorite method now that the factory dominates civilization.

America has not yet permitted the factory, officially, to take over the government. America still gives, officially, lip-service to the rights of the individual. But factory-dominated America is slowly but surely destroying its idealists by making laws, schools and all other popular institutions "practical." Already the factory has created a factory folkway. In America "business as usual" is not a mere slogan—it is a holy and patriotic virtue.

But look at Russia. In Russia proscription of the nonconformist is practiced—after socialization—on an even greater scale than in capitalistic America.

There the factory is supreme.

There the factory has taken over the government.

And there all men are being forced to conform to the needs of the factory, precisely as in ancient Sparta they were forced to conform to the needs of the State, and in the Middle Ages to the needs of the Church.

And now let me try to tell you why it is that I have come to the conclusion that it is the factory—the gross abuse of the factory—that has produced this ugly civilization.

For it *is* an ugly civilization.

It is ugly because of its persistent failure to concern itself about whether the work men do, and the things they produce, and above all the way they live, create the comfort and understanding essential if mankind is to achieve an adequate destiny.

And it will remain ugly and probably become uglier year by year until the men who are able to mitigate its ugliness free themselves to do so.

26. WALTER LIPPMANN

Planning in Time of Peace
(1937)

Walter Lippmann (1889-   ) was born in New
York City. At Harvard, where he received his degree
in 1909, Lippmann was an enthusiastic young radical.
In 1914 he became one of the original editors of the
New Republic and, after government service during
the war, he joined the staff of the *New York World*
as an editorial writer. With the coming of the New
Deal, he confessed a growing disillusionment over his
old pre-World War I optimism in regard to collectivism. In addition to his important books, Lippmann has
had a wide influence as the author of a nationally-
syndicated newspaper column on domestic and world
affairs.

Although all the known examples of collectivism have had their
origin in war or have as their objective the preparation for war, it
is widely believed that a collectivist order could be organized for
peace and for plenty. "It is nonsense," says Mr. George Soule, "to
say that there is any physical impossibility of doing for peace purposes the sort of thing we actually did for war purposes." If the
State can organize for war, it is asked, why can it not organize for
peace and plenty? If it can mobilize against a foreign enemy, why
not against poverty, squalor, and the hideous social evils that
attend them?

It is plain enough that a dictated collectivism is necessary if a nation is to exert its maximum military power: very evidently its capital and labor must not be wasted on the making of luxuries; it can tolerate no effective dissent, nor admit that men have any right to the pursuit of private happiness. No one can dispute that. The waging of war must be authoritarian and collectivist. The question we must now consider is whether a system which is essential to the conduct of war can be adapted to the civilian ideal of peace and plenty. Can this form of organization, historically associated with military purposes and necessities, be used for the general improvement of men's condition? It is a critical question. For in answering it we shall be making up our minds whether the hopes invested in the promises of the collectivists are valid, and therefore entitled to our allegiance.

We must remind ourselves again, not only why collectivism is necessary in war but why war is so favorable to collectivism. In wartime the political conditions fix the "imperatives" which Mr. Chase lays down: "the scrapping of outworn political boundaries and of constitutional checks and balances, where the issues are technical [sic]; centralization of government; the overhead planning and control of economic activity." Under the system of centralized control without constitutional checks and balances, the war-spirit identifies dissent with treason, the pursuit of private happiness with slackerism and sabotage, and, on the other side, obedience with discipline, conformity with patriotism. Thus at one stroke war extinguishes the difficulties of planning, cutting out from under the individual any moral ground as well as any lawful ground on which he might resist the execution of the official plan. The dissenter, the conscientious objector, the indifferent and the discontented, have no rights which anyone is bound to respect, and if they are dealt with leniently it is because the war administrators have scruples or regard them as negligible. In the degree of their interference with the prosecution of the war, they have no more standing against military authority than has been enjoyed by the victims of Lenin, Trotsky, Stalin, Mussolini, and Hitler. Mr. George Soule has found the polite name for all of this. He puts first among "the lessons from our war planning" that "we must have an objective which can arouse general loyalty and enthusiasm."

War easily provides such an objective, and it is incomparably suited to the creation of a collective sentiment in which all lesser purposes are submerged. A call to arms is specific and everyone understands it. The cry that the enemy is at the gates, even the cry that beyond the deserts and mountains of Africa lies the promised land, needs little explaining. This is a very different thing from blowing the bugles and summoning the people to the abundant life to be achieved by "capacity operation of its plant, on the balanced load principle." Anyone can imagine an enemy and hate him; but to talk about an abundant life is merely to begin an interminable argument. This is the reason, based on deep psychological compulsion, why the socialist propaganda has always relied more upon an appeal to class war than upon the vision of a socialist society, why the effective leaders from Marx to Lenin have always derided as "unscientific" and "utopian" any detailed concern with the nature of a socialist society. Their intuition has surely been sound. For it is the war-spirit that most readily imposes unanimity for collective action among masses of men. When men are at peace, they have an incorrigible tendency, if one likes collectivism, a noble tendency if one dislikes it, to become individuals.

For reasons of this sort war provides a congenial climate for the administration of a planned economy. It is no less favorable to the planners when they face the crucial problem of deciding what specifically they will plan for. "We must have," says Mr. Soule, "an objective which is capable of being so concretely defined that it can decide questions as to how much we need to produce and in what order of importance the requirements are to be arranged." In wartime, or when a nation is totally committed to preparation for war, Mr. Soule's planners go to the general staff for a schedule of war machines, ammunition, fuel and spare parts, uniforms, food and medical supplies, barracks and the transporation needed in order to train, equip, and supply an army of a specified size. With the demands of the general staff before them, they can take an inventory of their available supplies of men, materials, and technical skill. They can estimate the indispensable requirements of the civilian population. From these more or less known factors the planners can calculate the proportions and the priorities in the expenditure of men and materials and money.

An overhead planning and control of economic activity is feasible because the plan is calculable. It is calculable because there is a specific purpose to be achieved, the supply of a military force of known size with known requirements out of known resources, and to this concrete objective all other needs must conform. The planners know definitely what goods are needed and in what amount. There is no problem of how much can be sold. The problem is how much can be produced. There is no worry about the varying tastes of voluntary consumers; the consumer is rationed. There is no such thing as a choice of occupation; labor is conscripted. Thus, though war economies are notoriously inefficient, they can be administered by the method of overhead planning and control because, theoretically at least, there are no unknown factors, and there can be no resistance; it is possible, therefore, to calculate the relation of the means to the end and execute the plan whether people like it or not. . . .

The question of whether an economy can be planned for abundance, for the general welfare, for the improvement of the popular standard of life, comes down, therefore, to the question of whether concepts of this sort can be translated into orders for particular goods which are as definite as the "requisitions" of a general staff. An objective like "the general welfare" has to be defined as specific quantities of specific goods—so many vegetables, so much meat, this number of shoes, neckties, collar buttons, aspirin tablets, frame houses, brick houses, steel buildings. Unless this can be done there will not exist the primary schedule of requirements from which to calculate the plan. The general staff can tell the planner exactly how much food, clothing, ammunition, it needs for each soldier. But in time of peace who will tell the planners for abundance what they must provide? . . .

The difficulty of planning production to satisfy many choices is the rock on which the whole conception founders. We have seen that in military planning this difficulty does not exist. It is the insurmountable difficulty of civilian planning, and although advocates like Mr. Mumford, Mr. Chase, and Mr. Soule have never, I think, faced it squarely, they are not unaware that it exists. They show that they are troubled because they denounce so vehemently the tastes of the people and the advertising which helps to form those tastes. They insist that the people have foolish and vulgar desires, which may be true enough, and that altogether better standards, simpler, more vital, more aesthetic, and more hygienic, ought to replace them. I agree. But I do not see how the purification of the public taste is to be worked out by a government commission. I can see how and why the general staff can decide how soldiers should live under martial discipline; but I cannot see how any group of officials can decide how a civilian population shall live nobly and abundantly.

For the fundamental characteristic of a rising standard of life is that an increasing portion of each man's income is spent on unessentials; it is applied, in other words, to things in which preference rather than necessity is the criterion. If all income had to be spent on the absolute necessities of life, the goods required would be few in number and their production could readily be standardized into a routine. Now it should be noted that all known examples of planned economy have flourished under conditions of scarcity. In the war economies of 1914-1918, in the collectivist regimes in Russia, Italy, and Germany, the supply of necessary goods has never been equal to the demand. Under such conditions, as during a siege or a famine, the communist principle is not only feasible but necessary. But as productivity arises above the level of necessity the variety of choices is multiplied. And as the choices are multiplied, the possibility of an overhead calculation of the relation between demand and supply diminishes. . . .

By what formula could a planning authority determine which goods to provide against the purchases of thirty million families with seventy billions of free spendable income? The calculation is not even theoretically possible. For, unless the people are to be deprived of the right to dispose of their incomes voluntarily, anyone who sets out to plan American production must first forecast how many units of each commodity the people would buy, not only at varying prices for that commodity, but in all possible combinations of prices for all commodities. . . .

Out of all the possible plans of production some schedule would have to be selected arbitrarily. There is absolutely no objective and universal criterion by which to decide between better houses and more automobiles, between pork and beef, between the radio and the movies. In military planning the criterion exists: to mobilize the most powerful army that the national resources will support. That criterion can be defined by the general staff as so many men with such-and-such equipment, and the economy can be planned accordingly. But civilian planning for a more abundant life has no definable criterion. It can have none. The necessary calculations cannot, therefore, be made, and the concept of a civilian planned economy is not merely administratively impracticable; it is not even theoretically conceivable. The conception is totally devoid of meaning, and there is, speaking literally, nothing in it.

The primary factor which makes civilian planning incalculable is the freedom of the people to spend their income. Planning is theoretically possible only if consumption is rationed. For a plan of production *is* a plan of consumption. If the authority is to decide what shall be produced, it has already decided what shall be consumed. In military planning that is precisely what takes place: the authorities decide what the army shall consume and what of the national product shall be left for the civilians. No economy can, therefore, be planned for civilians unless there is such scarcity that the necessities of existence can be rationed. As productivity rises above the subsistence level, free spending becomes possible. A planned production to meet a free demand is a contradiction in terms and as meaningless as a square circle.

It follows, too, that a plan of production is incompatible with voluntary labor, with freedom to choose an occupation. A plan of production is not only a plan of consumption, but a plan of how long, at what, and where the people shall work. By no possible manipulation of wage rates could the planners attract to the various jobs precisely the right number of workers. Under voluntary labor, particularly with consumption rationed and standardized, the unpleasant jobs would be avoided and the good jobs overcrowded. Therefore the inevitable and necessary complement of the rationing of consumption is the conscription of labor, either by overt act of law or by driving workers into the undesirable jobs by offering them starvation as the alternative. This is, of course, exactly what happens in a thoroughly militarized state.

The conscription of labor and the rationing of consumption are not to be regarded as transitional or as accidental devices in a planned economy. They are the very substance of it. To make a five-year plan of what a whole nation shall produce is to determine how it shall labor and what it shall receive. It can receive only what the plan provides. It can obtain what the plan provides only by doing the work which the plan calls for. It must do that work or the plan is a failure; it must accept what the plan yields in the way of goods or it must do without.

All this is perfectly understood in an army or in wartime when a whole nation is in arms. The civilian planner cannot avoid the rationing and the conscription, for they are the very essence of his proposal. There is no escape. If the people are free to reject the rations, the plan is frustrated; if they are free to work less or at different occupations than those prescribed, the plan cannot be executed. Therefore their labor and their standards of living have to be dictated by the planning board or by some sovereign power superior to the board. In a militarized society that sovereign power is the general staff.

But who, in a civilian society, is to decide what is to be the specific content of the abundant life? It cannot be the people deciding by referendum or through a majority of their elected representatives. For if the sovereign power to pick the plan is in the people, the power to amend it is there also at all times. Now a plan subject to change from month to month or even from year to year is not a plan; if the decision has been taken to make ten million cars at $500 and one million suburban houses at $3,000, the people cannot change their minds a year later, scrap the machinery to make the cars, abandon the houses when they are partly built, and decide to produce instead skyscraper apartment houses and underground railroads.

There is, in short, no way by which the objectives of a planned economy can be made to depend upon popular decision. They must be imposed by an oligarchy of some sort, and that oligarchy must, if the plan is to be carried through, be irresponsible in matters of policy. Individual oligarchs might, of course, be held accountable for breaches of the law just as generals can be court-martialed. But their policy can no more be made a matter of continuous accountability to the voters than the strategic arrangements of the generals can be determined by the rank and file. The planning board or their superiors have to determine what the life and labor of the people shall be.

Not only is it impossible for the people to control the plan, but, what is more, the planners must control the people. They must be despots who tolerate no effective challenge to their authority. Therefore civilian planning is compelled to presuppose that somehow the despots who climb to power will be benevolent—that is to say, will know and desire the supreme good of their subjects. This is the implicit premise of all the books which recommend the establishment of a planned economy in a civilian society. They paint an entrancing vision of what a benevolent despotism could do. They ask—never very clearly, to be sure—that somehow the people should surrender the planning of their existence to "engineers," "experts," and "technologists," to leaders, saviors, heroes. This is the political premise of the whole collectivist philosophy: that the dictators will be patriotic or class-conscious, whichever term seems the more eulogistic to the orator. It is the premise, too, of the whole philosophy of regulation by the state, currently regarded as progressivism. Though it is disguised by the illusion that a bureaucracy accountable to a majority of voters, and susceptible to the pressure of organized minorities, is not exercising compulsion, it is evident that the more varied and comprehensive the regulation becomes, the more the State becomes a despotic power as against the individual. For the fragment of control over the government which he exercises through his vote is in no effective sense proportionate to the authority exercised over him by the government.

Benevolent despots might indeed be found. On the other hand they might not be. They may appear at one time; they may not appear at another. The people, unless they choose to face the machine guns on the barricades, can take no steps to see to it that benevolent despots are selected and the malevolent cashiered. They cannot select their despots. The despots must select themselves, and, no matter whether they are good or bad, they will continue in office as long as they can suppress rebellion and escape assassination.

Thus, by a kind of tragic irony, the search for security and a rational society, if it seeks salvation through political authority, ends in the most irrational form of government imaginable—in the dictatorship of casual oligarchs, who have no hereditary title, no constitutional origin or responsibility, who cannot be replaced except by violence. The reformers who are staking their hopes on good despots, because they are so eager to plan the future, leave unplanned that on which all their hopes depend. Because a planned society must be one in which the people obey their rulers, there can be no plan to find the planners: the selection of the despots who are to make society so rational and so secure has to be left to the insecurity of irrational chance.

27. ROBERT M. HUTCHINS

The Path to War—We Are Drifting into Suicide
(1941)

Robert M. Hutchins (1899-   ) at the age of thirty
was appointed President of the University of Chicago.
Even earlier, he had been briefly Dean of the Yale
Law School. Since his retirement from Chicago in
1951, he has been associated with the Ford Foundation and the Fund for the Republic. A long-standing
critic of American higher education, Hutchins also
has not hesitated to take the unpopular side of other
controversial issues.

I speak tonight because I believe that the American people are
about to commit suicide. We are not planning to. We have no
plan. We are drifting into suicide. Deafened by martial music, fine
language, and large appropriations, we are drifting into war.

I address you simply as an American citizen. I do not represent any organization or committee. I do not represent the University of Chicago. I am not a military expert. It is true that from
the age of eighteen to the age of twenty I was a private in the
American Army. I must have somewhere the very fine medal given
me by the Italian government of that day in token of my co-operation on the Italian front. But this experience would not justify me
in discussing tactics, strategy, or the strength to which our armed
forces should now attain.

I wish to dissociate myself from all Nazis, Fascists, Communists and appeasers. I regard the doctrine of all totalitarian regimes as wrong in theory, evil in execution, and incompatible with the rights of man.

I wish to dissociate myself from those who want us to stay out of war to save our own skins or our own property. I believe that the people of this country are and should be prepared to make sacrifices for humanity. National selfishness should not determine national policy.

It is impossible to listen to Mr. Roosevelt's recent speeches, to study the lease-lend bill, and to read the testimony of cabinet officers upon it without coming to the conclusion that the President now requires us to underwrite a British victory and apparently a Chinese and a Greek victory, too. We are going to try to produce the victory by supplying our friends with the materials of war. But what if this is not enough? We have abandoned all pretense of neutrality. We are to turn our ports into British naval bases. But what if this is not enough? Then we must send the Navy, the Air Force, and, if Mr. Churchill wants it, the Army. We must guarantee the victory.

We used to hear of "all aid short of war." The words "short of war" are ominously missing from the President's recent speeches. The lease-lend bill contains provisions that we should have regarded as acts of war up to last week. The conclusion is inescapable that the President is reconciled to active military intervention if such intervention is needed to defeat the Axis in this war.

I have supported Mr. Roosevelt since he first went to the White House. I have never questioned his integrity or his good will. But under the pressure of great responsibilities, in the heat of controversy, in the international game of bluff, the President's speeches and recommendations are committing us to obligations abroad which we cannot perform. The effort to perform them will prevent the achievement of the aims for which the President stands at home.

If we go to war, what are we going to war for? This is to be a crusade, a holy war. Its object is moral. We are seeking, the President tells us, "a world founded on freedom of speech, freedom of worship, freedom from want, and freedom from fear." We are to intervene to support the moral order. We are to fight for "the supremacy of human rights everywhere."

With the President's desire to see freedom of speech, freedom of worship, freedom from want, and freedom from fear flourish everywhere we must all agree. Millions of Americans have supported the President because they felt that he wanted to achieve these four freedoms for America. Others, who now long to carry these blessings to the rest of the world, were not conspicuous on the firing line when Mr. Roosevelt called them, eight years ago, to do battle for the four freedoms at home. But let us agree now that we want the four freedoms; we want justice, the moral order, democracy, and the supremacy of human rights, not here alone, but everywhere. The question is whether entrance into this war is likely to bring us closer to this goal.

How can the United States better serve suffering humanity everywhere; by going into this war, or by staying out? I hold that the United States can better serve suffering humanity everywhere by staying out.

But can we stay out? We are told it is too late. The house is on fire. When the house is on fire, you do not straighten the furniture, and clean out the cellar, or ask yourself whether the house is as good a house as you would like. You put out the fire if you can. The answer is that the house is not on fire. The house next door is on fire. When the house next door is on fire you do not set fire to your own house, throw the baby on the floor, and rush off to join the fun. And when you do go to quench the fire next door, you make sure that your bucket is full of water and not oil.

But, we are told, we are going to have to fight the Axis sometime. Why not fight it now, when we have Britain to help us? Why wait until we have to face the whole world alone?

Think of the mass of assumptions upon which this program rests. First, we must assume that in spite of its heroic resistance and in spite of the enormous supplies of munitions which it is yet to receive from America the British Empire must fall.

Second, we must assume that the present rulers of totalitarian states will survive the conflict.

Third, we must assume that if these regimes survive they will want to attack us.

Fourth, we must assume that they will be in a position to attack us. This involves the assumptions that they will have the resources to do so, that their people will consent to new and hazardous ventures, that their task of holding down conquered nations will be easily completed, and that the ambiguous attitude of Russia will cause them little concern.

Next, if Britain falls, if the totalitarian regimes survive, if they want to attack us, if they are in a position to do so, we must further assume that they will find it possible to do so. The flying time between Africa and Brazil, or Europe and America, does not decide this question. The issue is what will be at the western end of the line? This will depend on our moral and military preparedness. A lone squadron of bombers might conquer a continent peopled with inhabitants careless of safety or bent on slavery. We cannot assume that any combination of powers can successfully invade this hemisphere if we are prepared to defend ourselves and determined to be free.

On a pyramid of assumptions, hypotheses, and guesses therefore, rests a decision to go to war now because it is too late to stay out. There is no such inevitability about war with the Axis as to prevent us from asking ourselves whether we shall serve suffering humanity better everywhere by going into this war or by staying out.

The chances of accomplishing the high moral purposes which the President has stated for America, even if we stay out of war, are not bright. The world is in chaos. We must give our thoughts and energy to building our defenses. What we have of high moral purpose is likely to suffer dilution at home and a cold reception abroad. But we have a chance to help humanity if we do not go into this war. If we do go into it, we have no chance at all.

The reason why we have no chance to help humanity if we go into this war is that we are not prepared. I do not mean, primarily, that we are unprepared in a military sense. I mean that we are morally and intellectually unprepared to execute the moral mission to which the President calls us.

A missionary, even a missionary to the cannibals, must have clear and defensible convictions. And if his plan is to eat some of the cannibals in order to persuade the others to espouse the true faith, his convictions must be very clear and very defensible indeed. It is surely not too much to ask of such a missionary that his own life and works reflect the virtues which he seeks to compel others to adopt. If we stay out of war, we may perhaps some day understand and practice freedom of speech, freedom of worship, freedom from want, and freedom from fear. We may even be able to comprehend and support justice, democracy, the moral order, and the supremacy of human rights. Today we have barely begun to grasp the meaning of the words.

Those beginnings are important. They place us ahead of where we were at the end of the last century. They raise us, in accomplishment as well as in ideals, far above the accomplishment and ideals of totalitarian powers. They leave us, however, a good deal short of that level of excellence which entitles us to convert the world by force of arms.

Have we freedom of speech and freedom of worship in this country? We do have freedom to say what everybody else is saying and freedom of worship if we do not take our religion too seriously. But teachers who do not conform to the established canons of social thought lose their jobs. People who are called "radicals" have mysterious difficulties in renting halls. Labor organizers sometimes get beaten up and ridden out of town on a rail. Norman Thomas had some troubles in Jersey City. And the Daughters of the American Revolution refused to let Marian Anderson sing in the national capital in a building called Constitution Hall.

If we regard these exceptions as minor, reflecting the attitude of the more backward and illiterate parts of the country, what are we to say of freedom from want and freedom from fear? What of the moral order and justice and the supremacy of human rights? What of democracy in the United States?

Words like these have no meaning unless we believe in human dignity. Human dignity means that every man is an end in himself. No man can be exploited by another. Think of these things and then think of the sharecroppers, the Oakies, the Negroes, the slumdwellers, downtrodden and oppressed for gain. They have neither freedom from want nor freedom from fear. They hardly know they are living in a moral order or in a democracy where justice and human rights are supreme.

We have it on the highest authority that one-third of the nation is ill-fed, ill-clothed, and ill-housed. The latest figures of the National Resources Board show that almost precisely 55 per cent of our people are living on family incomes of less than $1,250 a year. This sum, says *Fortune* Magazine, will not support a family of four. On this basis more than half our people are living below the minimum level of subsistence. More than half the army which will defend democracy will be drawn from those who have had this experience of the economic benefits of "the American way of life."

We know that we have had until lately nine million unemployed and that we should have them still if were not for our military preparations. When our military preparations cease we shall, for all we know, have nine million unemployed again. In his speech on December twentieth, Mr. Roosevelt said, "After the present needs of our defense are past, a proper handling of the country's peacetime needs will require all of the new productive capacity— if not still more." For ten years we have not known how to use the productive capacity we had. Now suddenly we are to believe that by some miracle, after the war is over, we shall know what to do with our old productive capacity and what to do in addition with the tremendous increases which are now being made. We have want and fear today. We shall have want and fear "when the present needs of our defense are past."

As for democracy, we know that millions of men and women are disfranchised in this country because of their race, color, or condition of economic servitude. We know that many municipal governments are models of corruption. Some State governments are merely the shadows of big-city machines. Our national government is a government by pressure groups. Almost the last question an American is expected to ask about a proposal is whether it is just. The question is how much pressure is there behind it or how strong are the interests against it. On this basis are settled such great issues as monopoly, the organization of agriculture, the relation of labor and capital, whether bonuses should be paid to veterans, and whether a tariff policy based on greed should be modified by reciprocal trade agreements.

To have a community men must work together. They must have common principles and purposes. If some men are tearing down a house while others are building it, we do not say they are working together. If some men are robbing, cheating, and oppressing others, we should not say they are a community. The aims of a democratic community are moral. United by devotion to law, equality, and justice, the democratic community works together for the happiness of all the citizens. I leave to you the decision whether we have yet achieved a democratic community in the United States.

In the speech in which Mr. Roosevelt told us in effect, that we are headed for war, he said, "Certainly this is no time to stop thinking about the social and economic problems which are the root cause of the social revolution which is today a supreme factor in the world." But in the same speech he said, "The need of the moment is that our actions and our policy should be devoted primarily—almost exclusively—to meeting this foreign peril. For all our domestic problems are now a part of the great emergency." This means—and it is perfectly obvious—that if any social objective interferes with the conduct of the war, it will be, it must be instantly abandoned. War can mean only the loss of "social gains" and the destruction of the livelihood of millions in modest circumstances, while pirates and profiteers, in spite of Mr. Roosevelt's efforts to stop them, emerge stronger than ever.

The four freedoms must be abandoned if they interfere with winning a war. In the ordinary course of war most of them do interfere. All of them may. In calmer days, in 1929, *The New York Times* said, "War brings many collateral disasters. Freedom of speech, freedom of the press suffer. We think we shall be wiser and cooler the next time, if there is one; but we shan't." The urge to victory annihilates tolerance. In April, 1939, Alfred Duff-Cooper said that "hatred of any race was a sign of mental deficiency and of lack of a broad conception of the facts of the world." In April, 1940, Mr. Duff-Cooper said that the crimes of the German militarists were the crimes of the whole people and that this should be kept in mind when the peace treaty was written.

We cannot suppose, because civil liberties were restricted in the last war and expanded after it, that we can rely on their revival after the next one. We Americans have only the faintest glimmering of what war is like. This war, if we enter it, will make the last one look like a stroll in the park. If we go into this one, we go in against powers dominating Europe and most of Asia to aid an ally who, we are told, is already in mortal danger. When we remember what a short war did to the four freedoms, we must recognize that they face extermination in the total war to come.

We Americans have hardly begun to understand and practice the ideals that we are urged to force on others. What we have, in this country, is hope. We, and we alone, have the hope that we actually achieve these ideals. The framework of our government was designed to help us achieve them. We have a tremendous continent, with vast resources, in a relatively impregnable position. We have energy, imagination, and brains. We have made some notable advances in the long march toward justice, freedom, and democracy.

If we go to war, we cast away our opportunity and cancel our gains. For a generation, perhaps for a hundred years, we shall not be able to struggle back to where we were. In fact, the changes that total war will bring may mean that we shall never be able to struggle back. Education will cease. Its place will be taken by vocational and military training. The effort to establish a democratic community will stop. We shall think no more of justice, the moral order, and the supremacy of human rights. We shall have hope no longer.

What, then, should our policy be? Instead of doing everything we can to get into the war, we should do everything we can to stay at peace. Our policy should be peace. Aid to Britain, China, and Greece should be extended, on the basis most likely to keep us at peace, and least likely to involve us in war.

At the same time we should prepare to defend ourselves. We should prepare to defend ourselves against military penetration. We should bend every energy to the construction of an adequate navy and air force and the training of an adequate army. By adequate I mean adequate for defense against any power or combination of powers.

In the meantime, we should begin to make this country a refuge for those who will not live without liberty. For less than the cost of two battleships we could accommodate half a million refugees from totalitarian countries for a year. The net cost would not approach the cost of two battleships, for these victims, unlike battleships, would contribute to our industry and our cultural life, and help us make democracy work.

But most important of all, we should take up with new vigor the long struggle for moral, intellectual, and spiritual preparedness. If we would change the face of the earth, we must first change our own hearts. The principal end that we have hitherto set before ourselves is the unlimited acquisition of material goods. The business of America, said Calvin Coolidge, is business. We must now learn that material goods are a means and not an end. We want them to sustain life, but they are not the aim of life. The aim of life is the fullest development of the highest powers of men. This means art, religion, education, moral and intellectual growth. These things we have regarded as mere decorations or relaxations in the serious business of life, which was making money. The American people, in their own interest, require a moral regeneration. If they are to be missionaries to the world, this regeneration must be profound and complete.

We must try to build a new moral order for America. We need moral conviction, intellectual clarity, and moral action; moral conviction about the dignity of man, intellectual clarity about ends and means, moral action to construct institutions to bring to pass the ends we have chosen.

A new moral order for America means a new conception of security. Today we do not permit men to die of starvation, but neither do we give them an incentive to live. Every citizen must have a respected place in the achievement of the national purpose.

A new moral order for America means a new conception of sacrifice, sacrifice for the moral purposes of the community. In the interest of human dignity we need a rising standard of health, character, and intelligence. These positive goals demand the devotion and sacrifice of every American. We should rebuild one-third of the nation's homes. We must provide adequate medical care in every corner of the land. We must develop an education aimed at moral and intellectual growth instead of at making money.

A new moral order for America means a new conception of mastery. We must learn how to reconcile the machine with human dignity. We have allowed it to run wild in prosperity and war and to rust idly in periodic collapse. We have hitherto avoided the issue by seeking new markets. In an unstable world this has meant bigger and bigger collapses, more and more catastrophic war. In Europe and Russia the efforts to master the machine are carried out by methods we despise. America can master the machine within the framework of a balanced democracy, outdistance the totalitarian despotisms, and bring light and hope to the world. It is our highest function and greatest opportunity to learn to make democracy work. We must bring justice and the moral order to life, here and now.

If we have strong defenses and understand and believe in what we are defending, we need fear nobody in the world. If we do not understand and believe in what we are defending, we may still win, but the victory will be as fruitless as the last. What did we do with the last one? What shall we do with this one? The government of Great Britain has repeatedly refused to state its war aims. The President in his foreign policy is pledged to back up Great

Britain, and beyond that, to the pursuit of the unattainable. If we go to war, we shall not know what we are fighting for. If we stay out of war until we do, we may have the stamina to win and the knowledge to use the victory for the welfare of mankind.

The path of war is a false path to freedom. A new moral order for America is the true path to freedom. A new moral order for America means new strength for America, and new hope for the moral reconstruction of mankind. We are turning aside from the true path to freedom because it is easier to blame Hitler for our troubles than to fight for democracy at home. As Hitler made the Jews his scapegoat, so we are making Hitler ours. But Hitler did not spring full-armed from the brow of Satan. He sprang from the materialism and paganism of our times. In the long run we can beat what Hitler stands for only by beating the materialism and paganism that produced him. We must show the world a nation clear in purpose, united in action, and sacrificial in spirit. The influence of that example upon suffering humanity everywhere will be more powerful than the combined armies of the Axis.

28. CALEB FOOTE

Have We Forgotten Justice?
(1942)

Caleb Foote (1917-   ) was born in Cambridge, Massachusetts. He received his A. B. degree from Harvard in 1938, and his law degree from the University of Pennsylvania, where he has been a professor of law since 1956. During World War II, as youth secretary for the West Coast branch of the Fellowship of Reconciliation, he was one of the very first and few Americans to criticize publicly the United States government's decision to evacuate all persons of Japanese ancestry from the Pacific Coast.

If Army plans materialize, before this article is in print 112,000 persons, a majority of whom are American citizens, will have been evacuated from their homes on the West Coast!

Obviously this compulsory evacuation of those whose only crime is their Japanese ancestry is a flagrant violation of the Fifth and Fourteenth Amendments to the Constitution, and so a perversion of democracy itself. Obviously, too, it denies the Christian doctrine of the supreme worth of the individual. It is creating untold human suffering, both physical and psychological, and it is a serious blow at interracial understanding and Japanese assimilation into American life.

Even more serious than these, however, is the fact that the evacuation heaps fuel on the fires of racial distrust, and lends authenticity to Japan's claims that this is a racial war. By putting many of our native-born *citizens* into "assembly" and "reception" centers—which, allowing for some differences, are virtually concentration camps—purely because of their race, our Government has aped the totalitarianism it is supposedly fighting. The peace that will follow the war is being made during the war and this treatment of innocent persons will not facilitate the creation of the state of mind necessary for gaining a good peace.

The background of what *Life* [Magazine] calls a "great and unprecedented migration" has been a vicious campaign of race hatred conducted in the Pacific Coast states. The anti-Japanese feeling that gave rise to it goes back forty years to a time when Japanese immigration into California was at its height. At first, these immigrants had been encouraged to come. They furnished cheap labor, and so were useful in breaking strikes and for field work. But these very "advantages" caused labor and small farming groups to resent their competition bitterly, and as time went on and the new racial group became more Americanized and acquired some economic power, the big economic groups who first welcomed them joined in opposing them. They were charged with destroying our standard of living, bringing in disease, being un-American and anti-Christian, and endangering our control by their own high birth-rate.

All of this resulted in the "Gentlemen's Agreement" restricting emigration from Japan, a series of land laws preventing Japanese aliens from owning or renting land, and the passage of the Exclusion Act in 1924. It is this latent race prejudice that has been whipped up anew since Pearl Harbor. Newspapers and politicians who just before the war commented on the "loyalty of the great majority" of *Niseis* and *Isseis,* led the parade of intolerance a month or two later. The city of Los Angeles fired all of its American-born Japanese employees, and other cities followed its lead. The State Personnel Board discriminated against citizen as well as alien Japanese, and the American Legion, County Boards of Supervisors, California Congressmen and others, joined newspaper editorial writers and columnists in urging complete evacuation. Early in January, job discrimination against aliens had become so severe that President Roosevelt called the firing of "honest and loyal people who, except for accident of birth, are sincerely patriotic" as "playing into the hands of the enemies of American democracy."

Meanwhile, anti-Japanese rumors and stories ran rife, purporting that "every Jap is a damned Jap," that they were poisoning vegetables and engaging in sit-down strikes, that there had been much sabotage in Hawaii, that all the Japanese in California were part of a well-organized fifth column. There is every reason to believe that persons or groups who hoped to gain from the evacuation had a major part in stirring up these irrational forces of racial prejudice. Big land-holding groups, laundries, and plant nurseries, who felt the competition of the Japanese, had a stake in the "internment," as did those who hoped to gain cheap, forced labor.

The defeats in the Far East, the shelling of an oil field near Santa Barbara, and the supposed air raid over Los Angeles, had much to do with a rise in anti-Japanese feeling that just preceded the evacuation order. Against this pressure were arrayed the efforts of the Japanese community to prove its loyalty, evidenced in the vigorous patriotism of the Japanese-American Citizens' League and heavy Japanese contributions to the Red Cross, U.S.O., Defense Bonds, etc. Some white groups made a notable effort to calm public opinion, and during the first two and one-half months of war the Federal Government kept the hysteria somewhat within bounds.

On February nineteenth, a sweeping proclamation by the President gave the War Department the power "to prescribe military areas from which any or all persons may be excluded." On March third, General DeWitt issued the first of a sweeping series of proclamations resulting in curfews, travel bans, and evacuation from an extensive area reaching well inland from the Pacific Coast. In most of these actions, Japanese-American *citizens* were considered more dangerous than German or Italian aliens!

Explanations for the military necessity of the evacuation have assumed that sabotage was committed, that the Japanese as a racial group were a potential fifth column, or that the evacuation was necessary for the protection of the Japanese themselves.

Not until late in March were the widespread rumors of Japanese sabotage at Pearl Harbor disproved by the statement of the Honolulu Chief of Police, confirmed from other sources, that "there were no acts of sabotage committed in the city and county of Honolulu on December 7," nor have any been reported since. This report discounts all previous rumors, and the fact that three months elapsed before it was issued, when the Administration must have had access to the facts, is one of the strongest indictments of the Government. Likewise, no proved case of sabotage by a Japanese on the Pacific Coast, on or since December seventh, has come to public attention. These facts still have not been sufficiently publicized, and unfounded rumors continue to circulate.

Undoubtedly some of the alien Japanese and perhaps a few of the citizens are disloyal; these persons, presumably, are among those taken into custody by the F.B.I. On the other hand, it should be pointed out that most Japanese aliens are not aliens by choice, but have not been permitted to become American citizens. There is absolutely no evidence to support the rumors that the Japanese, *as a racial group,* were either disloyal or an organized fifth column. Certainly many of them live near defense plants, and vital harbors, highways, railways and power lines, but so do millions of Americans, regardless of race, and to deduce disloyalty from this is absurd.

That the Japanese on the West Coast have been in danger because of their race since December seventh, is acknowledged, and from that fact many believe that, however tragic it may be, the evacuation has been necessary for the protection of the Japanese themselves. Some murders, supposedly by Filipinos, naturally created great fear among the Japanese but, since the first of the year, the number of these incidents has dropped off, and steps were taken to protect the Japanese in a way they should be protected—by increasing local police and F.B.I. aid. Evacuation amounts to compulsory protective arrest, which sets a dangerous precedent in dealing with racial minorities and, in the long run, greatly adds to the problem of the protection of this particular minority. Meanwhile, the social, psychological, and human damage caused by the Government's policy is immensely more tragic than were the comparatively few cases of violence.

The economic loss to the Japanese and the Japanese-Americans has been tremendous. The estimated wealth of the group, $500,000,000 has diminished greatly, possibly by as much as 75 or even 90 per cent. The loss of business, agricultural, and professional positions, gained by slow and patient effort, means that the job of normal living in American communities once again has to be started almost from scratch.

Moreover, the effects upon our whole economy will be pronounced. The 23 per cent of the evacuees who are in agriculture produced 40 per cent of California's truck crops, and in Los Angeles County, where 25,600 of the county's 40,000 acres of producing farm land are affected, white replacements can be found to take over only a fraction of the land. In other fields, 5,000 gardeners in Greater Los Angeles and many nursery men and floriculturalists are irreplaceable; fish fanciers will miss the Nippon Goldfish Company, largest in the West; bacteriological research will miss the vital *agre* produced by a skilled young *Nisei;* school boards will have 20,000 fewer elementary pupils to plan for.

Some of the loss to the Japanese is directly attributable to profiteering, where expensive electric refrigerators, radios, etc., went for a song; more of it is due to the major unemployment and financial problem that has struck them as a racial group since December seventh, and to the losses naturally encountered in any migration.

Civil liberties have suffered a heavy blow, too, for, as the American Civil Liberties Union recently pointed out, this action undermines the very basis of constitutional government and means that the Bill of Rights is not applicable in any area declared military by the Government. The equal protection of the Government has been denied these people who should have equal rights for participation in community life, due process of law, and so on.

Psychological and physical suffering is the inevitable accompaniment of life in what is essentially a concentration camp. Some of the evacuees, particularly the idealistic *Niseis,* are resolved to make the most of this hardship, and are going through with it in a spirit of love and a determination to train themselves and others for a better future. But for more of the *Niseis,* the effect of having their property destroyed, their hopes for the future dashed, and chances for normal living ended is one of at least partial disintegration of personality. There is a fear that they will be moved out into the desert and left there for many years, forgotten by white Americans, and the moral problem that has arisen in most of the camps is an indication of the psychological frustrations that exist.

Living conditions are very crowded, with rooms twenty by twenty-five feet intended to accommodate ten people. Eating is communal, and privacy will be a thing almost unknown. A *Nisei* girl, commenting on the unpleasant climate at Manzanar, describes the dust that covers everything, the extreme heat that makes her dread the summer, and the lack of anything creative to do. First-hand reports of visitors to the camps and the *Niseis* who are in them do not bear out the romanticised stories that have appeared in the press, and emphasize the great suffering that results when so many persons are detained on the desert in close quarters.

Racial understanding has been dealt a severe blow, for increased segregation of the Japanese, with corresponding lack of assimilation into the American community, is a feature of the plan. Where whites were coming into contact with the Japanese, they were losing some of their prejudice, and these contacts are now cut off. For the *Nisei* it means being thrown back into a racial consciousness which he considers secondary to American citizenship, while the white American sees all Japanese lumped together as disloyal and tends to regard them as inferior as a group.

Racial intolerance is increased and its solution postponed by the evacuation. In the immediate future the resettlement authorities of the Government will be under great pressure to release some of the Japanese to do work in the fields as labor gangs, or to participate in other anti-social ventures. Some of the Rocky Mountain and Middle Western states already are taking action to prevent any permanent resettlement of the Japanese within their boundaries, and there is every reason to believe that resettlement will become more and more difficult as time goes on. Representative Rankin, of Mississippi, urges that these unfortunates be kept in detention for the duration and then be shipped back to Japan, while other reactionaries are advocating a Constitutional Amendment to take away from the *Niseis* their rights of citizenship.

A few of these evacuees are pacifists; a great many of them are Christian communicants; still more are American citizens; all are human beings needing our love and help and friendship. So, whether we call ourselves pacifists or Christian or American or humanitarian, the evacuation presents a tremendous challenge. So far, most of the attempts to help have been alleviatory in nature. Some have helped in evacuation problems, such as moving, the storage of goods, renting houses, and protection against profiteers. At least two religious groups set up hostels to which early evacuees could go, and there have been other indications of the expression of love toward these people, the importance of which cannot be overstated. Nevertheless, this is not enough, for more than alleviation of immediate suffering is needed, and it is encouraging to note some *Nisei* groups planning for future cooperative settlements, and white students trying to help evacuated students become relocated in other areas.

The sharp distinction between aiding the processes of evacuation and detention and helping those individuals who need love and assistance must be maintained, for the evacuation and continued detention of these people is wrong and as such should be consistently opposed. The Government should not have yielded to the pressure for evacuation, and should now change its policy with a view to arranging immediately for fair *public* hearings for all now in the camps. Where no concrete evidence of guilt exists, citizens should be given unconditional release, and the aliens treated as are other enemy aliens, not as a racial minority. The present policy, looking toward the release of those who can prove their innocence, must be reversed, for the whole tradition of Anglo-Saxon common law is the presumption that a man is innocent until proved guilty, and in the present case the burden of proof rests upon the Government, not upon the evacuee.

These actions should be taken now, for the solution of the problems the evacuation has created will not be made easier by waiting until later. If action is postponed until the post-war period, it will be greatly complicated by the problem of resettling millions of soldiers and war industry workers at the same time. In addition, by admitting its mistake and rectifying it, our Government could contribute an encouraging boost to the forces of racial understanding. In a time when we are seeking to prove to the Negro that this is not just a white man's war, and trying to counteract Axis influence on colored peoples the world over, no action could be more pertinent.

If this measure is not opposed, there is no guarantee what group will be next, for what can happen to a Japanese racial minority can happen also to a Negro or Jewish minority. By our opposition and our attempt to bring the truth to the attention of the public we can contribute to building the peace, as knowledge of the truth and an attitude of racial tolerance among American citizens are prerequisites of any better world. . . .

29. CLYDE EAGLETON

The Beam in Our Own Eye
(1946)

> Clyde Eagleton (1891-1958), an authority on inter-
> national law, was born in Sherman, Texas. For more
> than thirty years he taught at New York University,
> and during World War II he also served as a consult-
> ant in the State Department, working on the United
> Nations Charter and accompanying the United States
> delegation to San Francisco as a technical expert.

You can criticize the Russians all you want to (and we have already got ourselves into a frenetic state doing it), and at various
points I might be able to add some items to the indictment. But
not now. Russia may enter into this article by way of counter-
point; but what I am concerned with at the moment is to try to
show what others see as they watch us Americans at our democratic antics. This glimpse, I am afraid, will show us trying to
have our cake and eat it, too; or, to use another famous figure
of speech, it will show us riding our horse off in all directions
at one and the same time. We want peace and security in the
world, so we say, and we are inclined to blame others because we
do not feel sure that we have it; but what are we, the American
people, contributing to the sense of security and trust among
nations?

To begin with, we said that we wanted an international organization which would provide security; and we can fairly claim credit for having made the United Nations Charter what it is. This is not necessarily a compliment, for we deliberately made it as weak as we could. We rejected the international police force for which the Russians had asked at Dumbarton Oaks, and thereby left Russia with a security system not quite so strong as she had hoped for. We upheld the veto of the Great Powers in the Security Council, and thereby made it impossible for the Security Council to take action against the only states which could be dangerous to us, and the only ones able to make the atomic bomb. We did not do this to appease Russia, though doubtless she wants the veto as much as anyone does; we did it to appease the American Senate and the American people. It was one of the many places in the Charter where we gave with one hand and took away with the other.

We rejected the compulsory jurisdiction of the International Court of Justice, which means that we refused to obligate ourselves even to submit our legal disputes to impartial adjudication. We insisted that the security organization should not be allowed to deal with anything which a sovereign state might say was a "domestic question," and would not even consent to have it decided by any organ of the United Nations, or according to international law, whether or not a question is a domestic one—thereby practically nullifying the whole Charter. We agreed in principle to contribute armed forces for the Security Council to use against an aggressor, but only on condition (Article 43) that each state should reach an agreement some time in the future as to the exact number and kind of forces it should supply. Until the undetermined time when these agreements shall have been made, the Security Council will not be able to take military action against an aggressor, because it will have no forces to employ.

There can be no doubt that at San Francisco we did an excellent job of preserving and protecting our national sovereignty, if that was what we were after; but complete freedom of action is not the usual foundation upon which one builds a system of law and order such as we claimed to be building. The UN is too weak today to assure us of the security which we wish; and for this result the American people cannot pass the buck to Russia or to any other state; they cannot even pass it to the Department of State. The President and the Department of State were doubtless too timorous and might have shown more courageous leadership; but you cannot blame them for being timorous when you recall what the Senate and the American people did to the League of Nations in 1919 and to the World Court in 1935. The President has not dared to submit any treaty of importance to the Senate since the latter date, until the Charter of the United Nations came up; it is no wonder that he was careful to prune it down so that it would not be rejected as the others had been. It is no wonder; but it is a bad situation. This is a democracy, and the Executive cannot bind the American people to fundamental changes of policy without their consent; and the American people did not speak up for a strong UN, and they are not yet speaking up for a strong UN.

What have we been doing since San Francisco to encourage international peace and to support the United Nations? We used to talk about the United Nations as a joint enterprise in which we were all to consult and co-operate with one another, against a common enemy. The United Nations is by the Charter definitely excluded from anything to do with the enemy states; they are to be handled by "the governments having responsibility" therefor. Who are these governments? President Truman suggested some months back that it was time for the United Nations to handle things; and Secretary Byrnes went to the Council of Foreign Ministers in London and argued that the affairs of Europe ought to be handled jointly, and not by just one nation. That was fine, but unfortunately it was inconsistent with our own national policy. We had already made it pretty clear that we were going to run the Pacific area all by ourselves, and when various states demanded that we apply to Japan the same principle which we wished to see applied in Europe, we would not hear of it; and MacArthur is still settling the affairs of Japan all by himself—though graciously consenting occasionally to hear advice offered by the Far Eastern Advisory Council. If the United States is to have exclusive control in Japan, why should not Russia have exclusive control in eastern Europe, or in Manchuria?

Still on the line of joint and sympathetic United Nations cooperation, we were all upset a few months back at the way the British were using their armed forces in Greece and Indonesia, and practically frantic about the way the Russians were using their forces in Iran. At the same moment, we were caught in the same sort of a situation in China—that was when the Communists were howling into one ear, and ex-Ambassador Hurley was howling into our other ear. Britain and Russia and we had troops in these areas by common agreement; trouble was to be expected in each area, and the troops were there to maintain order. (It was sheer luck that it was the British rather than we who were on the hot spot in Indonesia, for the Combined Chiefs of Staff had only a short time before transferred control in that area from the United States to Great Britain.)

When the Soviet Union was brought up before the Security Council, she promptly countered by bringing Britain up on the same charges. Mr. Gromyko could, with as much reason, have hauled the United States before the Security Council because of what we were doing in China; he probably refrained only because the current policy of his government was to be tough with Britain and nice to the United States. If we can accuse Russia of using her forces in Iran to spread her communistic system there, Russia can—and she may do it yet—accuse the United States of using American forces to defeat communism and uphold our capitalistic system in China.

Try another viewpoint. One of the things for which we criticize Russia is the fact that she is trying to build up a sphere of influence—though of course we do not use so mild a term—in the Near East. At the same time, and for years back, the United States has been building up a sphere of influence reaching from the North Pole to the South Pole, and we are now talking of extending it from Dakar to Okinawa. Mr. Molotov at San Francisco, after watching how the United States worked with the other American republics to get Argentina admitted, intimated that Russia could anticipate a solid bloc of some twenty American nations, led by the United States, to vote against his country in future United Nations decisions. With half the world in our sphere of influence, the efforts of the Russians in their part of the world look positively puny!

Now, let's take a look at trusteeship. Trusteeship is surely anti-imperialistic; and if the American people are anything, they are anti-imperialistic. The Atlantic Charter began with the words "we seek no aggrandizement, territorial or otherwise"; and good Americans have been busy condemning British and Dutch and French imperialism, and demanding that the colonial possessions of these countries be put under trusteeship. They have not suggested, however—not loud enough to be heard—that any American possession be put under trusteeship. On the contrary, we are trying to grab more territory in the Pacific and not put even it under trusteeship. This issue is not officially decided; but the American people and members of Congress are saying "Our boys fought and died for those islands, didn't they? Well, then, they are ours!" That is imperialism as baldly as it has ever been put—might makes right!

It is bad enough to disregard the principles which we accepted in the Charter of the United Nations, but the proposal to take illegally the mandated islands of the League of Nations in the Pacific is really shocking. Of course, if we want to take those islands, no one is going to stop us—we are too big; and this, you may recall, is exactly what we complain about Russia's doing in eastern Europe.

Whether we are turning imperialistic or not—as some of our foreign friends are beginning to wonder—we are giving the Soviet propagandists an excellent opportunity to charge us with it. Inevitably, therefore, they present the Soviet Union as the champion of downtrodden peoples everywhere against the imperialistic, capitalistic nations. This should give even the most nationalistic of our patriots something to consider seriously.

There is another angle to all this. If we are going to claim Pacific islands on the ground that we conquered them and that we need them for national security, we could as well claim lands which we conquered elsewhere or which we need as bases, and which might be even more useful to us. How far—other states may be asking—does the United States intend to go with this strategic base idea? We are bargaining to get Iceland into UN, provided she will let us have bases there—another vote for us; Australia and New Zealand are worrying about bases in that part of the world; and what is going to happen with regard to the string of air bases across Africa? What are all these bases for? Of course, we Americans know that these bases are not for aggressive purposes, but how is Russia to know? I know that the dog is not going to bite me, but does the dog know it?

And what about the atomic bomb? The United Nations was not strong enough to provide security before the bomb came along; much less can it take care of this added and difficult problem. This was recognized in the ABC declaration, issued by President

Truman and Prime Ministers Attlee and King, in which they offered to turn over the bomb secrets to the UN provided adequate safeguards could be established. Presumably, such safeguards would mean a considerable strengthening of the United Nations security system; but there was no evidence to show that the United States, which had made the UN weak, was now ready to make it any stronger. While everyone was puzzling over this, and wondering if the United States could be stalling, the Secretary of State's Committee on Atomic Energy released a report which disregards the UN entirely as regards security.

The owner of so terrible a secret is bound to be looked upon with suspicion by his neighbors; so what might our neighbors think of this report? They would probably say that it contains novel and constructive and perhaps well-intended proposals; they would perhaps be a little skeptical as to the possibility of ownership and operation of atomic energy facilities by the UN; but surely they would ask: where is the security we are all looking for? All the report says is "strategic balance of power among nations," and "danger signals." It seems to mean that UN will locate its atomic materials and plants inside the borders of several nations, so that if one nation illegally seizes what is within its territory, other nations can illegally seize what is within their territories and, if they feel like it, can hit back at the aggressor with what they have seized. This does not sound like collective security through the United Nations; it sounds like the old game of national action and power politics. Doesn't the United States trust the UN, or intend to use it? It may well seem doubtful to those who note the care with which our proposal for the international control of atomic energy reserves to us the right to continue manufacture of the bomb—until we voluntarily decide to stop.

As this is being written, the Security Council has overridden the Russian request, and also a memorandum from the Secretary General of the United Nations, and has decided to leave the Iranian matter on the agenda. I helped in the making of Chapter VI, and I think the general position taken by the Secretary General was correct. Whether it was or not, the argument was disregarded by the Security Council on the general ground that the important work of the Security Council ought not to be impeded by slavish devotion to procedure. We taught those Russians a lesson this time! And what was the lesson? That the claim of the accused to constitutional procedures under the Charter will not even be considered; that the Charter is of no importance, and that the impartial and expert opinion of the Secretariat is to be spurned, whenever a big enough gang in the Security Council wants to put something across. These are precedents which may be used against us some day. Yes, we showed those Russians where they belong —and that place, they might conclude, is outside the United Nations. It may be even more important to show a Great Power, than to prove to a small state, that it will receive fair treatment under the Charter.

Which way are we going? If we are not going to strengthen the UN and increasingly rely upon it for security, why should we expect Russia to do so? If we are going to depend upon our own national efforts for security, and set up United States instead of United Nations bases, why should not Russia build up her national strength and claim Spitsbergen or Tripolitania, or such places? If we consider that our national safety requires the Panama Canal to be under our own instead of international administration, how can we expect Russia to want international control of the Dardanelles? We have committed ourselves to collective security through the United Nations by signature, but everything that we do indicates that we rely upon our national, and perhaps on our regional, strength rather than upon the UN. We seem to be trying to impress our strength upon the world: our Navy is sailing around displaying itself in various places; we are planning a tremendous demonstration with the atomic bomb, which no other nation could afford; our soldiers in various places manifest, sometimes in appalling fashion, the unrestrained might of the United States. Yet, at the same time, the unwillingness of the American people to go in for conscription—or even to extend the draft—makes it very doubtful whether we could actually, with any degree of safety, rely upon our own national strength to protect us.

You say that the statements made above are exaggerated and unfair? Naturally, you would. I think so, myself; I wrote them so. Nevertheless, they are no more exaggerated than the charges which we are making against other states, and very probably they underestimate what others are saying about us. But there is a much more constructive reason for saying these things than the mere pleasure of exposing our vagaries and inconsistencies. It is time to stand up firmly against the Soviet Union; we are, in fact, beginning to do so. But we cannot do it effectively unless we have a firm foundation of consistent policy upon which to stand; unless the policy offers reasonable security and a fair amount of justice to Russia; and unless our course of conduct is one which would give Russia some reason to trust us or the UN.

There is no use asking what Russia will do—that depends upon what we are going to do. The first question before us is not Russia, but ourselves. If we will take a responsible lead, a lead which clearly shows that we intend to give to the United Nations the support which it must have if it is to succeed, we can get most of the world to follow us; and if we show that the United Nations will not be used against Russia unfairly, there is little doubt whether Russia will continue to support it. It would be very difficult for her to stay out, with most of the world behind us. We have a definite advantage over her, for she needs security above all, and she does not have so many friends on her side; and she is quite well aware of these facts. She could not afford to stay out; if she did stay out, she would have the world organized against her. She would, that is, if the United States makes the United Nations into a real security system. If we don't do that, if each nation must depend upon itself for security, some of them will line up with Russia.

The problem is not Russia; the problem is us. Whatever Russia wants or does not want, nothing can be done until the American people make up their minds to a definite and consistent policy which they are willing to support and for which they are willing to pay the price. It is the United States which now blocks advance toward real security. That is our problem; the problem of Russia comes later. We are now in a vicious circle, and there is no use arguing whose fault it is or who began it; someone must cut through it. The responsibility for taking the first steps in this direction is ours; we are the strongest and most influential state in the world at the moment; the UN cannot be made stronger unless we do it; and we have the bomb.

30. RUSSELL KIRK

Conscription Ad Infinitum
(1946)

Russell Kirk (1918-   ), author of several works
outlining the history and philosophy of conservatism,
was born in Michigan, where he taught at the State
University in East Lansing. A senior fellow of the
American Council of Learned Societies, 1950-1952,
and a Guggenheim Fellow, 1954-1955, Kirk has been
more recently Research Professor of Political Science
at Post College, Long Island.

"Some one, I see, is lifting up his sweet voice in praise of Conscription," wrote George Gissing nearly half a century ago. A
threat of peacetime military training in England alarmed Gissing;
the lapse of more than four decades has been required to enable
the American advocates of a permanent draft to become so numerous and influential that the national administration is urging
enactment of a sweeping policy of conscripting boys in their
teens. "If now there were . . . a conscription of the whole youth-
ful population to form for a certain number of years a part of
the army enlisted against *Nature* . . . the military ideals of hardi-
hood and discipline would be wrought into the growing fiber of
the people. . . . We should be *owned,* as soldiers are by the army,
and our pride would rise accordingly." These phrases, which have
the ring of Adolf Hitler's, were written by William James in
1910; they are echoed in this troubled year by enthusiasts for

discipline who are recommending conscription, not only as a military measure, but as a social objective. The anxiety of the proponents of this system to obtain its adoption before postwar excitement subsides is obvious. We need to reflect deeply before we decide upon a policy which so deeply concerns the general happiness; we reflected very little three decades ago before adopting national prohibition.

There are two parallel, but separable, arguments in favor of peacetime conscription: that it is a military necessity and that it is a tool for forging a Brave New World—James's "moral equivalent of war." For nearly four years the writer was a conscript soldier, and military life has aroused in him an interest in the draft more than abstract.

The military excuse for the measure is being debated by persons better fitted than this writer to talk of it, but it is amusing to observe the embarrassed vehemence with which the Chief Executive and a parade of officers endeavor to convince us by a species of *ex post facto* reasoning that there is some intimate connection between the atomic bomb and the conscription project. The argument of military necessity is probably not convincing to the average soldier, who knows what his basic training amounted to. When General Eisenhower's declaration that every enlisted man with whom he had conversed was eager for permanent military training was read in this soldier's barracks, the laughter appeared to be derisive: a private does not bandy words with a general of the armies, but among his own kind. True, the question of military necessity must be decided upon its own merits, but if a hard fate should compel us to adopt the proposal, we should face the fact that conscription is advantageous only as a means of raising troops; otherwise, it is a cruel detriment. It is time we quashed the folderol that military training will "solve our juvenile-delinquency problem" and that a year of life in cantonments will build heroic muscles and minds. Any common soldier knows better. Not long ago the writer rode with a naval commander, a surgeon, who wanted a permanent draft so that his impetuous sixteen-year-old son would be taught to obey. One could not, without grave discourtesy, reply that if parental authority failed of beneficial effect, impersonal military authority could not be expected to accomplish more. It is a curious notion, that teaching a boy to make a bed and fire a Garand under compulsion will make him sober, self-reliant, and stable. If we are to believe the ubiquitous Dr. Gallup, this fancy is popular. Probably the first thought that comes to the mind of a citizen quizzed on the topic is that the draft would improve someone else's offspring. This topic will bear a little reflection.

> To coal and iron mines, to freight trains, to fishing fleets in December, to dish-washing, clothes-making, and window-washing, to road-building and tunnel-making, to foundries and stoke-holes, and to the frames of skyscrapers, would our gilded youths be drafted off, according to their choice, to get the childishness knocked out of them, and to come back into society with healthier sympathies and soberer ideas. They would have paid their blood-tax, done their own part in the immemorial human warfare against nature; they would tread the earth more proudly, the women would value them more highly, they would be better fathers and teachers of the following generation.

Thus wrote William James; and thus today some people are declaring that we need conscription to make young men the pure and lovely creatures their ancestors are alleged to have been—to teach them, among other things, to brush their teeth, scrub their faces, and cook their suppers. Abstract humanitarianism has come to regard servitude—so long as it be to the state—as a privilege. Greater self-love has no government than this: that all men must wear khaki so that some men may be taught to brush their teeth. Apologists for Negro slavery claimed for their peculiar institution the virtue which humanitarians now ascribe to the draft: that it instilled a healthful discipline. A humanitarianism which believes that boys can be filled with sweetness and light, strength and joy, through living communally under military force in training camps or work camps is very abstract indeed. Few will deny that the humanitarianism of Fascism was nothing if not abstract; such were the premises upon which Fascist youth organizations were established. Most interesting is the ignorance of the motives and desires of the common man displayed by academic psychologists, and William James was no exception. When a man can maintain that the basis of morality lies in the satisfaction of desire and remark, according to Hutchins Hapgood, "So long as one poor cockroach feels the pangs of unrequited love, this world is not a moral world," it is not surprising that he can think the nation requires conscription to satisfy its soul. Only under a thoroughly muddled system of ethics could the drafting of young people be called a moral measure.

The claims of enthusiasts for conscription are numerous. They may be consolidated under three heads: conscription builds character, it improves health, it educates youth to play its part in the world. The writer, who has been on the inside of conscription looking out, has not found himself ennobled, strengthened, or educated thereby. He is not aware that being ordered about has made him tread the earth more proudly or even, alas, more highly valued by women. The tendency of every movement to swing full cycle has brought some of us to the absurdity of believing that strength of will, private morality, courage, fidelity, and resolution can be nurtured by a military discipline so crushing to self-reliance that it prescribes the moment a man may shave his jowls, and by a communal existence that places in a lower bunk a boy from a Mississippi farm and in the upper bunk one from the San Pedro wharfs. The Progressivists in education have made so thorough a failure of their method of forming character through a neglect, allegedly salutary, that a half-conscious reaction has set in, as much a fallacy as the Progressivist notion. Kipling hit upon a profound truth: single men in barracks don't grow into plaster saints. Military discipline effects no more than the repression of disorder in camp; it does not attempt to shape men anew.

In military life, distant from home and most of the forces of social opinion, there is every inducement for an average young man to sink into indolence and indulgence and every reason for him to rely increasingly upon the state for very existence. Had James made the rounds with the military police on a Saturday night, he might have been a trifle startled. Independence and initiative often are stifled by rigid discipline; the army is no school for inner strength. Sudden precipitation into the rough comradeship of barracks often leaves its mark upon a boy; and it is to be hoped the time has not come when we are such fierce Spartans as to sneer at sensitivity of character. The necessities of war have forced us to introduce young men to such a life; but only great emergency can excuse it. It is common enough to see and hear a half-dozen foul-mouthed young sailors or soldiers, fancying themselves drunken on a few bottles of 3.2; this picture is natural enough, there being little in their life to make them otherwise and military existence being essentially rough; but the education they receive is no more admirable than is their public conduct.

As for health, military life offers no peculiar facilities for muscle-building, tooth-brushing, or bath-taking. Much of the strenuous training which soldiers undergo to harden them for combat would be unwise if utilized for any other purpose; the long-run physical effect is often quite the contrary of the ideal of sound and long life. "Damn you, be healthy!" might well be the slogan of those who think army life makes a man a Greek god. One is tempted to ask if he owns his own body. A society which looks upon the citizen as a unit of human energy, a cog in the wheel of the state, may well applaud this program, which sacrifices a great deal of liberty for a very small increase in health; but that is not yet our society.

What of the educational benefits of military existence? We are told that the boy and the state are to profit. Young men are to be made carpenters and cooks; they are also to learn how to create the good society. Sufficient manual labor is performed in the army; but contrary to the supposition of James, it does not appear to "knock the childishness" out of "gilded youth," or to send them "back into society with healthier sympathies and soberer ideas." The man with the hoe is not apt to become a philosopher. More often the men who toil most strenuously during the week drink the most whiskey on Saturday night. James's freight trains and fishing fleets have not played a conspicuous part in making better fathers and teachers. This is like the hoary nonsense about the virtues of working one's way through college; but military life does not inculcate even the frugality necessitated by self-support in school: the army guarantees a man three meals, clothing, shelter, and pay even though he be a sluggard. Let him who will call this training for social responsibility. There is no ennoblement in any sort of labor per se; the formation of mind and character are apart from the sort of work done. A soldier who has spent a year digging trenches is a better father only in the sense that he has learned to prize, by contrast, the pleasures of his own fireside— supposing him not to have acquired tastes anything but domestic. Nor is military discipline a means of teaching men to live with men. One wishing to learn how men behave unto each other should go not into the army, under the artificial restraints of military law, but into Ford's [River] Rouge Plant, with its polyglot multitude. The only way really to learn how to live with men is by living with them in the common ways of society. In the army a man is at once sheltered and bullied.

Just why boys should join the armed forces to learn carpentry or any other skill is a mystery to this soldier. Probably enough boys already are learning carpentry—chiefly from carpenters. Proposals that a part of the training of conscripts be in industrial plants appear to be based on the notion that there is a shortage of factory workers. But during the war, shortage of labor never seriously retarded military production and would not have been a factor at all worth considering had not many young workers been drafted into the army. Would not young men be conscripted out of the factories again in case of war? What point in industrial training? It is difficult to discern any advantage of the camp over the classroom and workshop. Our schools are poor enough all too often, but they are not yet so low as to do homage to the military method of instruction. The army classroom is distinguished for its deadly dullness, its narrowness of scope, and the ineptitude of its average unhappy, involuntary soldier-instructor. The army is no school for life and no substitute for school. The army is not calculated to make youth virtuous, healthy, or sagacious. It is a sorry makeshift to replace the influences of home and school. It can teach well only one thing—how to fight; and there are said to be higher accomplishments than that.

In addition to the alleged military and social values of a peace-time draft, there is one more reason for its proposal—one from which the draft's champions generally shrink, but which, very probably, is at the back of the mind of many who would like to see youth in uniform. The specter of unemployment is haunting every politician, economist, industrialist, and labor leader. Mr. Dewey said that he saw the solution in heroic production of gadgets, but as to the immediate means, was silent. Mr. Roosevelt announced that everything was planned and that no one need worry, but his details were nebulous. Mr. Truman thinks that there is magic in the phrase "full employment," but one suspects that his disappointment at Congressional refusal to put his whole program to the test is not unmixed with relief. That the problem is not hopeless should be obvious: when there are millions of appetites to be satisfied and hundreds of thousands of houses to be built, no one need be idle were it not that the wheels of the social machine have jammed and the frantic operators have embraced the economics of despair. Subsidies and counter-subsidies, planned shortages, limitations on production, diversion of labor to profitless channels are a few aspects of the fallacy of beneficial want. One of the most obvious palliatives for unemployment is to push a large number of young men into an expanded CCC or an expanded army on a subsistence basis and so make room for others in regular employment—one of the obvious palliatives and one of the worst.

It is one of the worst because it is a fleeting and insufficient remedy; it is one of the worst because it is a negation of the principles of liberty and hope which the nation has been trumpeting. If modern society can provide no better way of existence than crowding young people together like so many ants and keeping them in a state of servitude in return for sustenance, there is little reason for modern society to continue to exist. We are already painfully bound by the intricate system of law and life that must govern any close-knit economy, and need not add to our social miseries by concentrating boys behind M. P. gates.

The War Department is conscientiously urging a peacetime training because it would be of some military utility. A man who has been taught to fire a Springfield is a slightly more valuable recruit than one who has never before squeezed a trigger. Whether this military advantage be outweighed by disadvantages of another nature, it is not the business of the War Department to judge; that is the concern of the people and of Congress; it is incumbent upon the War Department to recommend measures that may increase military power. The Secretary of War and the Chief of

Staff are not social architects. They are not employed to calculate costs other than military. But there are games not worth the candle. Jew-baiting was contributory in some degree to German military prowess, for it hardened the mind and conscience of the average man, and, as Napoleon is said to have put it, "The worse the man, the better the soldier." We do not believe the moral cost of intolerance to be worth the military gain. The question of conscription may be parallel. Would the wasting of men in the unproductive field of military training and the disruption of the life of millions of young men be too high a price for a possible increase in armed strength? A builder may tell you truthfully that a house of stone is the most durable sort of house; it is not his business to judge whether you can afford a house of stone. Just so far is the War Department a judge of the desirability of conscription. In matters of social welfare, there can be no satisfactory authority but society *en masse*.

Not long ago no policy of the Nazis was more decried than their regimentation of young men and women. And yet, now that the Nazi is dead, there are those among us who would make of him an image, and, in defiance of the Decalogue, worship him. For the mass of men there is no tyranny more onerous than that of military life.

31. ROBERT A. TAFT

Equal Justice Under Law
(1946)

> Robert A. Taft (1889-1953), son of the President, after being graduated from Yale University and Harvard Law School, became a member of the family law firm in Cincinnati. In 1921 he began his political career in the Ohio House of Representatives. From 1939 until his death he was a United States Senator and a leader of the Republican Party. Although generally conservative, Taft was often liberal in matters where he felt important principles of individual freedom were at stake.

I wish to speak of the heritage of the English-speaking peoples in the field of government, and their responsibility to carry on that heritage, and to apply its tried principles to the entire world as rapidly as that can be done. The very basis of the government of the United States, derived through the Colonies from principles of British government, was the liberty of the individual and the assurance to him of equal treatment and equal justice. We cannot claim that these principles were original with the English-speaking peoples, because, of course, they existed in Greece and in the Roman Republic and in other nations before England became a nation. But to a large extent they disappeared during the Middle Ages and their revival was most marked in Great Britain, and even more in the establishment of the American Republic.

I desire today to speak particularly of equal justice, because it is an essential of individual liberty. Unless there is law, and unless there is an impartial tribunal to administer that law, no man can be really free. Without them only force can determine controversy, as in the international field today, and those who have not sufficient force cannot remain free. Without law and an appeal to a just and independent court to interpret that law, every man must be subject to the arbitrary discretion of his ruler or of some subordinate government official.

Over the portal of the great Supreme Court building in Washington are written the words "Equal Justice Under Law." The Declaration of Independence, the Constitution of the United States and every pronouncement of the founders of the government stated the same principle in one form or another. Thomas Jefferson in his first inaugural emphasized above everything the necessity for "equal and exact justice to all men of whatever state or persuasion, religious or political. . . ."

Unfortunately, the philosophy of equal justice under law, and acceptance of decisions made in accordance with respected institutions, has steadily lost strength during recent years. It is utterly denied in totalitarian states. There the law and the courts are instruments of state policy. It is inconceivable to the people of such a state that a court would concern itself to be fair to those individuals who appear before it when the state has an adverse interest. Nor do they feel any need of being fair between one man and another. Therefore they see no reason for presenting logical argument to justify a position. Nothing is more typical of the Communist or the Fascist than to assert and re-assert an argument which has been completely answered and disproved, in order to create public opinion by propaganda to the ignorant.

The totalitarian idea has spread throughout many nations where, in the nineteenth century, the ideals of liberty and justice were accepted. Even in this country, the theory that the state is finally responsible for every condition, and that every problem must be cured by giving the government arbitrary power to act, has been increasingly the philosophy of the twentieth century. It infects men who still profess complete adherence to individual liberty and individual justice, so that we find them willing to sacrifice both to accomplish some economic or social purpose. There is none of the burning devotion to liberty which characterized Patrick Henry and even the conservative leaders of the American Revolution.

We see the ignoring of justice internationally when a powerful nation takes the position that its demands must be complied with, "or else," and refuses to argue or discuss the question. We see it within this country in some labor groups and in some business groups who present ultimatums backed by economic force, and refuse to submit even to partial arbitration. It is present in the world so long as any nation refuses to submit its disputes to argument or adjudication.

Of course the new philosophy has been promoted by two world wars, for war is a denial both of liberty and of justice. *Inter arma leges silent.* We all of us recognize that justice to the individual, vital as it is, must be subordinate to the tremendous necessity of preserving the nation itself. Abraham Lincoln said, "Let reverence for the laws be breathed by every American mother to the lisping babe that prattles on her lap, let it be taught in the schools, in the seminaries and in colleges." But Lincoln suspended the writ of habeas corpus in Maryland in the early days of the Civil War, in violation of the Constitution. In this war we have granted arbitrary war powers without appeal to the courts, and now the people have become so accustomed to such powers that the government proposes to continue war powers unimpaired to meet some supposed peace emergency. We hear constantly the fallacious argument, "If you would surrender these rights to win the war, is it not just as necessary to surrender them to win the peace?" Unless we desire to weaken for all times the ideals of justice and equality, it is absolutely essential that our program of reconversion and of progress abandon the philosophy of war, that it be worked out within the principles of justice.

Take as an example of war legislation the Price Control Act. I considered price control essential for the conduct of the war and supported the Act. I am convinced, however, that general price control is impossible without the granting of arbitrary powers over every citizen's life to an executive board. Congress itself cannot fix the prices. No individual can be allowed to go to court and enjoin an unjust act, because to permit this would break down the entire system and so the law must give wide discretion to the Price Administrator without any effective appeal to the courts.

Also the spirit in which it has been administered has been arbitrary without any interest in assuring substantial justice. The administrator adopted the so-called "freeze" theory which, in effect, required that prices be unchanged regardless of increased costs, regardless of the destruction of many small businesses, and regardless of whether people in similar situations are given equal treatment. So, also, landlords have been forced to rent their property without regard to the fairness of their rents or the fact that others receive more for the same facilities. Wages have been held on an arbitrary formula and an injustice done to those groups who did not have the political power to force increases.

While I do not agree with the theory even in time of war, I could only regard these individuals as casualties of the war. But we cannot continue this course in time of peace unless we are prepared to repudiate our heritage and take a long step towards the destruction of liberty. The truth is that general price and wage

control, attempting to regulate from Washington a billion trans-
actions a day, is impossible without granting arbitrary power and
denying equal justice. I feel very strongly that its very existence
in time of peace would be an end to economic liberty, which I
believe to be essential political liberty. There is no compromise if
we are to return to a system of equal justice under law, except
to abolish general price and wage control.

There are other war powers still remaining which also are impossible to administer if they are subject to court appeal and
principles of justice, notably the priority powers under the Second
War Powers Act.

Even before the war we had drifted far from justice at home.
Expediency has been the key to the legislation of recent years and
many of the existing bureaus administer the law without any belief
in the principle that the government should be fair to every individual according to a written law. For instance, the National
Labor Relations Act was based on the sound principle that collective bargaining should not be interfered with by employers. But
wide discretion was given to the Board, and the first Board members, instead of trying to administer the Act fairly, regarded
themselves as crusaders to put a CIO union into every plant in the
United States without consideration of any element of impartiality.
I sat for weeks hearing the bitter complaints against the administration of that law, and the most violent complaints came from the
heads of the American Federation of Labor. The courts held that
the law did not permit them to interfere with the discretion of the
Board. I do not think that any more serious miscarriages of justice
have ever occurred in the United States than under that first
National Labor Relations Board. President Roosevelt was finally
forced to replace all the members of that Board, but only amendments to the Act can reverse some of the arbitrary practices and
decisions established by the first Board. Questions, for instance,

regarding the calling of elections, and freedom of speech, and the reinstatement of workers, are decided with little consideration of principles of justice.

The whole government policy has been so pro-labor in industrial disputes that few have any confidence in the impartiality of Federal action. It is essential not only that we have laws, but that we have a belief in the impartiality of our government boards and officials who administer the law. Industrialists are criticized because they do not always submit their disputes to arbitration by the President or his appointees. Obviously, they feel from experience that those appointees will be prejudiced against their position, and that the decision will be based not on principles of law but on government policy. The criticism is just, but it is our duty to see that our system of courts and arbitration boards assure impartiality. The fact-finding board in the General Motors case clearly stated that its decision was based on a wage-price policy without authority of law, declared by President Truman in a press release. If we establish fact-finding boards for labor disputes, they must at least be judicial in nature and we must declare by law the principles on which they must act.

Now we have the same kind of a plan in the Chavez Bill to set up a Fair Employment Practice Commission authorized to deal with every application for employment. Certainly no end can be more desirable than to remove the discrimination which exists, particularly in the employment of Negroes. But even for the best possible end, we cannot afford to proceed with the unfair labor practice technique, because it gives arbitrary power to a board necessarily prejudiced, because concerned with policy alone, and with no practical appeal to the courts. Other methods can be developed.

The practice of creating administrative boards has destroyed justice in many other fields. When government undertook to regulate the production of every farmer, telling him what he could sow and what he could reap, it had to set up an administrative machinery far beyond the capacity of any court to control. The enforcement of milk prices, production, and distribution by Federal milk boards has also been pursued without regard to any legal principle. Programs for general economic regulation are always inconsistent with justice because the detailed control of millions of individuals can only be carried through by giving arbitrary discretion to administrative boards. Such boards are always concerned with policy, but not with justice.

The law authorizing reciprocal trade treaties has a most desirable purpose of promoting foreign trade, but because no legal standards for granting tariff reductions are prescribed, the procedure again has departed from principles of justice. Hearings are held before boards which have nothing to do with making the final decisions, decisions which may destroy an American industry, without that industry even being advised what action is proposed to be taken. In this field, as in many others, we have delegated to the President powers to be exercised in his individual discretion, without the slightest requirement of any conformity to law or principle. Such power is not necessary to a sound program of promoting foreign trade.

These are only examples. But even more discouraging is the attitude of the people and the press. Government action which twenty-five years ago would have excited a sense of outrage in thousands, is reported in a few lines and if disapproved at all, is disapproved with a shrug of the shoulders and a hopeless feeling that nothing can be done about it.

To a large extent this feeling has been promoted by the attack on the Supreme Court, and the effort to make the courts instruments of executive policy. The old court may have been too conservative, but the judges believed they were interpreting the laws and Constitution as they were written, and most of the country believed that they were honestly impartial. Today the court regards itself as the maker of policy—no maker of policy can command respect for impartial dispensation of justice.

I believe more strongly than I can say that if we would maintain progress and liberty in America, it is our responsibility to see not only that laws be rewritten to substitute law for arbitrary discretion but that the whole attitude of the people be educated to a deep devotion to law, impartiality, and equal justice.

It is even more important to the entire world that these principles be established as the guide for international action. In my opinion they afford the only hope of future peace. Not only must there be a more definite law to govern the relations between nations, not only must there be tribunals to decide controversies under that law, but the peoples of the world must be so imbued with respect for law and the tribunals established that they will accept their decisions without an appeal to force.

Whether we have a league of sovereign nations, like the United Nations, or a World State, there cannot be an end of war if any important people refuse to accept freely the principle of abiding by law, or if truly impartial tribunals are not established.

Unfortunately, I believe we Americans have also in recent foreign policy been affected by principles of expediency and supposed necessity, and abandoned largely the principle of justice. We have drifted into the acceptance of the idea that the world is to be ruled by the power and policy of the great nations and a police force established by them rather than by international law.

I felt very strongly that we should join the United Nations Organization, but it was not because I approved of the principles established in the Charter. Those who drafted the original Dumbarton Oaks proposals apparently had little knowledge of the heritage of the English-speaking peoples, for in those proposals there was no reference to justice and very little to liberty. At San Francisco a good many declarations were inserted emphasizing the importance of law and justice, but they were not permitted to interfere with the original set-up of the Security Council. The Security Council is the very heart of the United Nations, the only body with power to act. The Charter gives it the power to adopt any measure, economic or military, which it considers necessary to maintain or restore international peace and security. The heritage of the English-speaking peoples has always emphasized liberty over peace and justice over security. I believe that liberty and justice are the only channel to permanent peace and security.

In spite of the fact that justice is mentioned in the Preamble to the Charter and as one of the guides for the Assembly, there is nothing in the Charter to make it a guide or even a consideration for the Security Council. In perfect accord with the Charter, the Security Council could decree the destruction of a nation simply because its location or its misfortunes make it a center of international contest, without regard to any justice or liberty for the nation concerned.

I offered an amendment on the floor of the Senate, directing our delegate not to vote for action against any nation unless he was satisfied that the result would be in accord with international law and justice as well as peace and security. The fact that this was rejected by the Administration shows the extent to which it has accepted the philosophy of force as the controlling factor in international action. When we consider also the veto power, we can see that the Charter tends to create an arbitrary rule of the world by the joint action of the great powers, which can only be overcome by the use of our veto power to insist always on law and justice. I do not favor the veto power in a properly constituted international organization, but it must remain until the underlying theory of the Charter is changed. But the question arises whether our delegate, and public opinion in this country, will insist on justice to all nations.

Only by pressure against a reluctant Administration did Congress agree to adhere to the decision of an impartial tribunal in the International Court of Justice. Such a willingness on the part of all nations, accepted by the public opinion of the world, is the basic essential of future peace. But the court and international law have been step-children to our government. Force, and a police force, similar to the police force within a nation, have been the keynotes, forgetting that national and local police are only incidental to the enforcement of an underlying law, that force without law is tyranny. This whole policy has been no accident. For years we have been accepting at home the theory that the people are too dumb to understand and that a benevolent Executive must be given power to describe policy and administer policy according to his own prejudices in each individual case. Such a policy in the world, as at home, can lead only to tyranny or to anarchy.

The Atlantic Charter professed a belief in liberty and justice for all nations, but at Teheran, at Yalta, at Moscow, we forgot law and justice. Nothing could be further from a rule of law than the making of secret agreements distributing the territory of the earth in accordance with power and expediency. We cannot excuse ourselves by declining territorial acquisition ourselves, or subjecting ourselves to unreasonable and illogical restriction on our sovereignty over uninhabited Pacific islands. We are just as much to blame if we acquiesce in unjustified acquisition of territory by others, such as the handing over of the Kurile Islands to Russia without trusteeship of any kind. Without a word of protest, we have agreed to the acquisition of Lithuania, Estonia and Latvia by the USSR. There is little justice to the people of Poland in the boundaries assigned to them. The extending of justice throughout the world may be and is beyond our powers, but certainly we need not join in the principles by which force and national policy is permitted to dominate the world.

During the war, and since, I have felt that there has been little justice in our treatment of the neutral countries. We took the position in effect that no nation had the right to remain neutral, and bullied these countries to an extreme restrained only by consideration of policy, but not of justice.

The treatment of enemy countries has seldom been just after any war, but only now are we beginning to get some justice into our treatment of Germany. Our treatment has been harsh in the American Zone as a deliberate matter of government policy, and has offended Americans who saw it, and felt that it was completely at variance with American instincts. We gave countenance to the revengeful and impracticable Morgenthau plan which would have reduced the Germans to economic poverty. We have fooled ourselves in the belief that we could teach another nation democratic principles by force. Why, we can't even teach our own people sound principles of government. We cannot teach liberty and justice in Germany by suppressing liberty and justice.

I believe that most Americans view with discomfort the war trials which have just been concluded in Germany and are proceeding in Japan. They violate that fundamental principle of American law that a man cannot be tried under an *ex post facto* statute.

The trial of the vanquished by the victors cannot be impartial no matter how it is hedged about with the forms of justice. I question whether the hanging of those, who, however despicable, were the leaders of the German People, will ever discourage the making of aggressive war, for no one makes aggressive war unless he expects to win. About this whole judgment there is the spirit of vengeance, and vengeance is seldom justice. The hanging of the eleven men convicted will be a blot on the American record which we shall long regret.

In these trials we have accepted the Russian idea of the purpose of trials—government policy and not justice—with little relation to Anglo-Saxon heritage. By clothing policy in the forms of legal procedure, we may discredit the whole idea of justice in Europe for years to come. In the last analysis, even at the end of a frightful war, we should view the future with more hope if even our enemies believed that we had treated them justly in our English-speaking concept of law, in the provision of relief and in the final disposal of territory. I pray that we do not repeat this procedure in Japan, where the justification on grounds of vengeance is much less than in Germany.

Our whole attitude in the world, for a year after V-E Day, including the use of the atomic bomb at Hiroshima and Nagasaki, seems to me a departure from the principle of fair and equal treatment which has made America respected throughout the world before this second World War. Today we are cordially hated in many countries. I am delighted that Secretary Byrnes and Senator Vandenburg have reversed our policy in many of the respects I have referred to. But abroad as at home we have a long way to go to restore again to the American people our full heritage of an ingrained belief in fairness, impartiality, and justice.

Peace in the world can only come if a law is agreed to relating to international relations, if there is a tribunal which can interpret that law and decide disputes between nations, and if the nations are willing to submit their disputes to impartial decision regardless of the outcome. There can be no peace until the public opinion of the world accepts as a matter of course, the decisions of an international tribunal.

War has always set back temporarily the ideals of the world. This time, because of the tremendous scope of the war, the increased barbarism of its methods and the general prevalence of the doctrine of force and expediency even before the war, the effect today is even worse and the duration of the postwar period of disillusionment may be longer.

As I see it, the English-speaking peoples have one great responsibility. That is to restore to the minds of men a devotion to equal justice under law.

32. HENRY MILLER

Remember to Remember
(1947)

Henry Miller (1891-   ) was born in Brooklyn. He
entered New York's City College, but quit almost
immediately and went to work. After the First World
War he joined the growing group of American ex-
patriates in Paris. There his first novel, *Tropic of
Cancer*, was published. The book, which was immediately banned in all English-speaking countries, made
him famous. When the Second World War broke out,
Miller returned to the United States to live at Big
Sur, California, where he continued his highly individualistic writing.

When I said a moment ago that America is a sad place, I meant
just that. It is sad to think that a country which has the greatest
advantages has so little to show for it. It is sad to think that
scarcely anyone believes in what he is doing, that almost no one,
barring the professional optimists, sees any hope in the future.
It is even more sad to observe that no real effort is made to do
anything about anything. Yes, I know that the workers are constantly organizing, constantly striking or threatening to strike, in
order to get better wages, better living conditions. But I also
know that, at this rate, they will never get sufficient wages to
meet the rising cost of living. The great bugaboo here in America
is "the dictatorship of the proletariat." Looking at the rank and

file, the so-called "masses," does anyone honestly believe that
these men and women will dictate the future of America? Can
slaves become rulers overnight? These poor devils are begging to
be led, and they are being led, but it's up a blind alley.

The war is over and, instead of the Four Freedoms, we have
all kinds of tyrannies, all kinds of misery, all kinds of privation.
The victors are divided, as always happens. Where are the leaders,
who are they, who will make the new world, or help to usher it
in? Can you call Stalin one, or President Truman, or de Gaulle,
or the Bank of England? Are these the men who incarnate the
time spirit? Are these the men who will lead us out of the wilderness?

The new world is being born of necessity, in travail, as all
things are born in this human realm. It is being born of forces
which we only dimly recognize. The elements which will make
the coming world comprise a whole which no political ideology
can hope to embrace. Only a new mentality, a new consciousness,
only a vision capable of embracing all the conflicting tendencies,
of seeing around, beyond and above them, will permit men to
adapt themselves to the order and the ambiance of this new world.
Once men become imbued with the idea that the "age of plenitude" is inevitable, all the current world views, petty, destructive,
mutually exclusive, will vanish like dust. There is not a single
political leader today who can see beyond his nose, not a single
scientist who can reckon with the forces which have already been
unleashed, much less marshal or control them. We are only faintly
beginning to realize that the world egg is truly shattered, that
this happened a few centuries ago, and that in its wake is a staggering cosmos in which men will be forced to play the role of gods.

The atomic bomb is only the first little Christmas present, so
to speak, from the blind forces which are shaping the new era.
Does any one suppose that we are going to be content with just

this one dazzling new toy? How antiquated already are the rail-roads, the steamships, the automobiles, the aeroplanes, the electrical dynamos! In a jiffy we can be in touch with China, India, Australia, darkest Africa; in a few hours (today, that is, but what about tomorrow?) we can be physically transported to any one of these distant places. And here we are lumbering along, millions and billions of us, as if paralyzed, as if deaf and dumb. With the proper will we in America could, almost overnight, supply the whole world with everything it needs. We don't need the support of any country. Everything exists here in super-abundance—I mean the physical actuality. As for our potential, no man can estimate it. Wars give only a slight intimation of what this country can do when it feels the vital urge. We are in possession of secrets which, if revealed and exploited, would un-leash incalculable power and energy. We could inspire such hope, such courage, such enthusiasm, that the passion of the French Revolutionists would seem like a mere breeze. I am thinking now only of what we actually possess, what we actually know, what we can actually visualize, myopic as we are. I say nothing of the suppressed, frustrated dreams of our inventors, our scientists, our technologists, our poets, of what would happen were they en-couraged and not discouraged. I say, taking stock of only that which we now know and possess, we could revolutionize life on this earth to an unthinkable degree, and in the space of a few short years. What Russia, for example, hopes to accomplish in the next twenty years would, from this viewpoint, appear childish. To the dreams of our wildest dreamers, I say—"Yes, entirely possible. Possible right now, tomorrow. Possible a thousand times over, and to an extent that not even the wildest dreamer imagines." The future is galloping towards us like a wild horse; we can feel her breath on our necks.

One does not have to belong to any party, any cult, any ism, to sense what lies ahead. One does not have to swear allegiance to this or that to make this new world feasible. If anything, we have to forego these allegiances—they have only been halters and crutches. Our allegiance is always given to dead things. What is alive does not demand allegiance; what is alive commands, whether one gives adherence or not. What is necessary is that we believe and recognize that which is asserting itself, that we put ourselves in rhythm with what is vital and creative.

Today the world is bound, cramped, stifled by those existing forms of government known as the State. Does the State protect us or do we protect the State? Whatever form of tyranny exists today exists by our consent. No matter into what corner of the globe we cast our eye today, we see the spectre of tyranny. Perhaps the worst tyranny is that which is created for our own good. There can be no common good unless the individual is recognized first and foremost—and until the last, the weakest, of men is included. Everything proceeds from the living individual. The State is an abstraction, a bogey which can intimidate but never convince us, never win us over completely.

In every State there is an element, like some mortal disease, which works to destroy it. And eventually, through a process of undermining, it does destroy it. No State ever had humanity in mind, only the interests of the State. When will we forget about the State and think of humanity, of ourselves, since it is we, all of us, who make up humanity? When will we think of all instead of just "our own?"

A new world is always more inclusive than the old one. A decadent, dying world is always jealous and possessive in all its parts. Since it can no longer live as a complex organism it strives to live cellularly, atomistically. Birth means disruption. It means the abandonment of one temple for another, the relinquishing of the known and the proven for the adventure of freedom and creation. It means above all—release. Those who are saying No! those who are defending the old order (the sacred temple, the sacred cow), those who are dubious and disillusioned, these do not want release. They want to die in the womb. To every urge they say "but," "if," or—"*impossible!*" Their motto is always the same: "Proceed cautiously!" Their talk is always of concession and compromise, never of faith, trust, confidence.

If the Russians are going to think only of Russia, and Americans of America, the hidden forces which direct the world, the forces which represent *all* humanity, will sooner or later put them in open conflict, incite them to destroy one another. When they talk of disarmament do they not mean stacking arms? If they mean peace, why do they wish to retain their weapons, their arsenals, their spies, their provocateurs? Wherever there is the jealous urge to exclude there is the menace of extinction. I see no nation on earth at present which has an all-inclusive view of things. I say it is impossible for a nation, as such, to hold such a view. Everyone will tell you that such a view would be suicidal. Yet it is as clear as the handwriting on the wall that the nations of this earth are finished, though they have not yet come to their end. The dissolving process may continue for a span, but the outcome is certain and definite. Nations will disappear. The human family does not need these water-tight compartments in which to breathe. There is nothing any longer which warrants the survival of the nations, since to be Russian, French, English or American means to be less than what one really is. . . .

We are only gradually shaking off the tyranny of the Church. Now we face another tyranny, perhaps worse; the tyranny of the State. The State seeks to make of its citizens obedient instruments for its glorification. It promises them happiness—in some distant future—as once the Church held out the hope of reaching Paradise. To preserve its interests, the State is perpetually obliged to make war. The chief concern of a State is to be ready and fit for the next conflict. The important thing, which is the enjoyment of life, now, this moment, every moment, is constantly postponed because of the necessity to be prepared for war. Every new invention is appraised from this standpoint. The last thing which any State thinks of is how to make its citizens comfortable and joyous. The wages of the average man barely suffice, and often do not suffice at all, to meet the cost of living. I am speaking now of the richest country on earth—America. What conditions are like in the rest of the world beggars description. One can say today without fear of contradiction that never since the dawn of civilization has the world been in a worse state.

To aid our fellow-sufferers throughout the world we are urged on the one hand to give all we can, and on the other hand, we are informed that no matter how much we give it will be but a drop in the bucket. The despair which seizes the sensitive individual, confronted with this dilemma, is fathomless. One knows that there must be a way out, but who holds the answer? The way has to be created. There must be a desire, an overwhelming desire, to find a solution. To think for one moment that it will be found by the representatives of our various governments is the gravest delusion. These men are thinking only of saving their faces. Each one is pitted against the other, is obliged to win some sort of petty victory over the other, in order to maintain his position. While these mouthpieces talk about peace and order, about freedom and justice, the men behind them, the men who support them and keep them up front, so to speak, are mobilizing all their forces to keep the world in a state of perpetual conflict. In China at this very moment America and Russia are playing the same game that was played in Spain a few years ago. There is no secret about it. Yet every day we are told through the news-

papers and over the radio that America and Russia are seeking
to understand one another, to live amicably in the same world.

It is not easy to see how the peoples of either of these great
countries can liberate themselves. The American people are
supine, the Russian people are acquiescent. In neither of them is
there the slightest revolutionary ardor. In opportunities for self-
development they are richer than any other people in the world.
They could not only support themselves comfortably, they could
between them assume the burdens of the starving nations of the
earth.

And what is it they are worried about? Why are these two nations still at loggerheads? Because each is fearful of the other's
influence upon the rest of the world. One of these countries represents itself as a Communist nation, the other as a Democratic
nation. Neither of them are what they pretend to be. Russia is no
more Communist than America is Democratic. The present Russian
government is even more autocratic than that of the Czars. The
present American government is more tyrannical than that of the
British in the time of the Thirteen Colonies. There is less feedom
now in both these countries than there ever was. How will such
peoples free the world? They do not seem to know the meaning
of freedom.

It seems almost inevitable now that these two countries are determined to destroy, and will succeed in destroying, one another.
And in the process of destroying each other they will destroy a
large part of the civilized world. England is weak, France is helpless, Germany is prostrate, and Japan will be only too delighted
to watch and wait, biding her time to make herself strong again.
Of all the countries which participated in the war, Japan learned
her lesson best. When the West is in ruins she will rise again, invade Europe, take it over.

"Nonsense! Ridiculous!" the critics will scream. And, burying their heads in the sand, they will whistle from their rear ends. For once, Democrats, Republicans, Fascists, Communists will agree. "Impossible!" they will shout. Well, this is a lone man's view. I have no axe to grind, no party to sustain, no ism to further. All I clamor for is that freedom, that security, that peace and harmony which all these conflicting groups advocate and promise. I don't want it when I'm dead. I want it now. Everything I do is with that purpose in mind.

I ask no one to sacrifice himself in order to promote my ideas. I demand no allegiance, no taxes, no devotion. I say—free yourself to the best of your ability! The more freedom you obtain for yourself, the more you create for me, for everyone. I would like you to have all that you desire, praying at the same time that you wish as much for the next man. I urge you to create and to share your creation with those less fortunate. If someone asks you to vote for him at the next election, ask him, I beg you, what he can do for you that you cannot do yourself. Ask him whom *he* is voting for. If he tells you the truth, then go to the polls and vote for yourself. Most anyone who reads this could do a better job than the man now doing it. Why create these jobs? Why ask someone else to regulate your affairs? What are you doing that is so important? Does the man who asks for your vote find you your job, does he provide your family with food and shelter, does he put clothes on your back, does he provide the education you need . . . does he even bother to see that you get a decent burial? The only time he is concerned about you is when you can make money for him. No matter how little you make he wants part of it. He keeps you poor on the pretext that he is doing something for your benefit. And you are too lazy to protest, knowing full well that he thinks about no one but himself. From childhood you were taught that it is right and just to delegate your powers to someone else. You never questioned it because everything you are taught in school has one purpose: the glorification of your country. Some-how, though it is *your* country, you seem to have no part in it until the time comes to surrender your life. Your whole life is spent in trying to get a hearing. You're always on the door-step, never inside.

Wherever one goes in this civilized world one always finds the same set-up. The little man, the man who does the dirty work, *the producer,* is of no importance, receives no consideration, and is always being asked to make the greatest sacrifice. Yet everything depends on this forgotten man. Not a wheel could turn without his support and co-operation. It is this man, whose number is legion, who has no voice whatever in world affairs. These matters are beyond his grasp, supposedly. He has only to produce; the others, the politicians, they will run the world. One day this poor little man, this forgotten son, this nobody on whose toil and in-dustry everything depends, will see through the farce. Unin-structed though he may be, he knows full well how rich is the earth, how little he needs to live happily. He knows, too, that it is not necessary to kill his fellow-man in order to live; he knows that he has been robbed and cheated from time immemorial; he knows that if he can't run his affairs properly, nobody else can. He is suffocated with all this bitter knowledge. He waits and waits, hop-ing that time will alter things. And slowly he realizes that time alters nothing, that with time things only grow worse. One day he will decide to act. "Wait!" he will be told. "Wait just a little longer." But he will refuse to wait another second.

When that day comes, watch out! When the little man all over the world becomes so desperate that he cannot wait another min-ute, another second, beware O world! Once he decides to act for himself, act on his own, there will be no putting him back in harness. There will be nothing you can promise him which will equal the joy of being free, being rid of the incubus. Today he is still yours, still the pawn which can be shuffled about, but to-morrow there may be such a reversal of all precedent as to make your hearts quake. Today you may still talk the absurd language of the Stone Age; today you may still coerce the young into prepared-ness for the next conflict; today you may still convince the blind and the ignorant that they should be content to do without the things you find indispensable; today you may still talk about your possessions, your colonies, your empires. But your days are num-bered. You belong in the museum, with the dinosaur, the stone axe, the hieroglyph, the mummy. The new age will come into being with your disappearance from the face of the earth.

At the dawn of every age there is distinguishable a radiant figure in whom the new time spirit is embodied. He comes at the darkest hour, rises like a sun, and dispels the gloom and stagna-tion in which the world was gripped. Somewhere in the black folds which now enshroud us I am certain that another being is gestating, that he is but waiting for the zero hour to announce himself. Hope never dies, passion can never be utterly extin-guished. The deadlock will be broken. Now we are sound asleep in the cocoon; it took centuries and centuries to spin this seeming web of death. It takes but a few moments to burst it asunder. Now we are out on a limb, suspended over the void. Should the tree give way, all creation vaults to its doom. But what is it that tells us to hasten the hour of birth? What is it that, at precisely the right moment, gives us the knowledge and the power to take wing, when heretofore we knew only how to crawl ignominiously on our bellies? If the caterpillar through sleep can metamorphose into a butterfly, surely man during his long night of travail must discover the knowledge and the power to redeem himself.

33. CHARLES A. BEARD

President Roosevelt and the Coming of the War
(1948)

> Charles A. Beard (1874-1948), one of America's
> most distinguished historians, maintained a life-long
> interest in matters of social welfare and public policy.
> His books, *An Economic Interpretation of the Consti-*
> *tution* (1913) and *The Rise of American Civiliza-*
> *tion* (1927), are outstanding works of analysis and
> synthesis. Beard's growing concern over American
> foreign and military policy was reflected in his criti-
> cism of United States diplomacy in the period before
> and after the Second World War.

The discrepancies between official representations and official realities in the conduct of foreign affairs during the year 1941, until
the coming of the war, stand out starkly in documents already
available. Other documents that bear on the subject, running into
the thousands, are known to exist, but they are still under the seal
of secrecy. What they will reveal, if all of them are ever unsealed,
can only be a matter of conjecture for the general public and students of history. But in any event several primary discrepancies are
established beyond question by the documents now published.

In the nature of things human and political, these established
discrepancies may be and are being turned to account in various
ways by politicians, publicists, and commentators. They may be,
for example, formulated into a bill of indictment against President

Roosevelt and his Administration. Or they may be incorporated in a brief of defense which, like a demurrer in a court of justice, concedes the facts and denies that they make a true case under superior and overriding principles, taken for granted in advance. Or they may appear to reflective minds as furnishing precedents material and relevant to the future and fortunes of constitutional and democratic government in the United States.

For these discrepancies a favorable interpretation has been and is still being offered by many American publicists in the following form. The great end which President Roosevelt discerned and chose justified the means which he employed. As a farsighted statesman he early discovered that unless the United States entered the war raging in Europe, Hitler would be victorious; and the United States, facing alone this monstrous totalitarian power, would become a victim of its merciless ideology and its despotic militarism. According to this interpretation, it was a question of democracy, the Four Freedoms, the noble principles of the Atlantic Charter, and world security on the one side; of totalitarianism, consummate despotism, and military subjugation on the other side. Since the American people were so smug in their conceit, so ignorant of foreign affairs, and so isolationist in sentiment that they could not themselves see the reality of this terrible threat to their own safety and a necessity to meet it by a resort to war, President Roosevelt had to dissemble in order to be re-elected in 1940 as against Wendell Willkie, then the antiwar candidate of the Republicans on an antiwar platform. Furthermore, as Members of Congress, Democrats and Republicans alike, continued throughout the year, until December seventh, their vigorous opposition to involvement in war, President Roosevelt, in conducting foreign affairs, had to maintain the appearance of a defensive policy until the Japanese attack on Pearl Harbor. But the means which President Roosevelt actually employed in the conduct of foreign affairs were justified by the great end which he, with peculiar clairvoyance, had early discerned and chosen for himself and his country.

Oblique but evident support for this interpretation was provided by the Department of State in Chapter I of its publication, *Peace and War, 1931–1941,* issued in July, 1943, prepared by or for Secretary Hull. In that chapter, the President and the Secretary of State are represented as convinced at some time "early" in that decade that "the idea of isolation as expressed in 'neutrality' legislation" was untenable, as having information about foreign affairs or foreseeing developments in foreign relations of which the public was not aware, and as compelled to move gradually "to a position in the forefront of the United Nations that are making common cause against an attempt at world conquest unparalleled alike in boldness of conception and in brutality of operation."

The interpretation that the end justified the means, like all other interpretations, depends upon the point of view of those who make or accept it; and though it be proclaimed as the settled truth, its validity is nonetheless open to tests of knowledge. Even a cursory examination of the thesis raises questions of time and consequences, foreign and domestic.

When did the end that justified the means actually come? With the surrender of Italy, Germany, and Japan? If not, when did it come or is it to come—in what span of time, short or long? By whom and according to what criteria is the question of time to be answered beyond all reasonable doubt?

If the time for the achievement of the end be postponed to some point in the indefinite future, the confirmation of the thesis must likewise be postponed indefinitely. In that case an effort to confirm it now becomes a matter of calculating probabilities, ponderable and imponderable. If, however, the results of the war—foreign and domestic—thus far known be taken into the reckoning, a question both logical and historical may be asked: Does it now appear probable that President Roosevelt did in fact so clearly discern the end—the consequences to flow from his actions in 1941—that he was in truth justified in his choice and use of means?

With regard to consequences in foreign affairs, the noble principles of the Four Freedoms and the Atlantic Charter were, for practical purposes, discarded in the settlements which accompanied the progress, and followed the conclusion, of the war. To the validity of this statement the treatment of peoples in Estonia, Lithuania, Poland, Rumania, Yugoslavia, China, Indo-China, Indonesia, Italy, Germany, and other places of the earth bears witness. More significant still for the fortunes of the American Republic, out of the war came the triumph of another totalitarian regime no less despotic and ruthless than Hitler's system, namely, Russia, possessing more than twice the population of prewar Germany, endowed with immense natural resources, astride Europe and Asia, employing bands of quislings as terroristic in methods as any Hitler ever assembled, and insistently effectuating a political and economic ideology equally inimical to the democracy, liberties, and institutions of the United States—Russia, one of the most ruthless Leviathans in the long history of military empires.

Since, as a consequence of the war called "necessary" to overthrow Hitler's despotism, another depotism was raised to a higher pitch of power, how can it be argued conclusively with reference to inescapable facts that the "end" justified the means employed to involve the United States in that war? If the very idea of neutrality with regard to Hitler was shameful in 1941, what is to be said of commitments made in the name of peace and international amity at Teheran and Yalta, where the avowed and endorsed principles of the Atlantic Charter for world affairs were shattered—in commitments which were subsequently misrepresented by President Roosevelt, publicly and privately?

Nor more than two years after the nominal close of the war did the prospects of "reconstruction" in Germany and Japan promise the achievement of President Roosevelt's great end in any discernible time ahead.

In respect of domestic affairs, the consequences of the involvement in the war are scarcely less damaging to the thesis that the end justified the means. Among the many dangers long emphasized by advocates of war in the name of perpetual or durable peace, none was described in more frightening terms than the prospect that Hitler would be victorious in Europe and that the result of his victory would spell disaster for the United States. It would mean the transformation of the United States into a kind of armed camp for defense, with all the evils thereunto attached: a permanent conscript army, multiplied annual outlays for armaments, a huge national debt, and grinding taxes. The expansion of American economy, so necessary for domestic prosperity, would be blocked by the impossibility of "doing business with Hitler," that is, by barriers to American commerce in the form of state-fostered cartels and state-controlled economies in Europe. Moreover, the promotion of beneficent reforms at home, from which President Roosevelt had been compelled to turn in military preparations for defense, would be permanently barred. Only by victory over Hitler, it was claimed, could these frightful evils be avoided.

But judging by results of participation in the war, and the prospects of evident tendencies, were these dreadful evils obviated by the victory at arms? While the war was still raging, President Roosevelt recommended to Congress the adoption of conscription as a permanent policy for the United States—under the softer name of universal service; and his successor, President Truman, continued to urge that policy upon Congress even after large-scale fighting had nominally stopped. Furthermore, it was now claimed by former advocates of war that huge armed forces were necessary in "peacetime" to "secure the fruits of victory" and "win the peace"—by extirpating the spirit of tyranny in Germany and Japan and by restraining the expansion of Russian imperial power.

As for military expenditures, they were fixed in 1947 at many times the annual outlays of prewar years, despite the cuts made by the Republican Congress in President Truman's budget demands. To the people of the United States, the war bequeathed a national debt, augmented from about $60,000,000,000 in 1940 to approximately $279,000,000,000 in 1946, or about $2,000 for every man, woman, and child in the country. To meet the annual interest on the national debt it was necessary in 1947 for the government to raise about $5,000,000,000, or more than the total peacetime outlay of the government for all purposes in any year before 1933—the advent of the New Deal; and the tax rates of 1947 made the tax rates of any year before 1941 look positively trivial in comparison. So stupendous was the debt and so heavy the tax burden that only Communists, looking gleefully to repudiation and a general economic crash, could envisage the future with satisfaction. Nor was the outlook for doing business with Stalin save on his own terms, or for that matter with several other European governments, any brighter than doing business with Hitler in the prewar years had been in fact.

With regard to the Democratic Party as the party offering beneficent and progressive reforms, the outcome of the war was little short of disastrous, at least immediately. Though entrenched in every department of the Federal Government and commanding the support of a bureaucracy numbering more than 3,000,000 officers and employees, enjoying all the economic perquisites therewith associated, the party was ousted from power in both Houses of Congress by Republicans triumphant at the polls in the Congressional elections of 1946.

Deprived of its "indispensable" leader through the death of

President Roosevelt in 1945, the Democratic Party broke immediately into belligerent factions, while internationalists quarreled over the proceedings, meaning, and utility of the United Nations. On the extreme right, gathered old-line Democrats bent on extinguishing all signs of the New Deal; on the extreme left, rallied the new-line "progressives," headed by Henry Wallace, pledged to innovations more radical, extensive, and costly than those of the New Deal; and in the middle a small number of reformers, claiming to be guardians of the true faith, established the Committee for Democratic Action, with which Mrs. Eleanor Roosevelt was affiliated. Hence, when the fortunes of the Democrats as the unified party of reform were considered, it was academic to raise the question whether the domestic consequences of the war for the new world order justified the means chosen by President Roosevelt to gain the end which he chose for himself and the United States.

Indeed, two years after the nominal close of the war for the end proclaimed, it was almost academic to discuss domestic affairs at all, for they were subordinate to overriding foreign commitments, known and secret, made by President Roosevelt and by his successor, President Harry Truman. In 1947, under President Truman's direction, the Government of the United States set out on an unlimited program of underwriting, by money and military "advice," poverty-stricken, feeble, and instable governments around the edges of the gigantic and aggressive Slavic Empire. Of necessity, if this program was to be more than a *brutum fulmen,* it had to be predicated upon present and ultimate support by the blood and treasure of the United States; and this meant keeping the human power and the economy of the United States geared to the potentials inherent in the undertaking.

In these circumstances, it was impossible for the Government or people of the United States to make any rational calculations as to economy, life, and work at home. Over young men and women trying to plan their future days and years hung the shadow of possible, in fact probable, calls to armed service. Congress could do no more than guess at the requirements of taxation and expenditures, domestic and foreign. Business enterprisers, with prospects of new war demands ahead, could lay out no programs for the production of civilian goods with any degree of assurance as to the future, immediate or remote. In short, with the Government of the United States committed under a so-called bipartisan foreign policy to supporting by money and other forms of power for an indefinite time an indefinate number of other governments around the globe, the domestic affairs of the American people became appendages to an aleatory expedition in the management of the world.

34. EDWARD C. KIRKLAND

Intellectual Freedom in a Time of Crisis
(1950)

Edward C. Kirkland (1894-   ), for thirty years professor of history at Bowdoin College, received his A. B. degree at Dartmouth and his Ph. D. at Harvard. In 1956-1957 he was Pitt Professor of American History at Cambridge University, England. President of the American Association of University Professors from 1946 to 1948, he was especially concerned with the preservation of academic freedom in the midst of the cold war.

At present the status of intellectual freedom for both teachers and learners is critical. Evidence comes from every quarter. Congressional insistence denies national scholarships to Communist students, and graduate students, who are not Communists, either steer away from fields of learning where restraints are likely to be imposed or resolve to keep their mouths closed on dangerous thoughts likely to imperil their future employment. Though in most institutions professors who desired the election of Henry Wallace or worked in his behalf were left administratively unmolested, in some they were cautioned or discharged for their political beliefs or activities. The number of rumored instances has been so numerous that organizations concerned with academic freedom have found it impossible thoroughly to investigate them all. From New Hampshire to Washington legislative committees have scrutinized institutions of higher learning in the light of standards alien and hostile to their chief purposes. The national Committee on Un-American Activities requested selected colleges and universities to send in lists of textbooks, a request that was answered by some flustered institutions, until a belated courage put an end to the procedure. Articles of weight about academic freedom have appeared in periodicals as polar as *The American Scholar* and *The Saturday Evening Post.*

These phenomena arise from a conjunction of causes. The ideological battle between democracy and communism, the strategic and national conflicts heightened by the spread of Russian influence in Asia, in central and, for a time, in western Europe, the regrouping of world power about Russia on the one hand and the United States on the other—this is but one, though the most colorful, explanation of the present crisis. Of greater importance are the more intimate bonds between educational institutions and the national government. The first steps were taken during World War II when such institutions participated in the war effort—and incidentally kept alive—by administering programs of military education and research. The tendency has been perpetuated and enlarged by the G. I. Bill of Rights, government-financed research, and by present and proposed programs of Federal scholarships. The value or inevitability of these arrangements is not here under discussion. Their upshot has been, however, to make educational institutions, even the private ones, in greater part than hitherto, agencies of the government and, through an easy and largely unnoticed osmosis, to foster the notion that what is proper in case of government is proper also in the case of a university or college. Furthermore the popularization and democratization of higher education, effected largely by governmental interposition, has been sudden. Institutions which once served only a minority of the population now minister to a much larger clientele. Practices—read heresies if you will—once tolerable since they influenced few now influence many. As yet there has not been time to educate this larger and newly-interested constituency in what colleges and universities are really for and in the part that freedom plays in their essential operations. Whatever the explanation for it may be, the current emergency is in no sense unique in human history. The assumptions and arguments of those who would interpret it to justify restraints or purges in higher education are, beneath the surface, very old ones, as dangerous as they always have been.

One source, already hinted, of our present confusion is the identification of governmental purposes with those of higher education. Whether government is properly only a policeman or the administrator of measures for the general welfare, widely conceived, most Americans would deny that its legitimate function included the determination of what is learned or taught. Stated thus baldly the idea is repulsive. Stated subtly—that higher education should exalt the American way of life and should mention Communism with a lack of enthusiasm—the idea is more ingratiating, at least to the commonalty and to some college presidents, if not to the scholar whose search for truth must be unimpeded and free. Incidentally, in this connection, the American intellectual should be as candid for himself as for others. He should not forget that the surrender of the German intellectuals, which he so much bewails, was a surrender to a fundamental government policy, stated by a regime legal enough to elicit from the United States recognition and an ambassador.

Imperceptibly the confusion of the State with the university shades into a second, the confusion of the university with an authoritarian Church. Like the latter the former has the truth. Admittedly college presidents and professors are in part responsible for this widely-cherished assumption. At least they have on baccalaureate and other important occasions habitually uttered this affirmation. College seals, emblazoned "veritas," give mute additional testimony. Actually anyone acquainted with the history of knowledge realizes how contradictory have been the fundamental concepts in such precise fields as science and medicine. All could not have been equally true; yet all have been taught as such, somewhere at some time. An examination of the more fallible matters of social science and good taste reinforces the observation. Members of academic communities should be both more modest and more accurate in their claims. What higher institutions are engaged in is the quest for truth. The process must be kept free so that the area of error, from which there is no complete escape, should be made as small as possible. All this is commonplace enough. Unfortunately one of the marks of a period of panic is the neglect of the obvious.

A second premise of our disturbed days is that it is both feasible and just to determine a man's fitness, either in matters of detailed belief or in matters of scholarly honesty and intellectual freedom, by the nature of the group, usually political, to which he voluntarily belongs. Few would deny the possible relevance of this information. But every careful thinker has learned long since to reject for individuals a determinism so crude and so absolute.

Sophisticated jurisprudence proceeds on the assumption that guilt is personal and is not a matter of association. If membership in the Ku-Klux Klan automatically meant exclusion from United States courts, the Supreme Court would have been deprived of the services of an Associate Justice who has been conspicuous in the support of freedom. The latest experiment of our government with guilt by association, the deportation of Japanese-Americans from their lawful homes and their confinement in concentration camps, is now widely regarded as a massive injustice and a national humiliation. No doubt individual Ku-Kluxers are blindly intolerant and individual Japanese-Americans dangerously subversive. Individual Communists, Progressives, and members of the American Legion, which revokes charters of its posts for "deviation," may be so hidebound intellectually or so disciplined from above as to be unfit to be members of a free company of scholars. But the decision must be made on an individual basis. Quotations from party platforms, theoretical works written over the period of a century, manifestoes and proclamations designed for particular historic contexts, pamphlets and instructions addressed to an inner circle do not in the nature of things reflect the opinion of individuals within the organization, particularly when it can be demonstrated that some of the culprits are acquainted with only a fraction of this documentation. It is a discouraging phase of the present attack upon political radicals that it has rarely been alleged and never proved that they have taught their sinister doctrine. In short they have not been "unloosed upon our boys and girls." Their unfitness consists in holding certain beliefs.

No doubt the vigorous defense of individuals holding unpopular beliefs is disagreeable—the issues are complicated—and costly. By sacrificing the extremist, adminstrators may hope to sustain the nourishing flow of appropriations, contributions, and endowments. Moreover the institution thus saved can continue to serve as a training school and vocational institute even if it can no longer aspire to the high title of university. Many will not know the difference. Furthermore to discard the radicals may well seem, to those wise in the ways of this world, the most effective protection of the liberals. Such adroitness may postpone the showdown; but, when it comes, the conditions favorable to defense have been gravely impaired. If the academic world surrenders its right to freedom, it is left to plead for a privilege. Already we have the spectacle of eminent scholars beseeching the foes of freedom to turn aside their wrath from the "true liberals." This unhappy outcome was implicit in the original capitulation.

35. WILLIAM O. DOUGLAS

Dennis *Versus* United States
(1951)

William O. Douglas (1898-   ), Associate Justice
of the United States Supreme Court since 1939, was
before that a member of the Law School Faculties at
Columbia and Yale. During the New Deal he was
chairman of the Securities and Exchange Commission.
In his opinions from the bench of the Supreme Court,
Justice Douglas has been a steadfast defender of individual rights and liberties.

If this were a case where those who claimed protection under the
First Amendment were teaching the techniques of sabotage, the
assassination of the President, the filching of documents from
public files, the planting of bombs, the art of street warfare, and
the like, I would have no doubts. The freedom to speak is not absolute; the teaching of methods of terror and other seditious
conduct should be beyond the pale along with obscenity and im-
morality. This case was argued as if those were the facts. The
argument imported much seditious conduct into the record. That is
easy and it has popular appeal, for the activities of Communists in
plotting and scheming against the free world are common knowledge. But the fact is that no such evidence was introduced at the
trial. There is a statute which makes a seditious conspiracy unlawful. Petitioners, however, were not charged with a "conspiracy

to overthrow" the Government. They were charged with a conspiracy to form a party and groups and assemblies of people who teach and advocate the overthrow of our Government by force or violence and with a conspiracy to advocate and teach its overthrow by force and violence. It may well be that indoctrination in the techniques of terror to destroy the Government would be indictable under either statute. But the teaching which is condemned here is of a different character.

So far as the present record is concerned, what petitioners did was to organize people to teach and themselves teach the Marxist-Leninist doctrine contained chiefly in four books: Stalin, *Foundations of Leninism* (1924); Marx and Engels, *Manifesto of the Communist Party* (1848); Lenin, *The State and Revolution* (1917); *History of the Communist Party of the Soviet Union* (B.) (1939).

Those books are to Soviet Communism what *Mein Kampf* was to Nazism. If they are understood, the ugliness of Communism is revealed, its deceit and cunning are exposed, the nature of its activities becomes apparent, and the chances of its success less likely. That is not, of course, the reason why petitioners chose these books for their classrooms. They are fervent Communists to whom these volumes are gospel. They preached the creed with the hope that some day it would be acted upon.

The opinion of the Court does not outlaw these texts nor condemn them to the fire, as the Communists do literature offensive to their creed. But if the books themselves are not outlawed, if they can lawfully remain on library shelves, by what reasoning does their use in a classroom became a crime? It would not be a crime under the Act to introduce these books to a class, though that would be teaching what the creed of violent overthrow of the Government is. The Act, as construed, requires the element of intent—that those who teach the creed believe in it. The crime then depends not on what is taught but on who the teacher is. That is to make freedom of speech turn not on *what is said,* but on the *intent* with which it is said. Once we start down that road we enter territory dangerous to the liberties of every citizen.

There was a time in England when the concept of constructive treason flourished. Men were punished not for raising a hand against the king but for thinking murderous thoughts about him. The Farmers of the Constitution were alive to that abuse and took steps to see that the practice would not flourish here. Treason was defined to require overt acts—the evolution of a plot against the country into an actual project. The present case is not one of treason. But the analogy is close when the illegality is made to turn on intent, not on the nature of the act. We then start probing men's minds for motive and purpose; they become entangled in the law not for what they did but *for what they thought;* they get convicted not for what they said but for the purpose with which they said it.

Intent, of course, often makes the difference in the law. An act otherwise excusable or carrying minor penalties may grow to an abhorrent thing if the evil intent is present. We deal here, however, not with ordinary acts but with speech, to which the Constitution has given a special sanction.

The vice of treating speech as the equivalent of overt acts of a treasonable or seditious character is emphasized by a concurring opinion, which by invoking the law of conspiracy makes speech do service for deeds which are dangerous to society. The doctrine of conspiracy has served diverse and oppressive purposes and in its broad reach can be made to do great evil. But never until today has anyone seriously thought that the ancient law of conspiracy could constitutionally be used to turn speech into seditious conduct. Yet that is precisely what is suggested. I repeat that we deal here with speech alone, not with speech *plus* acts of sabotage or unlawful conduct. Not a single seditious act is charged in the indictment. To make a lawful speech unlawful because two men conceive it is to raise the law of conspiracy to appalling proportions. That course is to make a radical break with the past and to violate one of the cardinal principles of our constitutional scheme.

Free speech has occupied an exalted position because of the high service it has given our society. Its protection is essential to the very existence of a democracy. The airing of ideas releases pressures which otherwise might become destructive. When ideas compete in the market for acceptance, full and free discussion exposes the false and they gain few adherents. Full and free discussion even of ideas we hate encourages the testing of our own prejudices and preconceptions. Full and free discussion keeps a society from becoming stagnant and unprepared for the stresses and strains that work to tear all civilizations apart.

Full and free discussion has indeed been the first article of our faith. We have founded our political system on it. It has been the safeguard of every religious, political, philosophical, economic, and racial group amongst us. We have counted on it to keep us from embracing what is cheap and false; we have trusted the common sense of our people to choose the doctrine true to our genius and to reject the rest. This has been the one single outstanding tenet that has made our institutions the symbol of freedom and equality. We have deemed it more costly to liberty to suppress a despised minority than to let them vent their spleen. We have above all else feared the political censor. We have wanted a land where our people can be exposed to all the diverse creeds and cultures of the world.

There comes a time when even speech loses its constitutional immunity. Speech innocuous one year may at another time fan such destructive flames that it must be halted in the interests of the safety of the Republic. That is the meaning of the clear and present danger test. When conditions are so critical that there will be no time to avoid the evil that the speech threatens, it is time to call a halt. Otherwise, free speech which is the strength of the Nation will be the cause of its destruction.

Yet free speech is the rule, not the exception. The restraint to be constitutional must be based on more than fear, on more than a passionate opposition against the speech, on more than a revolted dislike for its contents. There must be some immediate injury to society that is likely if speech is allowed. The classic statement of these conditions was made by Mr. Justice Brandeis in his concurring opinion in *Whitney v. California,* 274 U.S. 357, 376-77,

> Fear of serious injury cannot alone justify supression of free speech and assembly. Men feared witches and burnt women. It is the function of speech to free men from the bondage of irrational fears. To justify suppression of free speech there must be reasonable ground to fear that serious evil will result if free speech is practiced. There must be reasonable ground to believe that the danger apprehended is imminent. There must be reasonable ground to believe that the evil to be prevented is a serious one. Every denunciation of existing law tends in some measure to increase the probability that there will be violation of it. Condonation of a breach enhances the probability. Expressions of approval add to the probability. Propagation of the criminal state of mind by teaching syndicalism increases it. Advocacy of lawbreaking heightens it still further. But even advocacy of violation, however reprehensible morally, is not a justification for denying free speech where the advocacy falls short of incitement and there is nothing to indicate that the advocacy would be immediately acted on. The wide difference between advocacy and incitement, between preparation and attempt, between assembling and conspiracy, must be borne in mind. In order to support a finding of clear and present danger it must be shown either that immediate serious violence was to be expected or was advocated, or that the past conduct furnished reason to believe that such advocacy was then contemplated.

Those who won our independence by revolution were not cowards. They did not fear political change. They did not exalt order at the cost of liberty. To courageous, self-reliant men, with confidence in the power of free and fearless reasoning applied through the processes of popular government, no danger flowing from speech can be deemed clear and present, unless the incidence of the evil apprehended is so imminent that it may befall before there is opportunity for full discussion. *If there be time to expose through discussion the falsehood and fallacies, to avert the evil by the processes of education, the remedy to be applied is more speech, not enforced silence.* [Italics added.]

I had assumed that the question of the clear and present danger, being so critical an issue in the case, would be a matter for submission to the jury. It was squarely held in *Pierce v. United States,* 252 U. S. 239, 244, to be a jury question. Mr. Justice Pitney, speaking for the Court, said, "Whether the statement contained in the pamphlet had a natural tendency to produce the forbidden consequences, as alleged, was a question to be determined not upon demurrer but by the jury at the trial." That is the only time the Court has passed on the issue. None of our other decisions is contrary. Nothing said in any of the nonjury cases has detracted from that ruling. The statement in *Pierce v. United States, supra,* states the law as it has been and as it should be. The Court, I think, errs when it treats the question as one of law.

Yet, whether the question is one for the Court or the jury, there should be evidence of record on the issue. This record, however, contains no evidence whatsoever showing that the acts charged, *viz.,* the teaching of the Soviet theory of revolution with the hope that it will be realized, have created any clear and present danger to the nation. The Court, however, rules to the contrary. It says, "The formation by petitioners of such a highly organized conspiracy, with rigidly disciplined members subject to call when the leaders, these petitioners, felt that the time had come for action, coupled with the inflammable nature of world conditions, similar uprisings in other countries, and the touch-and-go nature of our relations with countries with whom petitioners were in the very least ideologically attuned, convince us that their convictions were justified on this score."

That ruling is in my view not responsive to the issue in the case. We might as well say that the speech of petitioners is outlawed because Soviet Russia and her Red Army are a threat to world peace.

The nature of Communism as a force on the world scene would, of course, be relevant to the issue of clear and present danger of petitioners' advocacy within the United States. But the primary consideration is the strength and tactical position of petitioners and their converts in this country. On that there is no evidence in the record. If we are to take judicial notice of the threat of Communists within the nation, it should not be difficult to conclude that *as a political party* they are of little consequence. Communists in this country have never made a respectable or serious showing in any election. I would doubt that there is a village, let alone a city or county or state, which the Communists could carry. Communism in the world scene is no bogeyman; but Communism as a political faction or party in this country plainly is. Communism has been so thoroughly exposed in this country that it has been crippled as a political force. Free speech has destroyed it as an effective political party. It is inconceivable that those who went up and down this country preaching the doctrine of revolution which petitioners espouse would have any success. In days of trouble and confusion, when bread lines were long, when the unemployed walked the streets, when people were starving, the advocates of a short-cut by revolution might have a chance to gain adherents. But today there are no such conditions. The country is not in despair; the people know Soviet Communism; the doctrine of Soviet revolution is exposed in all of its ugliness and the American people want none of it.

How it can be said that there is a clear and present danger that this advocacy will succeed is, therefore, a mystery. Some nations less resilient than the United States, where illiteracy is high and where democratic traditions are only budding, might have to take drastic steps and jail these men for merely speaking their creed. But in America they are miserable merchants of unwanted ideas; their wares remain unsold. The fact that their ideas are abhorrent does not make them powerful.

The political impotence of the Communists in this country does not, of course, dispose of the problem. Their numbers; their positions in industry and government; the extent to which they have in fact infiltrated the police, the armed services, transportation, stevedoring, power plants, munitions works, and other critical places—these facts all bear on the likelihood that their advocacy of the Soviet theory of revolution will endanger the Republic. But the record is silent on these facts. If we are to proceed on the basis of judicial notice, it is impossible for me to say that the Communists in this country are so potent or so stategically deployed that they must be suppressed for their speech. I could not so hold unless I were willing to conclude that the activities in recent years of committees of Congress, of the Attorney General, of labor unions, of state legislatures, and of Loyalty Boards were so futile as to leave the country on the edge of grave peril. To believe that petitioners and their following are placed in such critical positions as to endanger the Nation is to believe the incredible. It is safe to say that the followers of the creed of Soviet Communism are known to the F. B. I.; that in case of war with Russia they will be picked up overnight as were all prospective saboteurs at the commencement of World War II; that the invisible army of petitioners is the best known, the most beset, and the least thriving of any fifth column in history. Only those held by fear and panic could think otherwise.

This is my view if we are to act on the basis of judicial notice. But the mere statement of the opposing views indicates how important it is that we know the facts before we act. Neither prejudice nor hate nor senseless fear should be the basis of this solemn act. Free speech—the glory of our system of government—should not be sacrificed on anything less than plain and objective proof of danger that the evil advocated is imminent. On this record no one can say that petitioners and their converts are in such a strategic position as to have even the slightest chance of achieving their aims.

The First Amendment provides that "Congress shall make no law . . . abridging the freedom of speech." The Constitution provides no exception. This does not mean, however, that the Nation need hold its hand until it is in such weakened condition that there is no time to protect itself from incitement to revolution. Seditious conduct can always be punished. But the command of the First Amendment is so clear that we should not allow Congress to call a halt to free speech except in the extreme case of peril from the speech itself. The First Amendment makes confidence in the common sense of our people and in their maturity of judgment the great postulate of our democracy. Its philosophy is that violence is rarely, if ever, stopped by denying civil liberties to those advocating resort to force. The First Amendment reflects the philosophy of Jefferson "that it is time enough for the rightful purposes of civil government, for its officers to interfere when principles break out into overt acts against peace and good order." The political censor has no place in our public debates. Unless and until extreme and necessitous circumstances are shown, our aim should be to keep speech unfettered and to allow the processes of law to be invoked only when the provocateurs among us move from speech to action.

Vishinsky wrote in 1938 in *The Law of the Soviet State,* "In our state, naturally, there is and can be no place for freedom of speech, press, and so on for the foes of socialism."

Our concern should be that we accept no such standard for the United States. Our faith should be that our people will never give support to these advocates of revolution, so long as we remain loyal to the purposes for which our Nation was founded.

36. HENRY STEELE COMMAGER

Guilt—and Innocence—by Association
(1953)

Henry Steele Commager (1902-   ) received his
degrees from the University of Chicago. A well-
known author and historian, he has taught at New
York University, Columbia, and Amherst. Professor
Commager was one of the first members of the academic community to question the post-World War II
loyalty investigations.

When Bishop Oxnam was called before the Un-American Activities Committee it was charged not that he was himself a Communist or even a fellow-traveler, but that he had lent his name to
organizations that the Committee considered subversive. He was
guilty, in short, of the new crime of improper association. The
Bishop succeeded in clearing himself of this stain on his character, though not to the satisfaction of all. Not, for instance, to
the satisfaction of the Rev. Daniel Poling, editor of the *Christian
Herald,* who deplored, in *The New York Times,* the habit of ready
association with miscellaneous organizations, and concluded with
the observation that "a man is known by the company he keeps."

This crime of guilt by association made its first appearance in
Federal law in the Alien Registration Act of 1940; it became not
merely a crime but a disability and a sin by virtue of President
Truman's Loyalty Order of 1947—an order which set up as one

357

standard for employment or dismissal "membership in, association with, or sympathetic affiliation with any . . . organization, movement, group or combination of persons, designated by the Attorney General as . . . subversive." Since then this cloud no bigger than a man's hand has grown until it fills the whole horizon.

Soon not only the Attorney General but almost everybody else was busy compiling lists—Congressional committees, state Attorneys General, state legislative committees, and scores of private organizations as well. The lists themselves, needless to say, grew longer and longer, for increasingly their compilers followed the principle implicit in Franklin's story of the two Quaker sisters: "I know not how it is, sister, but the older I get the more I find that no one is right but me and thee, and sometimes I am troubled about thee." And the standard of "affiliation" grew vaguer and vaguer.

To the witch-hunters of our time no more plausible test was ever devised than this one, for sooner or later almost every man or woman who is active in public affairs joins some organization that somebody considers subversive. And the notion that "birds of a feather flock together," that "there is no smoke without fire," is so widespread that it affects even the most level-headed.

Yet no more pernicious doctrine has ever found its way into law or into popular acceptance than this doctrine of guilt by association. It is pernicious in principle, in application, and in consequences. It confesses a gross and palpable misreading of our history and subverts vital parts of our democracy and our constitutional system. It is essential that we examine this doctrine critically so that we may see what it has cost us and what it may yet cost us.

First, then, the doctrine of guilt by association is unsound in logic. It is unsound because it assumes that a good cause becomes bad if supported by bad men; perhaps it assumes the reverse as well—as it logically should—that a bad cause becomes good if supported by virtuous men. But truth stands on its own merits; it may be made more acceptable with proper sponsorship, but it is neither enhanced nor impaired by the authorities who support it. If all the subversives in the land asserted that two and two made four, two and two would still make four. If a particular cause is worthy of support, it does not cease to merit support because men we disapprove support it.

There is a persuasive reason why conservatives and liberals alike should subscribe to this principle, and that is a practical one. For if bad support could damage a good cause, then all that would be needed to tarnish the Declaration of Independence or destroy the Constitution would be the endorsement of these documents by the Communist Party; all that would be needed to ruin the Republican Party or the American Legion or the American Bar Association would be approval of their objectives by *The Daily Worker*. The doctrine that a good cause can be damaged by disreputable support means that all that is necessary to ruin a good cause is bad support.

Second the doctrine is wrong legally. In Anglo-American law guilt is personal, not collective. It does not spread, by a process of osmosis, from the guilty to the neighboring innocent. And guilt attaches itself to illegal acts, not to dangerous thoughts or suspicious associations. There is, of course, such a thing as collective guilt in a conspiracy, but the laws dealing with conspiracy are ample to take care of this. It is a far cry from joining the World Federalists or the Civil Liberties Union to a conspiracy, and a climate of opinion that befogs the distinction is one in which the most fundamental rights can be lost.

The Supreme Court has itself repeatedly repudiated the notion of guilt by association, and repudiated, too, the notion that any one man can decide what organizations are illegal. Furthermore, in our legal system, guilt is not retroactive, and the Constitution specifically prohibits the Congress from passing a bill of attainder or an *ex post facto* law. "An *ex post facto* law," the Supreme Court has said "is one which renders an act punishable in a manner in which it was not punishable when it was committed."

It would be difficult to find a more succinct description of the malpractices in which our Congressional committees are now engaged. To punish, either by law or by destruction of character or by forfeiture of job, the joining of an organization in 1937 or 1945 which was not held to be subversive or even suspect until 1950 is a violation of the spirit if not of the letter of the Constitution and revolts anyone familiar with the history of Anglo-American justice.

Third, the doctrine is wrong practically. It is, after all, neither possible nor desirable that we engage in a check of the membership, past as well as present, of all organizations to which we belong or which we are asked to join. What a shambles our society would be if we actually did this. We should be careful what we join, we are told; we should be careful in lending our name. But how do we go about being careful? Do we start with our church? with our labor union? with our fraternal society? with our veterans' organization? with our professional group? If the presence of subversives in an organization is enough to persuade us to drop our membership, all that the Communists need to do to destroy any society is to join it.

Perhaps the most curious thing about this principle of collective contamination is its selective character. It operates, indeed, on a double standard. No one suggests the danger of association with the Daughters of the American Revolution or the American Legion or the Democratic Party. Yet it is easy to make out a case against each of these—a case quite as plausible as that made out against such organizations as the Civil Liberties Union—for at one time or another each of these has been guilty of intolerance, or of encouraging the violation of the First or the Fourteenth Amendment. And, after all, if Republicans can associate with a McCarthy or a Velde and Democrats with a McCarran or a Talmadge, without ostentatious infection, it is difficult to know where we are to draw the line or establish our moral quarantine.

There are, needless to say, dangers in promiscuous joining or name-lending. But we must leave something to the individual judgment, something to common sense, something to the operation of the natural law of diminishing returns. Those who join organizations without proper inquiry into purpose or direction, or who lend their names indiscriminately to causes and organizations, will soon discover that they are tagged as "joiners," that they suffer embarrassment and confusion, and that they forfeit whatever influence they once commanded.

Certainly no one should give his name to an organization without some investigation or assurance of its character. But clearly there are practical difficulties here, for we cannot spend all of our time investigating each organization that appeals to us, nor do we want an official body to make investigations for us. On the whole, if we must err—as we will—it is probably better for society that we err on the side of generosity than on the side of caution.

And we must beware, too, lest we erect a double standard in this matter of lending our names and our support to causes and organizations. It ill becomes a society that applauds the stars of the film, television, radio, sports world when they "lend" their names—for a price—to the endorsement of breakfast food they do not eat, soap they do not use, whiskey they do not drink—to become indignant when misguided idealists lend their names to what they think are good causes.

A more serious problem arises in the divorce—or gap—between membership and responsibility. On the whole it is certainly desirable that those who join an organization take part in its activities and assume some share of responsibility for its direction. If its character is not what it purports to be, if its activities are not in fact those they had originally supported, they should either work to change it, or, if they are unable to do this or do not care enough to try, they should get out. If they fail to do either they may expect to be charged with irresponsibility.

Here again, however, we must beware of a double standard. When our whole society operates to divest membership from responsibility it is not fair to require that reformers or liberals be entirely different from the rest of us. After all, all those who own shares in a corporation—and there are millions of them—own the corporation and are ultimately responsible for its conduct. Yet how many shareholders interest themselves in the labor policies or the taxation policies of their corporations?

For that matter, how many of those who insist—and quite rightly, too—that those who join organizations should take an active part in them, themselves take an active part in the political party to which they belong, in their church or their professional organization? If we applied to the average person who belongs to many organizations the tests we are now asked to apply to a Bishop Oxnam or a Helen McAfee Horton, a great many of our parties, our churches, and our fraternal and professional organizations would collapse overnight.

Fourth, the doctrine is wrong historically, for it flies in the face of the whole of our experience. If there is a basic American principle and practice, it is the principle and practice of voluntary association. The voluntary association is at the basis of our constitutional system, of our democracy.

Our democracy has functioned through voluntary associations ever since the days of the Mayflower Compact and the Fundamental Orders of Connecticut.

Our churches are private voluntary associations. Our political parties, our labor unions, our professional societies, our fraternal orders, our educational and charitable societies, all are private voluntary associations. Most of our major reforms, political, social, moral, were carried through by private voluntary associations: women's rights, temperance, educational improvement, the attack on slavery, prison and penal reform, slum clearance—these and a hundred others all got their original impetus from such organizations.

But it is needless to elaborate on anything so obvious. We are a nation of joiners, and it is by joining that we get most of the business of democracy done. We have not yet learned to turn automatically to the Government to do what we want, though the McCarthys and the Jenners are the deadly enemies of private enterprise in the social, the intellectual, and the spiritual realm. A government that may decide what organizations are safe and what are unsafe must be strong enough to impose its ideas and principles on everyone. Is it that kind of government that we want?

Our great tradition of voluntary democracy is now in peril. For the logical consequence of the doctrine of guilt by association is of course that men will cease to join new organizations and will drop away from old ones. Already ordinary men and women are timid about joining—and who can blame them? Already college students refrain from political or reform activity—and who can blame them? You never know which organizations may be found subversive twenty years from now.

Nor need we delude ourselves that it is only the lunatic fringe, the expendable, organizations that will suffer. We are all of us members of many societies, and we may say with John Donne that when the principle of association is attacked we ask not for whom the bell tolls, it tolls for us. Already the Unitarian Church is suspect in some quarters; elsewhere it is the Civil Liberties Union or the World Federalists or the friends of UNESCO or the American

Library Association, which has courageously opposed book censorship, or the entire teaching profession. In time it may be a major church or a major party, for a committee that can hire a man who imagines seven thousand Communists among the Protestant clergy, is capable of anything.

Once the notion that joining may be dangerous is firmly established, all of our organizations will be affected, and the American democracy will dry up at the roots. For as Tocqueville said in one of the most astute of all his prophecies:

> When some kinds of associations are prohibited and others allowed, it is difficult to distinguish the former from the latter beforehand. In this state of doubt, men abstain from them altogether, and a sort of public opinion passes current, that tends to cause any association whatsoever to be regarded as a bold and almost illicit enterprise.
>
> It is therefore chimerical to suppose that the spirit of association, when it is repressed on some one point, will nevertheless display the same vigor on all others. . . . After having exhausted your strength in vain efforts to put down prohibited associations, you will be surprised that you cannot persuade men to form the associations that you encourage.

Thus our present-day wrecking-crew may knock out one of the props of our democratic system. And while they are about this, they are engaged in a related and equally subversive activity. That is the attack upon the right of petition, a right so important that it occupies an honored place in both English and American Revolutions. The right of petition is not openly attacked, to be sure; even the McCarthys are not quite that impudent. But the attack upon it is no less deadly for that. After all, if a petition for clemency for the Rosenbergs, for example, or for the abolition of the Un-American Activities Committee is to expose men and women to investigation, to the charge of subversion, they will think twice before signing anything.

A year or so ago a Wisconsin paper had the notion to get signatures for the preamble of the Declaration of Independence; it got precious few, for the majority of those approached regarded the request as dangerous and the document as subversive—which of course it was! If only George III could have inculcated that attitude of mind in the Americans of that day, there never would have been any nonsense about signing the Declaration of Independence.

Finally the doctrine of guilt by association is wrong morally. It is wrong morally because it assumes a far greater power in evil than in virtue. It is based therefore on a desperate view of mankind. It rests on what may be called the rotten-apple theory of society—the theory that one wicked man corrupts all virtuous men, and that one mistaken idea subverts all sound ideas.

Why is there no doctrine of innocence by association? Why is it that our present-day witch-hunters pay this matchless tribute to the power of Communism or radicalism, that they think its doctrines and its proponents irresistible?

It is, of course, because they are men consumed with fear and hatred, they are men who know nothing of the stirring history of freedom, they are men of little faith. We may go further and say that they are hypocrites in that they do not even believe in the doctrines that they proclaim. For if they did believe them, they would not need to fear counter-argument, but would be willing to submit their beliefs to the competition of the marketplace of ideas.

The doctrine of guilt by association is wrong morally for other reasons as well. It assumes that it is possible to divide mankind between the saved and the sinners (or, if you will, the loyal and the disloyal, the patriotic and the subversive, the Americans and the un-Americans), and that the saved must never associate with the sinners.

It is, needless to say, a very old attitude. It is the attitude which the Pharisees took when they asked of the Disciples "Why eateth your Master with publicans and sinners?" The Pharisees are still with us, even in the clergy; they are still prepared to divide us all into the saved and the sinners, and they are still sure that it is wicked to consort with sinners.

Who are these men to whom all truth is revealed? Who are they that know so surely which causes are good and which are bad, what motives are noble and what are ignoble?

There is one consolation here, and that is that the society of the saved gets more and more exclusive, and the society of the damned larger and larger. Just as each new party that came to power during the French Revolution thought it essential to send its predecessors to the guillotine for the lack of true zeal, so the hatemongers of our day are spreading their nets wider and wider until in the end hardly anyone can escape.

The doctrine of guilt by association, then, is deeply immoral. It rests on a low view of human nature. It confesses a lack of faith in truth and virtue. It makes us into the kind of men and women who are very conscious of their own importance and very careful never to expose that self-importance to the risks of battle or of life, the kind of men and women who never support any but the most respectable causes, read any but the most approved books, associate with any but the most distinguished people.

It is perhaps well to remember that in the beginning and for a longer time than the United States has existed, Christianity itself was the most disreputable of causes and it is well to remember what the Rev. Samuel J. May said of the Abolitionists:

"We Abolitionists are what we are—babes, sucklings, obscure men, silly women, publicans and sinners, and we shall manage this matter just as might be expected of such persons as we are. It is unbecoming in abler men who stood by and would do nothing, to complain because we do not do better."

It is time that we see this doctrine of guilt by association for what is it: not a convenient device for detecting subversion, but a device for subverting our democratic principles and practices, for destroying our constitutional guarantees, for corrupting our faith in ourselves and in our fellow-men.

37. C. WRIGHT MILLS

The Permanent War Economy
(1958)

C. Wright Mills (1916-1962), prominent younger critic of postwar American society, received his A. B. degree from the University of Texas and a Ph. D. from the University of Wisconsin. He taught sociology—first at the University of Maryland, and from 1946 until his death at Columbia University. His books, which include *White Collar* (1951) and *The Power Elite* (1956), have attracted widespread attention.

Since the end of World War II many in elite circles have felt that economic prosperity in the U. S. is immediately underpinned by the war economy and that desperate economic—and so political —problems might well arise should there be disarmament and genuine peace. Conciliatory gestures by the Russians are followed by stock-market selling. When there is fear that negotiations may occur, let alone that a treaty structure for the world be arranged, stocks, by their jitters, reflect what is called a "peace scare." When unemployment increases and there is demand that something be done, government spokesmen regularly justify themselves by referring first of all to increases in the money spent and to be spent for war preparations. Thus with unemployment at 4.5 million in January, 1958, the President proclaimed that war-contract awards will rise from the $35.6 billion of 1957 to the $47.2 billion of 1958.

These connections between economic conditions and war preparations are not obscure and hidden; they are publicly and regularly reported. And they are definitely among the causes for elite acceptance of the military metaphysic and hence among the causes of World War III.

Back of these well-reported facts are the structural connections between the privately incorporated economy and the military ascendancy. Leading corporations now profit from the preparation of war. Insofar as the business elite are aware of their profit interests —and that is their responsible business—they press for a continuation of their sources of profit, which often means a continuation of the preparation for war. As sources of political advice and as centers of power, higher business and higher military circles share an interest in the felt need for armament and for its continual and wasteful development. We cannot assay with accuracy the causal weight of this personnel and their interests, but the combination of a seemingly "permanent war economy" and a "privately incorporated economy" cannot reasonably be supposed to be an unambiguous condition for the making of peace.

I am *not* suggesting that military power is now only, or even mainly, an instrument of economic policy. To a considerable extent, militarism has become an end in itself and economic policy a means of it. Moreover, whatever the case in previous periods of capitalism, in our immediate times war in each country is being prepared in order to prevent another country from becoming militarily stronger. "There is much justification," E. H. Carr has noted, "for the epigram that 'the principal cause of war is war itself.' " Perhaps at no previous period has this been so much the case as now, for the means of war, and war as a means, have never before been so absolute as to make war so economically irrational.

But we must remember that true capitalist brinkmanship consists of the continual preparation for war, just short of it; and that such brinkmanship does have economic functions of important capitalist consequence. Moreover, it is by no means clear that the American elite realize the economic irrationality of war itself. In the meantime, an expensive arms race, under cover of the military metaphysic and in a paranoid atmosphere of fright, is an economically attractive business. To many utopian capitalists, it has become The Business Way of American Life.

I cannot here examine the economics of World War II, but it is relevant to understand that the corporate elite of America have ample reason to remember it well. In the four years following 1940, some $175 billion worth of prime supply contracts—the keys to control of the nation's means of production—were given to private corporations. Naturally enough, two-thirds went to the top one hundred corporations—in fact, almost one-third went to ten private corporations. These companies were granted priorities and allotments for materials and parts; they decided how much of these were to be passed down to subcontractors. They were allowed to expand their own facilities under extremely favorable amortization (20 per cent a year) and tax privileges (instead of the normal twenty or thirty years, they could write off the cost in five). In general these were the same corporations that operated most of the government-owned facilities and obtained favorable options to "buy" them after the war.

It had cost some $40 billion to build all the manufacturing facilities existing in the United States in 1939. By 1945 an additional $26 billion worth of high-quality new plant and equipment had been added—two-thirds of it paid for directly from government funds. Some $20 billion of this $26 billion worth was usable for producing peacetime goods. If to the $40 billion existing we add this $20 billion, we have a $60-billion productive plant usable in the postwar period. In 1939, the top two hundred and fifty corporations owned about 65 per cent of the facilities then existing; during the war, they operated 79 per cent of all new privately operated facilities built with government money; as of September 1944, they held 78 per cent of all active prime-war-supply contracts.

The economic boom of World War II—and only that—pulled the U.S.A. out of the slump of the 'thirties. After that war a flood of pent-up demand was let loose. To this was added the production of war materials of conventional and unconventional sort. The result, as everyone knows, was the great American prosperity of the last decade.

In the winter of 1957-58 another recession began in the United States. By late March, some six million were unemployed. The mechanics of this recession were generally familiar. There was an "overextension" of capitalist investment in the early 'fifties, perhaps due to favorable tax amortization; then the rate of capital formation dropped. There was an increase in the installment debt —a mortgaging of future income—especially during 1955. At the same time there has been an arrogant rigidity of prices set by corporate administrators. In fact some prices (for example, steel) were administered up rather than down—even in the face of declining demand—and production was cut.

To this old capitalist folly, Dr. John Blair has recently revealed, there has now been added a rather direct link between "the mode of compensation" for corporation executives and the rigidity or even the increase of the prices they administer. The stock options given these executives connect their income and wealth to dividends or to the market value of common stock, thus avoiding taxes payable on salaries. Price increases, it is well known, tend to raise stock prices. The long-term compensation of the business elite is thus tied to rising prices and to rising stock values, rather than to lower costs and lower prices.

The recession could of course be fought by vigorous price reductions, even imposed by government price controls; by a cut in taxes to increase purchasing power; and by a very large public-works program, perhaps for school facilities. Such means, which are theoretically at the disposal of the capitalist slump-fighter, are now generally accepted by liberal and by conservative economists. Perhaps such means would be economically adequate. They do not, however, seem to be politically acceptable to everyone involved in the decisions; they do not seem to be altogether acceptable to the capitalists of the Eisenhower Administration.

There is always another way open to them: expenditures for war as a capitalist subsidy and as a countervailing force to capitalist slump. Such expenditures have been most efficiently wasteful, and they often seem to be politically unarguable.

It is not relevant to my argument that this particular recession either deepen or be overcome. My point is that slump—for so long as it is felt as a threat—will further harden the militarist posture of the U.S. elite, and that this elite has attempted and will attempt to overcome it by still larger military expenditure. It is of course not that simple, but neither is it so complex as to be incomprehensible. International tensions, incidents, crises do not just happen. The definitions of world reality held by both sides of the encounter, as well as continual default, enter into such international affairs. Slump in America will stiffen these war-making definitions and will serve as additional excuse for the continued lack of decision; it will increase the tension; it will make more likely and more frightening the incidents; it will sharpen the perilous crisis. The fear of slump in America cannot reasonably be considered a context that will increase the American elite's contribution to the making of peace. In their interplay with Soviet decision-makers it is more likely to increase their contribution to the thrust and the drift toward World War III.

Yet it is a hard fact for capitalism that the new weaponry, the new kinds of war preparations, do not seem to be as economically relevant to subsidizing the defaults and irrationalities of the capitalist economy as the old armament and preparations. The amount of money spent is large enough, but it tends to go to a smaller proportion of employees, to the technician rather than to the semi-skilled. The people who make missiles and bombs will probably not put into consumption as high a ratio of their incomes as would the more numerous makers of tanks and aircraft. Accordingly, the new type of military pump-priming will not prime as much; it will not carry as great a "multiplier effect"; it will not stimulate consumption or subsidize capitalism as well as the older type. It is a real capitalist difficulty, and the military expenditures may indeed have to be great to overcome it.

Ten years ago, in *The New Men of Power*, I noted that "if the sophisticated conservatives have their way, the next New Deal will be a war economy rather than a welfare economy. . . . In the last transition from peace to war, WPA was replaced by WPB. . . . The establishment of a permanent war economy is a long-time trend. Its pace and tactics will vary according to the phase of the slump-war-boom cycle dominant at any given time. In the phase of inflated boom with great fear of slump, the practical rightists (of the smaller business classes) have the initiative, but in the longer historical perspective, they are merely advance shock troops of the big right. Carrying out the old-fashioned policies of the practical conservatives will lead straight to slump. Then the sophisticated conservatives will take over policy-making for the business class as a whole."

That, I believe, is what we have been witnessing in the Eisenhower Administration.

Many sophisticated conservatives, it would seem, have taken seriously the capitalist image of the world so widely set forth at the end of World War II. "We are asking the U. S. businessman," *Fortune* editorialists then wrote, "to think of Wendell Willkie's 'One World' not in fancy geopolitical terms, but merely in market terms." In describing the glories of capitalist expansion in terms of what father and son did, they ask: "Is this expansion from local iron-monger to 'national distribution' ordained to stop there? The task of expanding trade in stovepipe from a national to an international range is a tricky and often exasperating business, but there is money in it."

There must be: American export of goods and services amounted to $26 billion in 1957; in addition, twenty-five hundred U.S. firms with branches or subsidies abroad sold some $32 billion. The U.S. "foreign market" is $58 billion a year. "Foreign earnings," *Fortune* wrote in January, 1958, "will more than double in ten years, more than twice the probable gain in domestic profits." Moreover, "average foreign investment in 1956 and 1957" was probably close to $6 billion. The total invested in 1957 ($37.5 billion) was "roughly double what it was in 1950." Given present rates of increase, it seems likely that, a decade from now, private foreign investment will rise to nearly $60 billion.

Imperialism has generally meant the political and, if need be, the military protection of businessmen and their interests in foreign areas. The political protection need not include the conquest of colonies; the military protection need not involve the establishment of bases and garrisons. But regardless of the manner of the protection extended, imperialism by definition involves the interplay of economic, political, and military institutions and men. No event of significance can be understood without understanding how these interests come to points of clash or of coincidence. "The international system" of the world today cannot be understood without understanding the changing forms of their interplay.

In thinking about "imperialism" we must be prepared to develop different theories for different periods and for different kinds of political economies. The pre-1914 situation, for example, was quite different from the post-1945 scene, in which two super-states of quite distinctive structure confront each other around the world, and in which specific ruling coalitions of economic, political, and military agents are quite unique.

Both Russia and America are "imperialistic" in the service of their ideas and in their fears about military and political security. It is in the economic element that they differ.

The economic aim of Soviet imperialism is simply booty. Such imperialism consists of the political control of an area with the aim of (1) accumulating valuable capital goods or (2) extracting agricultural and other "surpluses"—as in the Stalinist exploitation of Eastern Europe. Such efforts, as in capitalist imperialism, result in keeping the "colonial" country from industrialization, in keeping it as a producer of raw materials. The economic nature of Soviet imperialism does not arise from any "contradiction" in the Soviet economy; economically, it is simply brutal conquest. But as the Soviet economy is further industrialized, this kind of imperialist temptation and drive loses its strength. The reverse is the case with capitalist imperialism.

The aim of capitalist imperialism is, at first, to open up markets for the export of "surplus" consumer goods, and to use the colonial country as a producer of raw materials which the industrial nation needs in its manufacturing. Manufactured goods, in turn, are sold to the backward country. In due course, however, the backward region becomes a sphere for the investment of capital accumulated by the advanced nation. Such export of capital requires, in the capitalist view, that the risk be limited by political guarantees. Only when the state will assure the capitalist that it will support and protect him can such risky investments be undertaken on any scale. After the investment is made there is naturally an expectation or a demand that it be backed up politically. Only a highly organized capitalist group can expect to exert such influence within and upon the state.

38. ERICH FROMM

May Man Prevail?
(1961)

Erich Fromm (1900-   ), psychoanalyst and author, was born in Frankfort, Germany. He received his Ph. D. degree from the University of Heidelberg in 1922, and ten years later came to the United States, where he has been a lecturer and faculty member at various colleges and universities. He is a Fellow of the New York Academy of Sciences and is the author of numerous studies in psychology, including the popular book *Escape from Freedom.*

The situation in which humanity finds itself is exceedingly grave. The policy of the deterrent will not ensure peace; it will most likely destroy civilization, and it will certainly destroy democracy even if it preserves peace. The first steps in avoiding a nuclear cataclysm and preserving democracy are to agree on universal disarmament, and, simultaneously, to arrive at a *modus vivendi* with the Soviet Union based on the acceptance of existing possessions of the two blocs.

These steps, however, are only a beginning in coping with the immediate danger of nuclear war. They do not solve the world problem in the long run. The central issue today is that of the future course of the underdeveloped nations, which comprise the majority of the human race. They insist not only on obtaining political independence but also on rapid economic development.

They will not wait two hundred years to achieve the economic level of Europe or the United States. The Communists have shown that by means of force and fanaticism it is possible to attain results; their method will become irresistibly attractive unless it can be demonstrated that similar results can be achieved without terror and without the destruction of individuality, through central planning along with economic and technical assistance from the industrialized countries. Such a policy requires the acceptance of a neutral bloc by both the East and the West and the strengthening of the United Nations as a supernational organization charged with the administration of disarmament and economic aid.

The pursuit of the policy suggested here requires such drastic changes in the American attitude that one cannot avoid having serious doubts whether such a policy is possible; in fact, its acceptance would seem to be impossible unless there is a growing conviction that it constitutes the only alternative to war.

First, such a policy would require that the President and Congress subordinate the special interests of the armed forces and of the big corporations (especially those with strong capital investments abroad) to the main goals of United States policy, peace and survival as a democratic nation.

Furthermore, this policy requires a material and spiritual reorientation in the West entailing the replacement of projective-paranoid attitudes toward Communism by an objective and realistic appraisal of the facts. Such realism is only possible if we take a critical view of ourselves and recognize the discrepancy that exists between our professed ideals and our actions. We claim that our present system is characterized by a high degree of individualism, and of religious or secular humanism. In reality we are a managerial, industrial society with a diminishing amount of individualism. We like to produce more and to consume more, but we have no goal—either as individuals or as a nation. We are developing

into faceless organization men, alienated from ourselves and lacking authentic feelings and convictions. This very fact leads us to
put so much emphasis on the lack of freedom and individualism
in Russia because we can then protest against features of the
Soviet society which in reality we are approaching in our own.

The Russians are today in some respects where Americans were
one hundred years ago; they are building a society, full of hope
and enthusiasm to go ahead and to accomplish what they have set
out to do. While in the United States, although there is still unnecessary poverty and unnecessary suffering, we are only filling
out what has been left to do; we are only doing more of the same.
We have no vision of something new, no aim that truly inspires
us. If this continues, we and the West will not survive. We will
lack the energy and vitality that are necessary for any nation or
group of nations to live and to survive in a world that is witnessing the awakening of nations that have been silent for hundreds
of years. Our weapons will not save us—at best they will drag our
enemies into the holocaust thirty minutes after we have perished.

What can save us and what can help mankind is a renaissance
of the spirit of humanism, of individualism, and of America's
anti-colonialist tradition. By our hesitant and often ambiguous
policy toward the underdeveloped peoples we have helped the
Communists realize one of their most significant successes: to become the leaders in the historical movement of the "New World,"
and to stamp us as the "reactionary" forces trying to arrest the
historical trend. We must, if not surpass, at least equal the Communists, by being wholly and unreservedly with the wave of
history, rather than half-heartedly and hesitatingly. As has been
said over and over again, the present struggle is a struggle for
men's minds. One cannot win this struggle with empty slogans and
propaganda tricks, which nobody except their own authors believe.

One can win it only if one has ideas to offer that are authentic because they are rooted in the realities of a nation's life.

The West is old, but by no means exhausted. It has shown its vitality by achievements in scientific thought that are unparalleled in history. We are suffering not so much from exhaustion as from the absence of goals, and from the "doublethink" that paralyzes us. If we ask ourselves where we are and where we are going, we shall have a chance to formulate new goals socially, economically, politically, and spiritually.

The Soviet system challenges us to develop a system that can satisfy the needs of man better than Communism does. But while we talk a great deal about freedom and the superiority of our system, we avoid the Soviet challenge and prefer to describe Communism as an international conspiracy out to conquer the world by force and subversion. The Russians hope to see the victory of Communism as the result of its superior performance. Are we afraid that we cannot meet the Communist competition, and is this the reason why we prefer to define the struggle as a military one rather than as a socio-economic one? Are we unwilling to make the necessary changes within our own society, and do we, for this reason, declare that no essential changes are necessary? Are we afraid to curb the political influence of our corporate investors in Latin America? By concentrating on the military threat against us and the resulting arms race we miss the *one* chance for victory: to demonstrate that it is possible to have at home—and in Asia, Africa, and Latin America—economic progress *and* individuality, economic and social planning *and* democracy. This is the answer to the Communist challenge—not the nuclear deterrent.

Our present thinking is a symptom of a deep-seated, though unconscious defeatism, of a lack of faith in the very values which we proclaim. We only cover up this defeatism by concentrating on the evils of Communism and by promoting hate. If we continue with our policy of the deterrent and with our unholy alliances with dictatorial states in the name of freedom, we shall defeat the very values we hope to defend. We shall lose our freedom and probably also our lives.

What matters today is preserving the world; but in order to preserve it, certain changes have to be made, and in order to make these changes, historical trends have to be understood and anticipated.

All men of good will or, rather, all men who love life must form a united front for survival, for the continuation of life and civilization. With all the scientific and technical progress man has made, he is bound to solve the problem of hunger and poverty, and he can afford to try solutions in different directions. There is only one thing he can *not* afford—and that is to go on with preparations for war, which, this time, will lead to catastrophe. There is still time to anticipate the next historical development and to change our course. But unless we act soon we shall lose the initiative, and circumstances, institutions, and weapons, which we created, will take over and decide our fate.

DATE

GAYLORD